Pastoral
Care

Pastoral Care

Telling the Stories of Our Lives

Karen D. Scheib
Foreword by Thomas G. Long

Abingdon Press

Nashville

Library of Congress Cataloging-in-Publication Data has been requested.

ISBN: 978-1-4267-6647-3

Scripture quotations unless noted otherwise are from the Common English Bible. Copyright © 2011 by the Common English Bible. All rights reserved. Used by permission. www.CommonEnglishBible.com.

Scripture quotations marked KJV are from The Authorized (King James) Version. Rights in the Autho-rized Version in the United Kingdom are vested in the Crown. Reproduced by permission of the Crown's patentee, Cambridge University Press.

Scripture quotations marked (NIV) are taken from the Holy Bible, New International Version®, NIV®. Copyright © 1973, 1978, 1984, 2011 by Biblica, Inc.™ Used by permission of Zondervan. All rights reserved worldwide. www.zondervan.com. The "NIV" and "New International Version" are trademarks registered in the United States Patent and Trademark Office by Biblica, Inc.™

Scripture quotations marked (ESV) are from The Holy Bible, English Standard Version® (ESV®), copyright © 2001 by Crossway, a publishing ministry of Good News Publishers. Used by permission. All rights reserved.

Scripture quotations marked RSV are from the Revised Standard Version of the Bible, copyright 1952 [2nd edition, 1971] by the Division of Christian Education of the National Council of the Churches of Christ in the United States of America. Used by permission. All rights reserved.

With kind permission from Springer Science+Business Media: *Journal of Pastoral Psychology,* "Love as a Starting Point for Pastoral Theological Reflection," volume 63, 2014, pages 705–17, Karen D. Scheib.

All personal names and stories have been modified and changed to protect the identities of the subjects. Any resemblance to actual persons, living or dead, or actual events is purely coincidental.

16 17 18 19 20 21 22 23 24 25—10 9 8 7 6 5 4 3 2 1
MANUFACTURED IN THE UNITED STATES OF AMERICA

*In memory of Liston Mills,
and in gratitude for story companions
in my life.*

Contents

Foreword

In this remarkable volume Karen Scheib, in her quiet and gentle way, guides the whole field of pastoral care in a new, bold, and refreshing direction. Practical theological disciplines—such as homiletics, liturgics, religious education, and pastoral care—by their very nature are the result of conversations with nontheological partners. Homiletics talks with communication theory, liturgics with ritual studies, and so on. These conversations can be marked by an uneasiness because the theological side of the discourse can quickly be dominated by the academically privileged nontheological field, causing theology to grow silent or to be relegated to muttering weak "amens" to the claims of the human sciences.

A generation ago, pastoral care received a burst of energy because of developments in clinical psychology. The clinical pastoral education movement was born, the language of psychotherapy became a new *lingua franca* among pastors, and courses in pastoral counseling became the hot ticket on seminary campuses. Eventually, however, the limitations of these new approaches to pastoral care became apparent. Pastors who hung out shingles as first-responder therapists increasingly felt the abrasion between this role and their other responsibilities as pastors. The psychotherapeutic focus of pastoral care often led to a cul-de-sac of individualism, a focus on pathologies rather than health, and views of human selves cut off from their large social, ethical, and ecclesial contexts.

Consequently, pastoral care and theology, as a seminary field, began to display signs of disorientation. Those in the field who soldiered on down the clinical path had trouble maintaining their theological identity, and those who charged off in the direction of social ethics found themselves hard pressed to explain how they were still doing "pastoral care."

What Karen Scheib has done in this book is reposition pastoral care as a theological activity performed in the context of the church. She draws deeply upon her Weslyan theological heritage, upon an understanding of life in its fullness as growth in love and grace, and upon a "communion ecclesiology" undergirded by a communal understanding of the trinitarian life of God. Thus grounded, she envisions pastoral care first as a rhythm of the life of the whole church and secondarily as a work of trained pastors. In her vision, pastoral care is rescued from a narrow understanding of it as exceptional acts of intervention performed only in moments of dire crisis. Instead, it becomes a "daily practice of pastoral care," an attending, in love, to the stories of others, and a "listening for ways God is already present in a lifestory."

One of the strong virtues of this book is that it insists on the particular and the local on the way to becoming general and universal. Scheib speaks not in abstractions but as a theologian, indeed as a *Wesleyan* theologian. She understands pastoral care not as a disembodied activity but as a part of the life of the church, indeed not the idealized church but the actual congregations down the street and around the corner. But once she has located pastoral care in a particular place and in a particular voice, the broader connections become visible. To listen to the narratives of persons is to be led to their larger narrative life in families, in society, in the wider culture. And to attend to narratives in Christian congregations already opens windows to other faith traditions, which have their own narrative textures.

One more virtue of the book is that it will be valuable on so many levels. Scholars in the field of pastoral theology will be challenged by her call to reenvision the field in theological hermeneutical ways. Pastors will find a new focus for their work. And students will discover a well-written and accessible volume with thoughtful discussion questions for each chapter.

This book by Karen Scheib is a great gift—solidly theological, grounded in the life of the church, and eminently teachable.

Thomas G. Long
Bandy Professor of Preaching, Emeritus
Candler School of Theology
Emory University
Atlanta, GA

Preface

*All human beings have an innate need to hear and tell stories and to have a story
to live by. . . . [R]eligion, whatever else it has done, has provided one of the main
ways of meeting this abiding need.*

—Harvey Cox, *The Seduction of the Spirit*

It is very likely that within the past week you told someone a story about yourself,
heard another's tale, or both. Perhaps you were applying for a job, catching up
with an old friend, making a new one, or providing pastoral care. Communicating
who we are and what matters most in our lives occurs through the sharing of stories. We not only have stories, our identities, our senses of self are composed by and
through stories—those we tell or choose not to tell, as well as stories others tell about
us. In crafting our own stories, we draw from a particular net of stories in which we
live, and this story net influences our view of the world. If you were raised in a religious tradition or community or have chosen to become part of one as an adult, the
narratives and stories of this tradition are also a part of the net of stories that holds
you and shapes your worldview.

Chances are quite high that you were first introduced to the beliefs of your
religious tradition though stories told or enacted through ritual. The Hebrew scriptures and the New Testament are full of stories, as are the sacred texts of many other
religious traditions. If Christianity is your faith tradition, perhaps you first heard
about God's promise to love and care for the world and all its inhabitants through a
picture book depicting Noah, the ark, and the rainbow. Stories of faith told in Sunday school, recounted in sermons, enacted through the sacraments, embodied in the
life of a friend, or lived out through the ministry of the church form all of us in the
Christian faith. These stories of our faith become a frame through which we interpret
our own lifestories.

In the pages that follow, I present a model of Christian pastoral care as a narrative, ecclesial, theological practice (NET). As a *narrative practice*, pastoral care attends
to the inseparable interconnection between our own lifestories, others' stories, the
larger cultural stories, and God's story. As a ministry of the church, pastoral care is
an *ecclesial practice* that derives its motivation, purpose, and identity from the larger
mission of the church to bear witness to and embody God's mission of love that

extends beyond the church for the transformation of the world. As a *theological practice,* pastoral care is grounded in God's love story. God's profound love for humankind heals our brokenness when human love fails and invites us into an ongoing process of growth in love of God, self, and neighbor. My primary intended audience is those who provide care with and on behalf of religious communities. Consequently, my focus is on the daily practice of pastoral care that occurs in the context and setting of congregations, from which care extends into the wider world.

My interest is the particular responsibility of the Christian church to proclaim and embody the narrative of the sacred story of love. This is the tradition to which I belong and to which I am committed. Still, neither Christianity nor the church has exclusive rights to this story: it is God's story and divine love may be revealed in multiple ways. Love, compassion, mercy, justice, and other related qualities are central to many of the world's religions. While I focus on pastoral care shaped by the stories of the Christian tradition and practiced on behalf of the church, I do believe a narrative approach to pastoral care can be adapted for use in other religious traditions. I am also convinced that a narrative approach to pastoral care can be very effective in interfaith conversations, since it begins by listening to the others' stories and is aware of how our own stories may bias what we hear.

Developing these two dimensions of narrative pastoral care in depth is beyond the scope of this book. While the focus of this text is on the role of those in leadership positions of the church as pastoral story companions, with practice and intentionality anyone can become a story companion. While the church proclaims and lives out the story of God's love, love begins with listening for the ways in which God is already present in a lifestory.

The first part of the book lays out the foundation of a narrative, ecclesial, theological model of care. Chapter 1 examines *how* we are storied beings and the formation of narrative identity. This chapter also reviews a range of narrative theories that inform the NET model of pastoral care. Chapter 2 considers the church's story, which includes our understanding of the nature and purpose of the church and pastoral care as an ecclesial practice through which this mission is embodied. Chapter 3 explores the stories we tell about God. *Who* do we imagine God to be, and *how* does God act in the world? Our answers to these questions are often embedded in the metaphors we use to talk about God. This chapter also explores how our metaphors shape our theology. Chapter 4 takes one metaphor for God—love—and examines in depth how we construct a story of God who is love. *Why* we engage in practices of pastoral care is also connected to the *what*: we are called to love because God has first loved us (1 John 4:11). The *purpose* of pastoral care is to generate stories that promote growth in love of God, self, and others.

What happens when pastoral caregivers are engaged in the coauthoring or revising of stories that promote healing and growth in love? The second part of the book addresses this question and explores how the narrative, ecclesial, theological (NET) model facilitates pastoral care through listening to and participating in the creation, revision, and coconstruction of lifestories. Chapter 5 develops the metaphor of pastoral story companions introduced in part 1, looking specifically at ways of narrative knowing, practices of listening, the unique nature of pastoral conversation, and the ethical responsibilities of pastoral story companions. Chapter 6 explores larger factors that shape our stories, the narrative environments of family, religion, and culture that often communicate rules regarding what stories can be shared, rules of storytelling, and what makes for a good story. Chapter 7 examines practices of close reading, including exegesis, and examines the parallels between exegesis of a biblical text for the task of preaching and the exegesis of a lifestory in the practice of pastoral care. Chapter 8 considers the role of pastoral story companions in the process of restorying when a lifestory no longer works, becomes foreclosed, or gets off track in times of transition, trouble, or trauma. A brief afterword considers the strengths and limitations of a NET model of care, followed by exercises and discussion questions for each chapter.

Acknowledgments

I am grateful first to my colleague and friend Tom Long, who has written the foreword to this book and has been a supporter of my work and particular approach to practical and pastoral theology. I wish as well to express my gratitude to Dean Jan Love for her support and for the research time to complete the volume. I am deeply appreciative of my colleagues at Candler School of Theology, who contribute to a rich intellectual environment supportive of creative scholarship. I wish to thank those colleagues (current and former) who read portions of the manuscript, suggested resources, engaged in extended conversations about this work, and provided general encouragement: Ian McFarland, Joy McDougall, Ed Phillips, Emmanuel Lartey, Carl Holladay, Liz Bounds, Luke Timothy Johnson, Roberta Bondi, and E. Brooks Holifield. The Center for Faculty Development and Excellence at Emory University provided a grant from the Scholarly Writing and Publishing Fund in support of a developmental editor, for which I am most thankful.

I also wish to thank to the editors and staff at Abingdon Press, particularly Kathy Armistead, who initially invited me to write this volume; David Teel, who has seen it through, extending encouragement and prodding when needed; and the entire team who made the idea of a book a reality. I could not have completed this work without the partnership of Uli Guthrie, who served as my developmental editor and writing coach, providing great advice and support. My thanks is also extended to several able student assistants who have assisted me with research, including Eunil David Cho, Mary Williams, Mona Pineda, and Lauren Bowden.

My colleagues in the New Directions in Practical Theology Group engaged in critical and constructive conversation on a paper I presented before that group, "Love as a Staring Point for Pastoral Theological Reflection," subsequently published in *Pastoral Psychology.* The work on this paper and the input from colleagues laid the foundation for key ideas and themes developed in this volume, especially the material in chapter 4. I am eternally grateful to Robert Dykstra who extended the invitation to the group. I am also grateful for the support of my colleagues in the Society of Pastoral Theology, which has been my intellectual and professional "home base." So many in this group have been a part of conversations leading to this work, that I risk leaving some out. However, I want to specially thank Angella Son, Carrie Doehring, Nancy Ramsey, Christie Neuguer, Horace Griffin, Ryan LaMothe, and Pamela Cooper-White. Liston Mills, one of the founders of this group, and my former teacher, is largely responsible for drawing my attention to the importance of ecclesiology for pastoral theology and has significantly influenced my approach to pastoral theology.

One's life as a scholar is only one part of a life, but one that is made easier by the support of friends and family. My thanks are extended to those outside of the academy who have encouraged my life within it: Peggy Hesketh, Anne Carey, Marcia Abrams, Ellen Shepard, and my husband, Jonathan Spingarn, for the innumerable ways he provides support and encouragement.

Part I

A Net of Stories

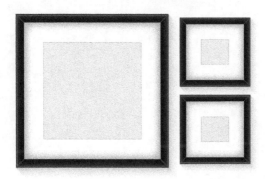

Chapter 1

Telling the Stories of Our Lives: Narrative Pastoral Care

If you want to know me, then you must know my story, for my story defines who I am. And if I want to know myself, to gain insight into the meaning of my own life, then I, too, must come to know my own story.

—Dan P. McAdams, *The Stories We Live By*

Imagine you are in a group setting, such as a classroom or a retreat, and are asked to introduce yourself to one other member of the group. At the end of the conversation you will introduce each other to the rest of the group. Instead of beginning with biographical facts, you are instructed to share a story about yourself that communicates something of who you are. What story would you choose to tell? Would it be the story of the summer you went to live in a small village in Peru? Perhaps it would be the story about falling into a trashcan headfirst while chasing a squirrel off the porch when you were seven. Or maybe you would tell about how much you loved leaving your city home for the summer and visiting your grandparents' farm. What might your listener learn about you from whatever particulars from this story you choose to tell? Perhaps it would be something about your adventurous spirit, your single-mindedness despite risks, or your love of nature. You might be surprised at how much you communicate about yourself through a familiar story. Stories are powerful.

Narrative pastoral care assumes that we not only tell stories, but that our sense of self, the meaning we assign to life events, and our understanding of the world are composed through stories. We do not experience our lives as a collection of "naked facts or strings of raw events," but rather as *stories*.[1] We are "hermenueutical beings," that is, we continually interpret our experience to make meaning out of the vast barrage of sensory perceptions, emotions, and thoughts coursing through our minds every moment.[2] And the primary way we make meaning is through stories.[3] As gerontologist William Randall asserts, "*The story of my life* [is] far more than a figure of

3

speech. It is not that life is *like* a story. On some extremely basic level, it *is* a story—a *lifestory*."[4]

Moreover, our lives are not singular stories, but collections of stories, or a *narrative* composed of multiple story strands of our experiences. When we claim *Christian* as part of our identity, we also claim this larger story as part of our own. Our lifestories are not a single-authored work, but the result of conversations, spoken and unspoken, with multiple coauthors. We live within a network of stories, held by our families, our local communities, and our religious communities and traditions. We weave our own stories out of this net of stories.

Narrative Pastoral Care: NET

A narrative approach to pastoral care invites us to become pastoral story companions in the dialogical coauthoring of lifestories. Accompanying others in authoring or editing a lifestory requires a range of practices and skills, including listening to and fully hearing the stories of others, being curious about how stories are formed, noting what is included and what is left out, identifying multiple story strands, and assisting a person in revising his or her life (and story) when needed. It is not only other people's stories or narratives we need to attend to, but our own as well. We, as well as those for whom we care, are called to shape lifestories that are not only good, but also are faithful stories that foster growth in love. In order to become effective story companions, we need to know something about how our lives are shaped by story.

Narrative pastoral care draws on research from a broad range of disciplines that have adopted a narrative approach and hold a view of human beings as hermeneutical, or interpretive beings—storytellers who seek to make meaning out of life. Some of the narrative approaches I explore in this volume include narrative psychology, therapy, gerontology, medicine, and theology, all of which draw on larger developments in literary and narrative studies. Narrative pastoral care, like the disciplines informing it, assumes that we are not the sole authors of our lifestories, but rather coauthors, developing our stories in the context of interpersonal, communal, and cultural contexts. Distinctive to narrative pastoral care is attending intentionally to God's role as coauthor of our lifestories. Narrative pastoral care is a communal practice that emerges from the stories and practices of a particular religious tradition or community. By encouraging active engagement in writing the stories of our lives, narrative pastoral care seeks to increase our ability to not simply construct a good story, but a good life.

While my approach to narrative pastoral care draws from other narrative disciplines and builds on previous work in pastoral care, it is distinctive. I define *narrative pastoral care* as an ecclesial, theological practice through which we listen to lifestories in order to discern the intersection of human stories and God's story in the context of community and culture. By claiming that pastoral care is an *ecclesial* practice, I assert that its motivation, purpose, and identity derive from the larger mission and ministry of the church to form persons and communities in a life of love made possible by God's love in Christ through the Spirit (Rom 8:9-10). A central purpose of the Christian church is to proclaim, interpret, and live out this story of God's profound healing and redeeming love, which restores our brokenness and invites us to respond through continued growth in love. The nature of love is that it does not keep to itself. Narrative pastoral care is intended to extend beyond ecclesial community, though the church has a particular responsibility to live out God's love story. Not just any story will do. From the perspective of narrative pastoral care, a good lifestory also engenders growth in love.

Narrative pastoral care is also a *theological* practice. Christian pastoral care is grounded in the biblical and historical narratives of God's unfolding love story. Understanding the larger role of theology in pastoral practice and being aware of one's own particular theological perspective allows us to discern how theological convictions are embodied in our practices. A narrative, ecclesial, theological, or a NET approach to pastoral care carefully attends to the network of stories bequeathed to us by our families, our communities, our cultures, and our faith—a network in which we write and live out our own lifestories.

Story-Shaped Lives

We are story-telling beings.[5] Whether in the form of folk tales, myths, legends, classic literature, popular fiction, movies, YouTube videos, or accounts of exploits shared between friends, stories are widely present in human culture.[6] Scholars from a range of disciplines who study story and narrative share the conviction that our sense of our selves, our lives, and our world is shaped and communicated through story.[7] Philosopher Paul Ricoeur asserts that the impulse to tell stories and construct a narrative reflects our human condition.[8] Discoveries in neuroscience confirm that our brains are wired for story, meaning "the human brain is designed to construe experience in narrative terms."[9] As neurobiologist Antonio Domasio has shown, consciousness and our sense of self, our "autobiographical self," are linked.[10] Psychologist Dan McAdams states it plainly: "Human beings are story tellers by nature."[11] According to sociologist Anthony Giddens, it is "the capacity to keep a particular narrative going," rather than behavior, that shapes identity in the modern world.[12]

We become more consciously active in the construction of our lifestories as we progress from childhood through adulthood.[13] Our narratives lengthen, we add more story strands, and our own stories become increasingly entwined with a multiplicity of other stories and narratives as we move through life.[14] We know from our general experience of hearing and reading stories that some seem better to us than others; some seem truer, more honest, more satisfying, and they provide us with a deeper understanding of life. Drawing from psychology, sociology, as well as philosophy and ethics, William Randall proposes that having a *"good lifestory"* enables us to live "in a sensible, responsible, more or less satisfying manner."[15]

The Nature of Story

Stories do many things: they entertain, educate, inspire, persuade, and motivate, but above all, they make sense of our lives, they convey meaning.[16] Stories teach us about the world.[17] But what exactly is a story? Are stories communicated only in words, or can they be enacted or performed even without words? The term *story* can have multiple meanings. For some a story connotes something fictional or made-up, while in a legal context, it can refer to "an argument, angle, or alibi."[18] In the usual everyday sense in which we use the term, a story is generally understood "as a particular arrangement of events, real or imagined, in the realm of space and time."[19] In simpler terms, stories are told by somebody "about somebody doing something."[20] Stories, then usually have at least these elements: (1) the storyteller or *author* who tells the story from a particular point of view; (2) one or more *characters*, or somebodies doing something; and (3) the *plot* in which the actions, conflicts, and concerns of the characters are laid out; and (4) the *setting* or the "temporal and spatial context in which the characters do something."[21]

While the terms *story* and *narrative* are often used interchangeably, they can have distinct meanings. Literary theorists who study narrative define it as the "showing or telling of . . . events and the mode selected for that to take place."[22] So defined, poems, songs, movies, scientific theories, rituals, or performed action without words may be considered different modes of narrative. As I use the terms here, narrative refers to what we mean by the "story of my life," or a lifestory, a larger framework that provides a more or less cohesive, thematic organization of the multiple stories we have lived in the past, are living in the present, or imagine we may live in the future.

Stories Shape Time and Identity

One of the things stories do is structure our sense of time.[23] Stories generally have some temporal sense, meaning they occur and unfold over time. Philosopher Paul Ricoeur's exploration of the interconnection between temporality and narrative has had a significant influence on the study of story and narrative.[24] Stories interpret our past, make sense of the present, and project a future. While most human cultures have a sense of time, not all understand time in terms of the sequence of past, present, and future that we tend to assume as normal in Western culture. Stories, however, require a sense of time. Stories move through time in some way, whether in a straightforward or a circuitous way.

If we were able to pay attention to every sensation, every experience, and every person encountered in a day, we would feel quickly feel overwhelmed. We generally do not experience the world in such a direct, unfiltered way. What we define as *experience* has already been filtered through "a complex interpretive process, commencing with initial sensory perceptions and culminating in emotion, thought, and action."[25]

A primary function of stories is to give meaning and shape to what might otherwise seem like random, unconnected events. By arranging the episodes of our lives into stories occurring over time, we provide meaning and coherence to our lives that otherwise might feel scattered and confusing.[26] We notice some details and filter out others, interpreting and translating the raw data of life through an implicit narrative framework; construct a story, even as we are in the midst of living it. We notice what we have interpreted as important to us, experiences we have deemed meaningful, whether positive or negative. Narratives are not some abstract idea we impose on our lives from afar, but rather "something we look through."[27] In fact, we don't just *have* stories; we *are* story-shaped beings.[28]

Culture's Influence on Story

We do not write our lifestories on a blank page. Our lives take on meaning "to the extent that they conform to or express culturally meaningful *stories*."[29] We interpret our life experiences and shape them into *our stories* through the narratives we construct from the various stories available to us, including our own life experiences, stories others tell about us, and stories from the larger culture, including religious traditions.[30] For Christians, the stories of our faith are a prominent source from which we draw in the construction of our life narratives.[31] These various story sources may help us construct coherent and life-giving stories or they may constrain or limit our lifestories.

The culture may also decide who is allowed to tell what kind of stories and which stories count as acceptable. We often see this dynamic played out in movies or television, as well as in real life. Are we more prone to believe the coherent story of a prominent surgeon and civic leader who says he did not commit abuse or sexual assault, or a distraught woman whose story is fragmented by the trauma she has endured? Likewise we may have grown up in religious traditions with stories that confirm our sense of self as beloved children of God, or we may been deemed unfit for certain roles in the life church due to our gender or sexual identity.

Ways of Knowing

Stories are not the only way we make sense out of the world, but they are the primary way we make sense of ourselves and other people. Psychologist Jerome Bruner argues that we come to understand the world either through *paradigmatic* or *narrative* knowing.[32] Paradigmatic knowing explains phenomena through rational argument and the scientific method. In paradigmatic knowing we rely on our senses and our intellect to make sense out of what we see in the world. Narrative knowing, on the other hand, is what we learn through stories. It is through stories that we make sense of human conduct and make meaning of our own lives.[33] If I want to know how my computer functions, I rely on paradigmatic knowledge. If I want to know why my friend, now nearing fifty, has never learned to drive, or why another friend volunteers with the Sierra Club, I need to know something of their stories. It is through stories that we understand one another's identity and motivations.[34] Narrative psychologists assert that our identity is shaped by stories as well as communicated through them.

The Construction of Identity through Story: Narrative Personality Theory

Narrative personality theory describes the formation of personality and identity. In a way, it presents an imagined ideal process of narrative identity formation, the way it ought to enfold if everything goes right.[35] Narrative personality psychologist Dan McAdams argues that identity is not only communicated through a lifestory, but that in a very real sense, I *am* my story.[36] Although we compose our sense of self throughout our lives, the period of late adolescence and early adulthood is a crucial time in this process. McAdams also argues that the "main psychological challenge" in contemporary culture for those in "emerging adulthood," or the ages between seventeen and twenty, is the formation of narrative identity.[37] While we are able to tell stories about our experience from an early age, it is only in late adolescence or emerging adulthood that we begin to consciously to arrange our lives into coherent narratives with a remembered past, a perceived present, and an imagined future.[38] In this period of our lives we begin to ask identity questions: Who am I? Where am I going? What do I believe in? What do I want to do with my life? What gives my life meaning, purpose, and coherence? These questions begin to form in our minds at this life stage "because the cultural conditions and expectations of modern society are such that *we have to ask them*."[39]

Questions of narrative identity may have been less pressing in earlier historical periods where who one was and what one did were often determined by one's place in the society. Contemporary society, particularly in the United States, offers us a wide variety of life choices and possibilities. We are faced with the freedom and dilemma of choice and it is our stories that help us hold our disparate choices together, as McAdams describes.

> There is no single one-size-fits-all "correct" way to live in a society like ours. There are many things we can do and be, many choices we can make. And we have to make them. We cannot do everything and believe everything. . . . And if an individual does manage to do and believe many different things . . . she is likely to wonder what it is that ties these different things together. What makes her life coherent? The answer is, the story she lives by—that is, narrative identity.[40]

During the period of emerging adulthood, we begin to form our narrative identity, which is "the internalized and changing story" of our lives.[41]

Narrative identity provides a means to hold together our various beliefs, hopes, dreams, and roles in a coherent way. The story you tell about yourself, for example at that church retreat or in the classroom, interprets your past, conveys beliefs about

8

how you have developed over time into the person you are now, and projects an anticipated future. This story also communicates your convictions, values, and commitments.[42] While this story begins to take shape in early adulthood, it not yet finished, it is "complex, contradictory," and it undergoes considerable revision over our lives.[43] Does the shape of our narrative or the themes prominent within it matter? According to research psychologists who study narrative identity, the answer is yes. Narrative psychologists have noted variances in the "dimensions of plot, image, theme, tone, and complexity" between one person's story and another's, linking these differences to "important psychological and social outcomes."[44] The primary motive communicated through a narrative may also reveal psychological differences between people.

Through analysis of hundreds of lifestory interviews, McAdams and his colleagues have identified two primary motives embedded in the plots and themes of our narratives: *agency* and *communion*.[45] *Agency* they define as "a broad tendency to expand, assert, defend, control, or express the self."[46] *Communion* is defined as "the broad tendency to connect the self to others, even to the point of giving up self for the benefit of others," loving and caring for others, and feeling a sense of commitment and belonging to a group.[47] The protagonist of a narrative emphasizing agency is trying to get ahead, influence others, or achieve a goal, often one that improves his or her own stature.[48] The lead character in a narrative that emphasizes communion may sacrifice himself for his beloved or herself for some greater good of her community. Human beings experience and express both motives in our narratives and we often live in the tension between these two motives, which at times can compete with one another. Sometimes one is emphasized over the other and the theme of agency or communion may dominate a life narrative. And our preference for one theme over the other, as well as the way in which we seek to balance these themes, can reveal something about our psychological makeup.

Think for a moment of your favorite movie or narrative. Are you drawn to action and adventure in which a hero or heroine relentlessly pursues some goal over all odds to achieve great personal success? James Bond comes to mind for me. Ostensibly he is serving his country, but he usually comes out ahead. Or do you like the stories in which people care for and tend to one another, even if it requires self-sacrifice? The film *The Sound of Music*, in which Maria von Trapp and her husband leave a comfortable home and their homeland to secure the safety of their children, comes to mind for me in this category (but this example may simply show my age!). Perhaps you are drawn to a film like *Cabaret*, in which the main character struggles between agency and communion.[49] Perhaps you can imagine other examples from contemporary films or novels that emphasize either agency or communion, or the tension between the two.

Life narratives that place a significant emphasis on agency and the main character's striving to get ahead with little regard for others or concern for friendship or love may suggest narcissism.[50] An overemphasis on communion over agency may also be problematic. Lacking the sense that one can act on one's own behalf or that one has some control over one's life may lead to depression, low self-esteem, a negative

9

evaluation of the self, or overdependence on others.[51] These core themes can provide a sense of coherence to our stories and help us evaluate the adequacy or functionality of our lifestories.

Criteria for Evaluating Lifestories

While the process of narrative identity construction may be become more self-conscious in emerging adulthood, our identities are not set at this point, nor do they stop when we reach a certain age. We continually work on our stories "consciously and unconsciously" throughout our lives.[52] We update, revise, edit, and often rewrite our lifestories as we move through adulthood, ideally moving "in the direction of increasingly good narrative form" in our middle and later years.[53] McAdams proposes six criteria of "good life-story form" expressed in how we talk and write about our lives: coherence, openness, credibility, differentiation, reconciliation, and generative imagination.[54]

Coherence means that the story hangs together and makes sense.[55] It has a certain story logic so that we can follow the plot or thread of the story. The themes of agency or communion may provide the connecting thread that allows us to follow the story. *Openness* in a lifestory refers to flexibility, the ability to allow the story to unfold, to incorporate new experiences, and to change course if needed.[56] For a story to be *credible*, it must give a reasonably full account of our lives, not omitting great chunks.[57] For McAdams, "the good, mature, and adaptive lifestory cannot be based on gross distortion," nor can the identity fashioned from this lifestory be "fantasy."[58] The concept of *differentiation* for McAdams echoes the concept, mentioned earlier, of lifestories as rich, complex, and multistranded.[59] Another way to describe this is to think of how our stories broaden and thicken with age: the longer we live, the more we have to tell. Some lifestories we hear, however long, may seem thin to us, leading us to wonder what was left out or how a life became so narrowed. Besides that, what is true in literature is also true in life: a good story has conflict. As the story progresses, however, we look for some resolution to conflict. *Reconciliation* is the term McAdams uses to describe this process in our lifestories in which the "tough issues and dynamic contradictions" are met by "narrative solutions that affirm the harmony and integrity of the self."[60] As we age, reconciliation can become increasingly challenging; we may face greater contradictions between what we can imagine and what is possible. Crisis and trauma can also challenge our ability to reconcile certain kinds of events with the lifestory we have constructed so far.[61] The concept of *generative imagination* reflects McAdams's use of Erik Erikson's developmental theory, combining Erikson's seventh and eighth stages: generativity and integrity.[62] A good lifestory is not simply inner directed but also extends beyond the self and "should eventually be oriented toward the wider world" and benefit others, including one's community and the larger society.[63] We will discuss these criteria further as they inform what we consider a good, life-giving, faithful story from the perspective of narrative pastoral care.

Narrative personality theory provides a description of the process of narrative identity formation and emerges from the larger field of personality theory developed within the context of research psychology in universities primarily in the United States. Narrative psychologists conduct quantitative and qualitative research studies in order to describe the processes of narrative identity development. *Narrative therapy* emerged from clinical practices of counseling and psychotherapy for treating persons in situations of psychological distress. While significant points of connection exist between the two theories, they developed more or less simultaneously and initially without much mutual influence.

Narrative Repair: Narrative Therapy Theory

The beginnings of narrative therapy can be traced to Michael White, from Australia, and David Epston, from New Zealand, who were initially trained in family systems theory. Steven Madigan, a student of White and Epston, has built on their work and promoted narrative therapy theory in the United States and Canada. Narrative therapy theory and practice are now well established in the United States and around the world.[64] The goal of narrative therapy is to repair limiting and disabling dysfunctional stories.

Narrative therapy theory is a distinctly postmodern approach to therapy. The therapist is considered not an expert, but a consultant. A key practice of narrative therapy is distinguishing between the person and the problem.[65] The idea here is that we tell the story of the problem in a way that takes over our lives, so that the "*problem-saturated*" story becomes the defining story.[66] We lose track of the rich, multi-stranded narrative of our lives. A principal goal of narrative therapy is the "deconstruction" of problem stories and in their place, identifying alternative story strands, then thickening and strengthening this "alternative" story into one that is more functional and life-giving.[67]

A key process in narrative therapy is naming and *externalizing* the problem a person brings to therapy.[68] Externalization separates the person from the problem. For example: Consider the difference between saying, "Ed is an alcoholic" or "Joy is a drug addict" and saying, "Ed is a person who struggles with alcohol" or "Drugs have a hold on Joy and she can't seem to get free." These represent different ways of telling the story between the person and the problem. In the first case, the person is labeled and defined completely by the problem. The problem story eclipses additional dimensions of a lifestory. Though Ed may struggle with the power of alcohol over his life, he may also be a loving father and loyal brother. Joy is a brilliant artist and a doting aunt, as well as a woman struggling to free herself from the grip of drug addiction. Through the processes of naming and externalization, the person seeking help begins to identify her or his relationship to the problem and can begin to recognize the influence that the problem exercises over his or her life. In addition, the care seeker begins to identify her or his influence over the problem and begins to gain a greater sense of agency.

The therapist and client work in a collaborative process to name the problem, but the naming is ultimately up to the client. Perhaps Ed will name his problem "Al," almost personalizing it, and will begin to see how Al talks him into drinking and will identify the false promises he makes, thus allowing Ed to see himself making choices about how he relates to Al rather than seeing himself as a helpless victim, or a hopeless alcoholic, and nothing more.[69] The narrative therapist is not interested in identifying pathology or diagnosing the problem according to DSM-5 (*Diagnostic and Statistical Manual of Mental Disorders*).[70] The narrative therapist believes that such diagnostic labels totalize the problem story and identify the person too much with the problem.

Additional tasks of narrative therapy include deconstructing damaging cultural narratives that contribute to the problem narrative, identifying unstoried or under-storied parts of a person's life, and assisting in the reconstruction of a more complex, coherent, multistoried, life-giving narrative. This is a dialogical process that occurs between the participants in the therapeutic process. Unlike many other forms of therapy, narrative therapy makes significant use of questions. It also draws heavily not only on psychological ideas but also on the postmodern philosophy of Michel Foucault, particularly his analysis of the constraining role of dominant cultural narratives.[71]

Both narrative personality theory and narrative therapy theory can make contributions to a narrative approach to pastoral care. While the two theories have somewhat different starting points, they are nonetheless compatible. Both have in common a nonpathologizing approach that focuses on identifying and building on people's strengths and increasing agency. While this approach is helpful with any number of persons, it is particularly helpful with persons who have been marginalized or labeled as pathological. It is also consistent with an approach to narrative pastoral care that emphasizes growth in love.

Restorying: Narrative Gerontology

Constructing a lifestory is a lifelong process. As a consequence we are often revising or "restorying" our lives.[72] Various practices of narrative care, including forms of life review and reminiscence, have been developed in the field of gerontology to assess the relative goodness or functionality of our lifestories and to provide a basis for revising these stories as we age.[73] *Restorying* practices a close reading of our lifestories, revising chapters that no longer work or reinterpreting memories from a new perspective. Gerontology, or the study of aging, may seem like an odd discipline to inform pastoral care. If we are at all familiar with gerontology, we may associate it with the study of older adults, or with the illnesses of old age such as Alzheimer's disease. This is partially correct, given that gerontology is a broad and interdisciplinary field encompassing a range of approaches. One approach to the study of aging that may be familiar to us is "a biomedical model that essentially equates aging to what happens to our bodies," or another perspective we may have encountered is "a social policy perspective" that deals with Social Security, Medicare, or other programs for the elderly.[74] An unfortunate side effect of these approaches to aging is that they contribute to a cultural narrative of aging in the United States as a time of loss and inevitable decline. Rather than portraying aging as a process of "actively growing old," this cultural narrative portrays aging as a passive process of "getting old."[75] Many older adults actively resist the sense of invisibility and obsolescence this narrative assigns to them.[76]

Narrative gerontology presents a different story of aging, one that is more interested in how human beings interpret the experience of aging from the inside out, rather than describing aging bodies aging from the outside in, as we might find in a biological or biomedical model of aging.[77] Narrative gerontology views human beings as "hermeneutical beings" who interpret and make meaning out of experience.[78] This view of human beings is consistent with the views presented earlier and coincides with the perspective of narrative personality theory and narrative therapy. As an interdisciplinary endeavor, narrative gerontologists draw on these disciplines as well as others in both the social sciences, such as sociology and anthropology, and the humanities, including literary theory and philosophy. Like narrative psychology, narrative gerontology seeks to describe certain human processes, specifically aging, which is a lifelong process. And like narrative therapy theory, narrative gerontology may develop interventions, such as life review, to assist persons in examining and revising a lifestory so that it becomes a better story, reflecting the criteria of good stories discussed earlier. Narrative gerontology is often more concerned with how we interpret the normal process of aging and less concerned with what we might call *narrative repair*, as is narrative therapy.

Narrative Pastoral Care (NET) in the Larger Story of Pastoral Care

A narrative approach to pastoral care is not entirely new and other pastoral theologians have proposed various forms of it. Edward P. Wimberley draws on indigenous storytelling practices in the Black church to inform care.[79] Others have adapted narrative therapy theory for use in pastoral care and counseling and spiritual formation.[80]

First, it is my intention to contribute to the growing literature on narrative approaches to pastoral care by presenting the NET (narrative, ecclesial, theological) model, which draws on a broad range of narrative disciplines and holds a view of humans as relational, meaning-making, story-telling beings. Second, I hope to reclaim strengths of various approaches to pastoral care throughout Christian history, from the early church, through the rise of modernity, to our current post-modern context.[81] The NET model reclaims fostering individual and communal spiritual formation as a central task of pastoral care. While spiritual formation has been a significant dimension of pastoral care throughout the history of the church, less attention has been paid to this element in those expressions of twentieth-century pastoral care that have been focused primarily on psychological healing.[82]

The NET model I propose is deeply grounded theologically and viewed as an ecclesial practice, which resonates with key emphases of the "classical" model of care.[83] A theological narrative of love, which is enacted by the community of love at the heart of the Trinity, runs through the NET model. The relational context of narrative formation is crucial in the NET model, thus reflecting the centrality of relationship as a means of care, which is in line with a key emphasis of the "clinical pastoral" model.[84] Given the centrality of love in the theological narrative that informs this model, however, it rejects hierarchical notions of an expert caregiver and a passive care recipient, which are limitations of the clinical pastoral model. Storyteller, listener, and the ever-present spirit of God are all coauthors of our stories. Because we author our stories in a particular narrative environment, the stories told around us and about us shape our own stories, requiring us to pay attention to cultural stories, as does the "communal-contextual" paradigm.[85]

The influence of postmodern thought on the communal-contextual model is evident in the NET model's understanding of story formation as an ongoing social process. Our stories are not fixed at some point in our lives but are constantly being developed and edited. A narrative model (NET) values diversity as divine gift and insists that love and justice are inseparable, critiques the abuse of power, and seeks to enourage positive transformation of the world through fostering growth in love.

As Dan McAdams reminds us in the opening quotation, we come to know ourselves and others through sharing the stories of our lives. We become fully our selves, fully human, and enter fully in relationship with another only as we coauthor life together. Implied in this shared narrative of care is a calling to reconfigure our storied lives in the context of a faith community implicated by and discerning God's presence in tales of love told and lived. We encounter a myriad of potential coauthors in every single day and our stories are continually being revised. Anyone can be a story companion, but those who choose to become story companions on behalf of a religious community commit to reading and authoring lifestories that honor and affirm the religious and spiritual narratives of that community, attend to God's presence in the midst of a life narrative, and promote good, strong, and hopeful stories. We become story companions by extending an invitation to sit awhile and tell a tale.

Chapter 2

The Church's Story: Called to Live Out Love

Every human community will disappoint us, regardless of how well-intentioned or inclusive. But I am totally idealistic about God's redeeming work in my life and in the world.... We [the church community] will let them down or I'll say something stupid and hurt their feelings. I then invite them on this side of their inevitable disappointment to decide if they'll stick around after it happens. If they choose to leave when we don't meet their expectations, they won't get to see how the grace of God can come in and fill the holes left by our community's failure, and that's just too beautiful and too real to miss.

—Nadia Bolz-Weber, *Pastrix*

One Sunday morning, during the children's time, the most dangerous and unpredictable part of the worship service from the pastor's point of view, I was trying to explain the abstract concept of God to a small group of children. Most of these children were under the age of eight and had yet to develop the capacity for abstract reasoning. I said something about the church being a place where we try to love each other. Then I made the rather fuzzy statement that God is present when we love and care for each other, even through we can't see God. Young children don't have much tolerance for fuzzy explanations; they want concrete answers. "Why?" asked a girl of about four. A bit flustered, I replied rather definitely, "Well that's just the way God is." Seemingly satisfied, the curious questioner said no more, but the congregation, of course, laughed. It wasn't a very good answer, but it wasn't all that bad either.

I do believe a love story is at the heart of the Christian faith and that the church is called to proclaim and enact this story. God's love is freely and fully given to us, made flesh for us, and we are called to respond by continually growing in love. Jesus proclaims love of God as the first and greatest commandment and loving one's neighbor as oneself as the second (Matt 22:34-40). The writer of the first letter to John declares that "God is love" and though we may not see God, "if we love each other, God remains in us and his love is made perfect in us" (1 John 4:16, 12). In the very last chapter of the Gospel of John, the resurrected Jesus appears to Simon Peter and asks him three times, "Do you love me?" Each time, he answers, "Yes Lord, you know I love you." After each affirmation of Peter's love, Jesus simply says, "Feed my sheep" (John 21:15-18). Jesus makes it clear that Peter's love for him must be expressed through active caring. Love is to be practiced as well as declared.

The church is called to be the place where love is lived out. One of the ways this happens is through the ministry of pastoral care, which I have defined as narrative, ecclesial, theological (NET) practice intended to foster growth in love of God, self, and others. As Nadia Bolz-Weber reminds us, however, the church as a human community does not always live out its vocation of love very well. We can find more than enough examples in history of the church actively opposing love, or not loving all. During the civil rights struggles of the 1960s in the United States, the rise of the Nazi movement in Austria and Germany following World War I, and apartheid in South Africa, individual Christians, church leaders, and entire church communities quoted scripture to maintain the status quo of inequality and turned a blind eye or condoned violence to maintain it. On a smaller scale, we see the difficulty the church has in loving when a person who is homeless or mentally ill is escorted out of a worship service or simply ignored. Failures in love occur when congregations split over politics, social issues, or how to spend an endowment.

Why such a somber note? While the church bears witness to the in-breaking of the reign of God, we live with the heartbreaking reality of human sin and brokenness, which reminds us of the here and not-yet-fully-here character of God's reign. There are those all too willing to point out the imperfections of the church and its leaders, readily dismissing the church for its human failings as reasons to give up on it.

Fortunately for us, the church is not only a human community but also one called into being by God and through which God acts to bring healing and redemption. In the same historical situations in which we find examples of the church's failure, we also see God working through the church, despite human brokenness. We find individual Christians, church leaders, and entire communities loving in the name of Christ, risking their lives in the face of hatred and resistance during the civil rights movement, in opposition to the Nazi regime and apartheid. Likewise we witness the church rising to be a community of love when we see hundreds of volunteers packing boxes of food and cleaning kits for a flood-stricken area or opening its kitchen every Sunday to feed neighbors who are underfed. When a congregation works through a difficult conflict while respecting all involved, love is present. As Bolz-Webber observes, when the church loves it is by the grace of God and "that's just too beautiful and too real to miss."[1]

A Story Stronger than Death: Living the Church's Story despite Human Imperfection

One day while in the church office, I heard a knock at the door. I opened it to find a young man in his early twenties. He was not a member of the congregation, but he wanted to see the pastor. I immediately found myself tensing up, thinking, "Here we go again: one more request for a handout." This church was not in a prosperous community and we often had folks asking for various kinds of assistance. I had nothing left in our emergency fund and dreaded telling him so, since some who hear that message do not react very well. Neither did I want to take the time involved in referring him to other agencies only to find he had no way to get there. Despite my reluctance, I asked him to come in, sit, and tell me how I could help him.

His words stopped me in my tracks and immediately pushed against the wall I had already begun to construct between us. He told me that he and his wife lived next door and had just had a baby. He stopped talking for a moment and looked down. The baby had died after being delivered and he wanted to arrange a funeral. "Will you do it?" he asked.

Reflection

He was not asking for a handout. He and his wife wanted the familiar rituals of the church to comfort them in their grief. Though the story of their child's life was short, it had begun the moment they knew they were expecting. The vision they had of their future, of becoming parents, and of cradling their newborn child had been shattered. Perhaps they came to me because they wanted someone else to witness the unwritten story of their child. Only the mother, father, and I stood at the graveside. No one else was physically present. Still, the Spirit hovered and the church was present, through ritual, prayer, and the words of scripture that proclaimed the story of a love stronger than death, a story entrusted to the church.

I am not claiming God's grace is confined only to the church, or that pastoral care happens only within the church or is offered only to church members. God's grace is more expansive than that. I am asserting that Christian pastoral care, wherever it is given and whoever gives it, is an ecclesial practice witnessing love. It all begins with stories: listening to the stories of those who seek care, and telling and enacting the story of God's love. Claiming that pastoral care is an ecclesial practice requires us to articulate exactly what we mean by *church* and what kind of community we envision as the church.

Love at the Center of the Church

To claim that the church is called to be a community of love is to make certain theological claims about the church. *Ecclesiology* is the theological category through which we express our convictions about the nature and purpose of the church. Many Christian denominations define the nature of the church in keeping with the historic creeds of the church as one, holy, and apostolic. Convictions about the purpose or mission of the church vary widely among various Christian denominations and individual churches. Theologian Avery Dulles identified five different models of the church, reflecting differing views throughout Christian history of the purpose of the church: the church as institution, sacrament, mystical communion, herald, and servant.[2] Two of these models are quite familiar to Protestants: the church as herald, emphasizing the proclamation of the word, and the church as servant, focusing on service to and engagement with the world.[3]

A sixth model, which Dulles initially called the "community of disciples," sought to harmonize the strengths of the five other models.[4] In developing this integrative model, Dulles drew not only on biblical images of the church but borrowed the phrase from the first encyclical of Pope John Paul II.[5] As this view of the church became predominant in both Roman Catholic and ecumenical ecclesiology, it came to be known communion or *koinonia* ecclesiology.[6]

Communion ecclesiology presents a vision of the church in which love is at the center and the life of the church is characterized by a "web of interwoven relationships" marked by "love, acceptance, forgiveness, commitment, and intimacy."[7] Thoroughly trinitarian, communion ecclesiology characterizes the church as sharing in the "life and love of three persons in one God."[8] The divine love evident in the Trinity, which is also expressed between Jesus and his disciples, becomes the foundation of the church. The character of this divine love is such that the church cannot remain turned inward but is called to spread divine love within and beyond the Christian community. Such love becomes the mark of the Christian life and of the Christian community.[9]

Centered on love, communion ecclesiology challenges the notion prevalent in United States culture that "the individual is the basic unit of human reality and that all types of community are secondary and accidental."[10] When religion becomes privatized, the communal dimensions of the church are minimized and the church is at risk of resembling other social organizations or clubs within the community whose primary goal is to meet personal or perhaps family needs. Such a church thinks of itself as providing various activities,[11] and it typically understands pastoral care to be a private, therapeutic activity meant to deal with personal crises. In such a church, the focus of ecclesial life easily shifts to encouraging the successful adjustment of individuals to the challenges of life, rather than communal spiritual formation.[12] By contrast, an ecclesiology in which love and communion are at the center helps us to imagine how the church might be a place where we are formed to live out love and continually grow in love.

Fostering Growth in Love

In the NET model of pastoral care, the primary purpose of pastoral care is to foster growth in love. Putting love at the center reclaims a historical emphasis on individual and communal spiritual formation as a central purpose of ministry. At the same time, the NET model of care is a relational model influenced by modern psychological and theological perspectives on the healing power of intersubjective relationships in which the full humanity of each participant is recognized and affirmed. The NET model's perspective on reality and identity, as not given but socially constructed, reflects a postmodern perspective, as does the significant role assigned to interpretation of experience and meaning making. The interdisciplinary nature of pastoral care is revealed in the NET model's use of insights from theology, the social sciences, and the humanities in the development of theory and practice. Given these multiple perspectives and influences, what does growth in love look like in the NET model of care?

Growth in Grace: Theological Perspectives

One of the ways the church has told the story of growth in love is through the doctrine of grace. Grace refers to God's activity in Jesus Christ and "expresses the character of God," which is love.[13] In Christian theology human beings, though created by God, are in need of divine grace because the intended loving relationships between God and human beings and among humans have been disrupted by sin. Sin has been defined in a number of ways throughout the Christian tradition, including disobedience to God's law and broken relationship. However it is defined, sin, both individual and corporate, distorts the image of God in us. As a result, our ability to love freely and fully is constricted, damaging our relationship with God, others, and ourselves. Grace, given freely by God and made manifest in Jesus Christ, restores the image of God within us, enabling us to love God, one another, and ourselves as we have been loved. God's abundant freely given grace restores our ability to love and allows reconciliation between God and humankind and among human beings. The nature of divine grace *is* love.

Salvation and grace are inextricably linked, since redemption comes only through God's grace and not human effort. Historically, the way the church has talked about salvation and the work of grace is through the language of *justification, regeneration,* and *sanctification.* Through God's justifying grace we are restored to right relationship with God. Justification is often referred to as the work God does *for* us. Sanctification is often referred to as the work God does *in* us through grace. Growth in love is our response to the gift of God's generous, healing, restoring, and empowering love.

Sanctification inaugurates a transformative relationship through which the image of God is restored in us and prompts an ongoing process of regeneration and renewal. Growth in grace, as a central dimension of the life of faith, "is a living, moving, dynamic existence" that occurs through the accompaniment of the Holy Spirit.[14] Our whole beings are transformed by grace, "our minds, bodies, feelings, judgments, social relationships," and our imaginations.[15] Growth in grace is a lifelong process through which we experience the "inexhaustible richness of the mystery of God and God's love, ever more deeply and profoundly."[16] Growth in grace is expressed through our growth in love, by intentional action, in response to the love we have received for the flourishing of all.[17]

The doctrine of grace is central to the Christian faith, though views of how it operates differ somewhat within various strands of the Christian tradition. In the

Eastern Orthodox tradition, the term *deification* is used to describe the process of the restoration of the image of God in us.[18] John Calvin called the lifelong process of growth in grace "regeneration."[19] Calvin held that this process occurs for God's elect and cleanses them of guilt, "renewing all their minds to true purity that they may practice repentance throughout their lives and know that this warfare will end only in death."[20] John Wesley referred to the process of growth as sanctification and viewed regeneration as a different process that precedes sanctification, yet he held justification, regeneration, and sanctification closely together.

Wesleyan Perspectives

The Wesleyan tradition is the one in which I stand and it significantly shapes my perspective on grace. Love plays a central role in Wesley's theology of grace. Indeed, Wesley understood divine grace as love. He believed that "authentic Christian life flows out of love, and that genuine human love can exist only in response to an awareness of God's pardoning love to us."[21] So extensive and pervasive is God's love that it is God's grace that makes us aware of our need for God through *prevenient grace*, the grace that goes before. Prevenient grace allows us to acknowledge our need for the gift of "grace provided in justification," which leads to regeneration and inaugurates the process of sanctification through which the image of God is restored and wholeness is brought to human life.[22]

Influenced by the teaching of the Eastern Church, Wesley understood grace as a "co-operant."[23] Divine pardoning love is revealed to humanity through the atoning work of Christ, while our loving response is made possible through the work of the Holy Spirit. The partnership that God initiates begins with prevenient grace but continues throughout the process of salvation. God's prevenient grace makes our response to God's love possible. When we receive and respond to God's grace, a bond is created that allows us to share in God's nature and be renewed in God's image.[24]

Sanctification restores the human-divine relationship broken by sin and leads to a life of health and wholeness through a restored communion with God and neighbor. God not only provides the possibility of a new life through justification but also makes growth in grace possible. Wesley talked about sanctification as "perfection," by which he meant not the absence of human limitations, but rather the restoration of God's perfect love in us.[25] It is only through grace that this perfect love can be restored.

Sanctifying grace, which enables growth in love of God, neighbor, and self, is also a relational and transformational process through which the image of God is restored. While God makes growth in grace possible, our cooperation through participation is required. Wesley suggests that we participate in this process through the means of grace, works of piety, and works of mercy.[26] Works of piety include what we might call *spiritual disciplines* such as prayer, worship, communion, and reading and hearing scripture. Through works of piety, we grow in our relationship with God as we meditate on God's word and enter God's presence in prayer. Through works of mercy we extend the love we have experienced to neighbor and enemy, by feeding the hungry, clothing the naked, and visiting those who are sick or in prison (Matt 25). We, who are loved into a new life, are called to love as we have been loved (John 13:34-36).

Therapeutic metaphors of healing are predominant in Wesley's theology of grace. Salvation may absolve us of the guilt of sin through divine forgiveness, but grace also initiates a "*truly holistic salvation*, where God's forgiveness of sin is interwoven with God's gracious healing of the damages that sin has wrought" (emphasis in original).[27] Healing includes the restoration of individual physical soundness as part of God's plan for the redemption of the whole of creation. Wesley was convinced that God intended both "inward and outward health" and, distinctively, that "*both* dimensions of divine healing can be experienced in the present" rather than only after the resurrection from the dead.[28] Love, which is the nature of grace, brings healing to the soul, mind, and body.[29]

Love and Growth: Psychological Perspectives

The characterization of mental health or psychological maturity as the capacity to work and love is deeply embedded in popular culture.[30] Modern psychology and psychotherapy, which trace their beginnings to the late nineteenth century, are well established as fields of inquiry in which love is a prominent topic. Psychological investigations of love focus primarily on human relationships, though some researchers have extended the study of love to other species.[31] The answers to key questions about the nature of love, including its biological origins and expressions, the development of love as a relational capacity over the life course, and how disorders in loving can be treated therapeutically, depend on the psychological perspective taken.

From the perspective of evolutionary psychology, love is adaptive; we need other human beings to survive.[32] Researchers interested in the biological basis of love have identified oxytocin, which increases in response to expression of affection, as a key hormone "associated with social bonding" and feelings of intimacy.[33] Other researchers have focused on various expressions of love, such as "passionate" love, defined as "an intense longing for a beloved," and "compassionate" love, associated with affection, companionship, friendship, and long-term commitment."[34] One researcher, Ellen Bersncheid, who has sought to provide an overview of the psychology of love, points to the difficulties in doing so because "love is not a single distinct behavioral phenomenon."[35] Rather love is "a huge and motley collection of many different behavior events" connected to each other because "they all take place in relation to another person," and is evaluated as positive emotional experience.[36] Researchers in psychology continue to explore the human experience of love, but much remains contested.[37]

From the perspective of narrative psychology, specifically the work of McAdams, growth in love can be viewed as a moving toward a greater balance between the themes of communion and agency in one's lifestory.[38] The theme of communion is expressed through care, and love for others, while the theme of agency can be seen as care for the self.[39] Growth is also measured in the movement toward greater coherence, openness, credibility, differentiation, reconciliation, and generative imagination.[40] The criterion of generative imagination is closely allied to theological meanings of growth in love. A good lifestory in which generative imagination is substantial extends beyond the self and is expressed in a life concerned with the well being of others.[41] This view of love in narrative psychology fits well with the theological view of love, discussed previously, in which love is expressed through intentional, empathic action in response to love received, with the intention of promoting the flourishing of all.[42]

Narrative Psychology: A Postmodern Perspective

Narrative psychology, in its various forms, is postmodern in its guiding assumptions of reality and identity as not fixed or given, but socially constructed. A primary goal of narrative therapy is the deconstruction of problem stories shaped by dominant cultural narratives that constrain and control, but that often operate outside of our awareness.[43] Narrative gerontology is less concerned with the biological aspects of aging than developing strategies for revising and maintaining life-affirming stories as a part of the ongoing process of adult development in a culture in which aging is seen primarily in terms of physical decline.[44]

A shared assumption of various approaches to narrative care is the central role of meaning making in human lives and stories as the primary vehicle for doing so. A form of narrative care emphasizing meaning making and insisting on the inseparability of mind and body is *narrative medicine*. Narrative medicine was developed primarily by Dr. Rita Charon. Charon asserts that physical symptoms cannot be understood apart from the meaning assigned them by the person who is ill.[45] Not only do people who are ill assign meaning to the illness and tell a story about it, an illness itself can be understood as an embodied story, one that cannot or will not be spoken aloud.[46] In order to fully treat a person's illness and promote physical and psychological well-being, the physician must attend to the larger life narrative in which the story of the illness is situated.[47]

Another shared assumption among narrative psychologies is the critical role of language and symbol in the social construction of reality. The self, as the lens through which we experience reality, is constructed through dialogical and linguistic practices, that is, through the telling of stories in the context of relationship. Narrative perspectives on identity are sometimes considered postpsychological because they locate a person's difficulties in terms of the relationship between the person and culture or society, rather than focusing on internal conflicts.[48] Narrative therapists are not interested in diagnostic categories; rather, the counselor encourages the care receiver to name the problem, and recognize her capacity to influence the problem, thus increasing personal agency and a sense of well-being.

Narrative care in all its forms is hermeneutical, that is, the focus of care is on reading and interpreting the text of a life. Once the text is understood as possible in its uniqueness and complexity, the coauthors, caregiver and care receiver, work together revising and rewriting when needed to develop a good, strong story that is life-giving. All forms of narrative care have implicit norms of what a healthy narrative looks like as well as embedded ethical assumptions about the kind of relationships fostered by healthy narrative development and identity.

The Limits of Modernism

Postmodern psychological theories developed in response to modernist theories of the nineteenth and twentieth centuries that tended to apply universal assumptions to human psychological development. Postmodernism also challenged modernist commitments to progress, whether scientific, or economic, or in terms of an emphasis on personal improvement.[49] Postmodernists argued that the advances of modern culture came with costs, including bureaucratic forms of organization with an emphasis on rational procedures accompanied by pressure "to rationally control the expression of feeling."[50] In the midst of the anonymity of modern society and the breakdown of various forms of community, conformity was achieved through "internal and psychological" controls rather than "external and collective" strategies[51] Within this context, various forms of therapy proliferated in the twentieth century, most of which reflected the "values of modern culture: rationality, progress, consumption, and safety."[52]

Despite modernist attempts to impose rationality and order in society, the tragedies of human existence continued: war, famine, new diseases, and other forms of catastrophe.[53] As a consequence of the advances and discontinuities of modern life in the industrialized Western world, therapy became necessary as a space to deal with the "implications of modernity...in response to the unique dilemmas and situations of the individual client."[54] Generally, the focus of much modern therapy is on the self through introspective processes in which a person examines his or her inner life, often with specific attention to internal conflicts, and the behaviors that express these unconscious conflicts.[55] Modernist approaches to psychotherapy give less attention to the relationship between therapy and society.

Narrative psychologist John McLeod argues that many approaches to psychotherapy may come to be viewed as "distinctly modern cultural inventions" of the twentieth century.[56] By using the language of "medicine and psychology," modern practices of psychotherapy gained legitimacy while ignoring their roots in older forms of religious practice, art, and drama.[57] Psychotherapy "eventually expanded to fill the gaps left behind as traditional forms of problem-solving and meaning making, such as religion, lost credibility."[58] As historian E. Brooks Holifield has argued, language of the soul, once used to talk about the inner life, was replaced with language of the self.[59] As a consequence, psychotherapy often competes with or displaces religion as a form of meaning making for many individuals.

NET (Narrative, Ecclesial, Theological) Growth in Love

Both theological and narrative psychological perspectives inform the practice of narrative pastoral care and the process of growth in love. Implicit in a NET approach to pastoral care is a relational theological anthropology. Emerging from the relationship of love within the Trinity, God's love is extended to humanity through the incarnate Christ, whose death and resurrection enable restoration to a loving relationship with God, self, and others, and promotes ongoing growth in love through the accompaniment of the Holy Spirit. While narrative psychologies do not have a *theological* anthropology, they do have an implicit anthropology and hold a similar relational view of human beings. Narrative psychologies provide more in-depth understandings of human behavior and are also compatible with the theological narrative of growth in love.

Narrative pastoral care, like narrative psychology, understands human beings as hermeneutical or interpretive beings, storytellers who seek to make meaning out of life. Like the narrative approaches we have reviewed, narrative pastoral care also assumes that we are not the sole authors of our lifestories, but rather coauthors, developing our stories in interpersonal, communal, and cultural contexts. Narrative *pastoral* care assumes that God is a principal coauthor of our lifestories. While various forms of narrative care pay attention to the role of narrative in shaping self-identity and developing a good, strong lifestory, narrative pastoral care is concerned with more than psychological health. Drawing on theological understandings of growth in love, narrative pastoral care views healing as part of the process of growth. Indeed, there are times in the practice of pastoral care when healing involves identifying and revising harmful theological and psychological narratives. In many cases healing precedes growth, at other times healing and growth in love are intertwined.

A NET approach to pastoral care draws on a variety of narrative theories, yet has distinctive features. Narrative pastoral care is a communal practice, emerging from the narratives of a particular religious tradition or community. Christian narrative pastoral care is an ecclesial practice reflecting the mission and ministry of the church to foster growth in love of God, self, and others. The NET model is rooted in a theological narrative of love, embodied through the church, which is called to be a community of love. The church has a particular responsibility to live out God's love story by extending narrative pastoral care beyond the boundaries of its own community. Love cannot keep to itself; therefore, the church is called into the world to embody divine love in myriad ways: through conversation, counsel, prayer, worship, preaching, service, and prophetic witness.

When we think of what love actually looks like in practice, we might bring to mind Paul's list of the gifts of the Spirit in 1 Corinthians 12:8-10: wisdom, knowledge, faith, healing, miracles, prophecy, discerning of spirits, speaking in tongues, and interpretation of tongues. Or perhaps growth in love leads to the gifts of prophecy, evangelism, teaching, or pastoring (Eph 4:11-12). But as Paul reminds us, the greatest spiritual gift is love, and he goes on to describe the character of love (1 Cor 13:4-13).

The definition of love that informs a NET approach to pastoral care is one developed by theologian Thomas Jay Oord: "To love is to act intentionally, in sympathetic/empathic response to God and others, to promote overall well-being."[60] This definition is discussed in depth in chapter 4, so for now I want to highlight only the last part of the definition. Growth in love is not self-focused but promotes the well-being of others, facilitating love as a central theme in our lifestories and a way of living. As we grow in love, we become agents of love, facilitating communion with God and each other.

Perhaps you have been fortunate enough to be part of a Christian community with love at the center. As Bolz-Weber indicates, it does not happen all the time, but when it does it is beautiful and real. I have been fortunate enough to experience this from time to time in my life in the church, in the roles of both parishioner and pastor. When my mother was diagnosed with a debilitating degenerative disease when I was a teenager, I found solace and companionship in the church. One couple in particular embodied love by listening to my stories, letting me cry, and feeding me dinner. As a pastor, I witnessed Jenna's and Jim's church community surrounding them with love following the death of their baby.[61] After becoming a professor, finding myself on the other side of the pulpit again, I was privileged to witness a congregation "pursue love" (1 Cor 14:1) as they surrounded the pastor, Ed, his wife, Lucy, and their family with love after his wife's cancer returned with virulence as it spread throughout her body.

When Lucy's cancer returned, the congregation was as devastated as her family. Very quickly, many in the congregation stepped up to preach, lead, worship, and attend to other daily matters in the life of the congregation, leaving Ed free to care for Lucy. Members of the congregation offered pastoral care and support to the pastor's family, and many kept watch with the family at the hospital. I have reflected on this experience elsewhere and an excerpt is presented here.[62]

> The apostle Paul's images of communal ecclesial life echoed our experience: "To each is given the manifestation of the Spirit for the common good" (1 Cor. 12:7 RSV). We felt the Spirit move among us, binding us together as one body in prayer, grief, and love. "Make love your aim," Paul declares (1 Cor 14:1 RSV), encouraging us to open our selves to the greatest spiritual gift of love not meant for us alone but for "building up the church" (1 Cor 14:12 RSV).[63]

Becoming Pastoral Story Companions

Those caregivers who choose to provide narrative pastoral care become pastoral story companions to others in the dialogical coauthoring of lifestories. Drawing on narrative psychologies, pastoral story companions learn how to listen to and read closely the stories of others and be curious about how stories and identity are formed and intertwined. Because lifestories are coauthored, we also must be attentive to our own lifestories, since we will hear the stories of others through the filter of our own.

As pastoral story companions, we are called to shape lifestories that are good, stories that meet the criteria of coherence, openness, credibility, differentiation, and generative imagination.[64] As pastoral story companions engaged in the ecclesial practice of pastoral care, we also seek to bear witness to the intertwining of God's love story with lifestories. In order to be faithful and effective pastoral companions, we need to know something about God's love story as it is recorded in scripture and has been handed down through the teaching of the church. We turn to this task in the next chapter.

Chapter 3
Stories about God

To be a Christian at all is to be a theologian. There are no exceptions.

—Howard W. Stone and James O. Duke, *How to Think Theologically*

The story goes that when Karl Barth, the famed Protestant theologian and author of the voluminous *Church Dogmatics,* was asked to sum up his theology in a single sentence, he reportedly replied by quoting the first line of the children's hymn, "Jesus Loves Me."[1] I have heard this story numerous times, and from what I can tell, it has been repeated many more times in sermons and church newsletters. No doubt the number of people who have heard this story is far greater than those who have actually read Barth's systematic theology. The image of a brilliant theologian quoting a children's song when asked about his own erudite work captures our imagination because *it's a good story, a story about God's love, and a story told in everyday language.*

Our basic theological convictions are most often expressed in such everyday language, even if they are derived from more formal doctrines or the creeds of the church. The primary place we learn the language of faith and hear stories about God is through our participation in the life of the church. Though few us may write volumes of systematic theology, as Christians we all have our stories about God, a theological narrative about who God is to us and how God works in the world. In a real way, a story is all we have. We primarily know God through the stories of the Bible, the history and traditions of our faith, and the rituals and practices of the church.

What is the shape or the central theme of our story about God? Do we see God as a loving parent or a judgmental ruler? Our story about God also tells us something about ourselves: who we are in relation to God, and perhaps most important, how God is disposed toward us. Our story might be that if we are good and obedient, God will keep us safe from harm and never give us more than we can bear. But when crisis or tragedy strikes, that story about God may be challenged. In a crisis, is our story about God strong enough to sustain us, or will we despair and feel abandoned by God? This question is not about God's adequacy, but rather about the adequacy of our *story* about God.

Narrative pastoral care (the *n* of narrative, ecclesial theology or NET) attends to the stories we tell about God, as well as the stories we tell about ourselves, and it understands these stories as being inextricably interwoven. As story listeners, pastoral companions, and coauthors, we can learn something about the person doing the telling by learning to listen to the way in which people compose and tell their lifestories and their God stories. Narrative *pastoral* care is grounded in the biblical narrative as a primary source of revelation about who God is and how God works in the world. The history and tradition of the church and the unfolding narrative of God in human lives in and through culture are additional sources of revelation regarding God's nature and purposes.[2]

When our stories about God are not adequate to provide hope and to foster growth in love, they need to be challenged. We must be well informed about the Christian story through theological study and reflection in order to assist others in coauthoring faithful, hopeful stories and to grow in love, even in the midst of difficult circumstances. In the story that follows, Jenna and Jim found themselves questioning the adequacy of their stories about God in the midst of a profound loss.

A Good Enough Story about God?

I rushed to the hospital as soon as I got the call that Jenna was in labor. I was worried because her labor had begun too soon. As I made my way through traffic, I recalled the excited, joyful announcement of their pregnancy to the rest of the young adult group just a few months ago.

Jenna was no longer in labor when I arrived, and something was wrong. The delivery had been physically and emotionally difficult; the baby had died during labor. Jenna lay on the bed, exhausted emotionally and physically from the ordeal, while Jim held her hand in shocked silence. I offered prayer when it seemed appropriate but largely felt speechless in the face of their tragedy.

Jenna and Jim had access to other caregivers in the hospital but called me, a familiar pastoral companion, a representative of their faith community, to help them make sense of this unexpected twist in their lifestory. After the loss of their baby, Jenna and Jim continued to attend worship regularly and to participate in the young adult ministry. We met and talked on several occasions. Their suffering challenged their faith, which until then had been adequate to their experience. Jenna in particular began to struggle with the image of the God in whom she had believed, a God who rewarded the good. The death of their child raised critical *theological* questions about God's will and God's presence or absence in the midst of suffering and tragedy.

A death of a loved one plunges us into grief. An unexpected death, especially the death of a child, often triggers a psychological crisis. We do not expect children to die. When Jenna and Jim headed to the hospital, even though it was before the due date, they had imagined the outcome as being new parents, holding their newborn as he or she greeted the world with a lusty cry. Their anticipated future story changed in an instant, challenging their stories of themselves. The theological and psychological challenges posed by this loss were intertwined in Jenna and Jim's stories about the death of their baby. Faithful and effective pastoral care had to call attention to the theological and psychological dimensions of their experience and how both would be woven into the larger ongoing narrative of Jenna and Jim's lives.

Theological Reflection in Narrative Pastoral Care

Though we may not encounter the kind of tragedy that Jenna and Jim experienced, most of us do face situations in life that cause us to reflect on the theological and personal narratives through which we interpret events in our lives. Examining the adequacy of our theological narratives is a part of our Christian vocation. When tragedy strikes, we may declare it to be God's will, or we may proclaim God's solidarity with us in our suffering. Both are theological claims. Whether we are conscious and intentional about it or not, when we act out of our Christian beliefs and convictions, we are being theologians. Many of us believe that theology is for experts and academics, beyond the reach of ordinary church members and pastors. Theologians Howard Stone and James Duke remind us that theological reflection is a part of our human response to the divine gift of faith.[3] To think theologically is to think about our lifestories in the light of our faith stories.[4]

Constructing Theological Narratives: Embedded and Deliberative Theology

"Jesus loves me! this I know, / For the Bible tells me so" is the first line of the hymn "Jesus Loves Me."[5] When asked to speak of our faith, we often use the confessional language of hymns, as the great theologian Karl Barth did, or refer to a favorite scripture, or words we have heard repeatedly in our home or church, such as "God is good." Much of the time we rely on the theological narratives we have absorbed growing up in our families, our faith traditions, and the culture around us. Theological statements, such as "The Lord is my shepherd " (Ps 23) or "Lord have mercy" are couched in confessional language, the language of witness, testimony, scripture, or prayer, and are expressions of "embedded" theology.[6] Embedded theology is "first order religious language" that communicates our understanding of "the way in which a person or community's life is related to God."[7] Embedded theology shapes our theological narrative and is an important part of our faith formation and spiritual practice. We also live out of this implicit theological story in our daily lives, as we face ethical decisions or as we strive to love our enemies. It is through the preaching and teaching of the church and through its embodied practices (like hymn singing) that we learn the content of our faith.

We assume that faith statements and practices have easily understood, shared meanings. In reality, many factors shape our embedded theologies and the assumed meanings of faith statements and practices. For example, if I am familiar with the worship practices of African American Protestant churches, I may know that the response to the statement "God is good all the time" is "All the time, God is good." If I have grown up in a predominantly white, middle-class Protestant church I may know that we don't clap after the choir has "performed." If I have grown up in a Korean or Korean American church, I will not be startled in the 5:00 a.m. prayer service when everyone begins praying out loud at the same time.[8] If I have been raised in a church that proclaims the Eucharist as a sacrament in which the real presence of Christ is manifest, I will have a very different understanding of what happens in the ritual of Communion from someone who has grown up in a church that views Communion as a memorial meal of God's past action. All of these differing views also reflect various interpretations of the Christian story.

Likewise, our theology shapes our practices of care. Speaking from an embedded theology I may seek to comfort a grieving friend with the words "God never gives you more than you can bear."[9] But instead of comfort, my friend may hear my words as judging her faith to be inadequate, or she may feel God has abandoned her. Unless I reflect further on the possible multiple meaning of these words and where they come from, I may close off opportunities to comfort my friend. In times of crisis our embedded theology often fails us. In such cases, we may need to reexamine long-held convictions.

Such reflection requires us to engage in "deliberative theology."[10] Deliberative theology is "second order" theological reflection, which explicates and evaluates the implicit meaning of embedded theology.[11] Deliberative theological reflection is not the sole province of academic theologians or Christian professionals. Growth in faith requires each of us to examine beliefs we have taken for granted. Certainly this deepens our understanding of the Christian narrative.

Theological reflection through deliberative theology is also crucial for faithful and effective ministry, including the ministry of pastoral care. The stakes can be high. If Jenna and Jim had not been able to reflect, they might have concluded that God had abandoned them or simply did not exist. Forming a theological narrative that asserted God was with them in the midst of their grief, that God, who also lost a beloved child, would understand their loss, was an essential part of the process of moving through grief. Jenna and Jim had access to caregivers at the hospital trained in grief counseling, but they also wanted *pastoral* care. They wanted to interpret and make meaning out of tragedy in light of their faith.

To provide religious leadership or engage in ministry in any form, we are required to assist others in deliberative theological reflection. Together we examine embedded theological narratives, which may no longer be sustaining. Deliberative theological reflection is not simply an "academic task," if we mean something arcane and not linked to lived faith. Such theological reflection helps us to construct a hopeful and faithful narrative that promotes growth in grace and love, and this in turn prepares us for a more effective, compassionate, and faithful ministry. It is not only our own and others' lifestories we need to understand, but also stories about God: the two are intertwined.

The Language of Theology

Part of seminary education is about engaging in theological reflection on our embedded theological narratives by studying the richness and complexity of the larger Christian narrative. This can be unsettling and disorienting. At times you may feel as if you have lost your faith, or that somebody has taken your Jesus. At times the task requires learning a new vocabulary, a new language. Think of the following section as Theology 101: a quick overview of theological disciplines, doctrines, sources of theological reflection, and theological method. Having some basic knowledge of these helps us to construct our theological narratives.

Theological Disciplines

Theology, in its broadest sense, is "the study of God and the relations between God and the universe."[12] *Theology* can also refer to our doctrine of God, or our specific convictions about God's nature and activity. In this sense of the term, you may refer to "my theology" when expressing a particular set of beliefs about God. You may use theology in the first meaning of the term when Great-Aunt Florence asks what you are doing now and you answer, "I am studying theology." In this sense, theology is inclusive of a range of theological disciplines included in theological education.

Within this larger definition of theology as a field of study, we find various disciplines, including practical and pastoral theology. Other theological disciplines include biblical, historical, and systematic or doctrinal theology. *Biblical* theology articulates the theology contained in the biblical text.[13] *Historical* theology refers to both the provision of "a historical and critical account of the development of Christian ideas, doctrines and beliefs" as well as "a theological analysis of the sources of Christian thought."[14] *Systematic, doctrinal,* and *constructive* theology all refer to the study of the doctrines or teachings the Christian church, including those about God, human beings (anthropology), salvation (soteriology) and the church (ecclesiology).

Within the larger category of doctrine we find dogma or normative statements of Christian belief that the church adopts as its official teaching.[15] These dogmatic statements or teachings are frequently contained in the official creeds of the church and officially sanctioned affirmations of faith. We find an example of a dogma about the nature of the church (doctrine of ecclesiology) in the statement "We believe in the one holy catholic and apostolic church."[16] *Systematic* theology strives to present the major doctrines of the Christian faith in an organized, coherent overview or "system" that remains faithful to the biblical witness.[17] *Constructive* theology "rejects closed systematic frameworks in favor of more open-ended reflections."[18] Both systematic and constructive theologians may use insights and perspectives from culture to provide an organizing perspective on the basic teachings of the church.

Practical theology reflects critically and constructively on religious practices, such as preaching, worship, care, and practices of formation. The purpose of practical theology is a deeper understanding of the theological convictions (theories) enacted through these practices. *Pastoral* theology, a form of practical theology, focuses its

31

critical and constructive reflection on the church's practices of care. Practical theo-logians examine the alignment between our embedded or enacted theology and our stated or professed theology. Sometimes what we say we believe is not reflected in our actual religious practice. For example, a congregation may print "All are welcome here" on its church bulletin or church sign and yet an otherwise well-meaning usher escorts an unkempt, presumed homeless person out of the sanctuary. Practical theo-logians bring theological theories into conversation with theories of human behavior from the social sciences in order to understand and revise practices, closing the gap between theory and practice

Doctrines or Other "-ologies" within Christian Theology

One way to think about how our theological narratives are constructed is to look at some of the major doctrines of the Christian master narrative. Our doctrine of God, or how we understand God's nature and God's activity in the world, is also referred to as *theology*. Our theology articulates our convictions about God's nature, how God acts, how God relates to human beings. Christian theology begins with the scriptural account of God's creative activity, is revealed through "the history of ancient Israel and in Jesus," and is expressed in the present life of the church.[19] The doctrine of the Trinity is an example of a theological claim about God affirmed regu-larly by the church in the recitation of the creeds.

Theological anthropology articulates beliefs about human beings in the world as they relate to God,[20] such as the origin of human beings, what it means to be created in God's image, and what it means for this image to be distorted or lost by sin. Views of how complete this loss is or how radical this distortion is may differ according to various theological perspectives. While our Christian understanding of human beings is drawn largely from "narratives, creeds, and doctrines," these beliefs are also shaped by the larger historical and cultural context in which they are developed.[21]

Christology articulates what we believe about the person of Jesus Christ—who he is and what difference he makes in the world. The central christological dogma of Jesus's full divinity was affirmed at the Council of Nicea in 325 CE against the backdrop of competing views of Jesus's divinity, particularly those of Arius and his followers.[22] The Council of Chalcedon in 451 CE reaffirmed this conviction and emphasized the full humanity of Jesus, thus establishing Jesus Christ's dual nature as fully human and fully divine as a basic dogma of Christian faith within the doctrine of Christology.[23] Whenever we recite the Nicene Creed we affirm the dogmatic con-sensus reached by the early church regarding the dual nature, human and divine, of Christ.

Soteriology is the area in Christian theology that communicates our understand-ing of Christ's saving work. I was once asked once by a third-grade Sunday school student, "How does Christ dying on the cross save us?" It is a very good question and not easy to answer simply. A consensus that Christ saves is central to Christian-ity. *How* Christ saves has received more than one answer throughout the Christian tradition. To take just three examples of many, Irenaeus, Anselm, and Abelard, early church theologians, have given quite different answers about how and from what Christ saves us. Each of these answers is embedded in its own theological narrative.

In his work *Against Heresies*, Irenaeus depicts human beings as held in bondage to the powers of evil, or in his words "sin, death, and the devil."[24] We are freed from this bondage as we attach ourselves to Christ through baptism, die to sin, and rise to a new life in Christ. Irenaeus and other patristic theologians sometimes used the image of ransom to refer to the price that Christ paid for human freedom. Liberation theologians later picked up on this view of atonement to describe Christ's power to liberate us from the bondage of oppression.[25]

In the medieval period (eleventh century) Anselm proposed a different view of atonement in his work *Cur Deus Homo* (why God becomes human).[26] Anselm's view reflects the feudal world in which he lived and he draws on images from it to explain the saving work of Christ. God, depicted as a king, demands obedience to divine rule and requires either punishment or satisfaction of divine justice in the face of disobedience. Humans are finite, sinful creatures and are unable to satisfy the demands of divine justice. Christ, who is perfectly obedient to the divine law, takes the place of (substitutes for) sinful humanity and thus satisfies the demands of the king's divine justice. Anselm's view is sometimes referred to as *substitutionary atonement.* Reform theologians generally held to Anselm's view of atonement but placed emphasis on Christ's sacrifice as satisfying God's wrath, rather than God's justice or honor.[27] *Satisfaction theory* is the term often applied to this version of atonement.

Later in the eleventh century, Peter Abelard wrote of the cross as an expression of God's forgiving love of humanity, even in the face of human rejection of Christ, love incarnate. Salvation effects a change in the human heart and our way of being in the world. Abelard's view, which is also echoed in much modern theology, emphasizes a change in human beings, rather than in the structure of the cosmos (Irenaeus) or in the divine court of justice (Anselm).[28]

Ecclesiology describes our convictions of the nature and purpose of the church as the body of Christ. The church, a community of human beings, is called into existence by God and charged with carrying out God's salvation in this world, guided by the ongoing presence of the Hoy Spirit. In classical ecclesiology the nature of the church is summed up in the Apostles' Creed as "one holy catholic (universal) and apostolic," a view that holds across the Christian church and a variety of theological narratives.[29] There are many different understandings of the purpose or mission of the church. Some of these are drawn from different biblical images, including the body of Christ (Eph 1:22-23), the household of God (Rom 8:29; Heb 2:10-18), or a vineyard (Mark 12:1-2).

Eschatology expresses our understanding of God's vision and final purposes of creation. Because the church is seen as the body of Christ in the world through which God's purposes are being carried out, eschatology and ecclesiology are closely linked. Eschatology is also about the temporality or timing of the reign or kingdom of God, variously as something fully present, as partial and not yet fulfilled, or as only fully revealed in the future or the afterlife.

Sources of Theological Reflection and Theological Method

The particular faith traditions, communities, and cultural contexts in which we have been raised and the sources and methods on which we draw for theological reflection together shape our interpretation of Christian doctrines. Four commonly identified sources of Christian theological reflection are scripture, tradition, reason, and experience.[30] How much authority we ascribe to each source reveals our convictions about the nature of God, human beings in relation to God, and God's activity in the world.

Our theological method is influenced by which source we choose as the starting point for our theological reflection.[31] Do we begin with scripture or with human experience? Is one source more authoritative than others? How are different sources in conversation with each other? One source may become a lens through which we interpret the other sources. Our assessment of the revelatory authority of these sources and the sources' relationships to each other reveals something of the theological method through which we connect our theological beliefs and the practice of ministry. Let's take a quick look at each of these four sources before turning to pastoral theological method.

Scripture

Christian theology begins with the sacred texts contained in the Hebrew scriptures (Old Testament) and New Testament.[32] The sacred texts of scripture are the primary means through which God's nature and activity in history are revealed to us. While the canon of scripture is closed, the revelation communicated through it is ongoing. Differing views of the authority of scripture influence how it functions in our theological reflection. For some, scripture is the sole and final arbiter of theological claims. For others, scripture may be the primary, but not the only, source of theological insight. Other sources of revelation may include tradition, reason, and experience.

Tradition

The tradition of the church is comprised of teachings of the church developed over time and handed on to subsequent generations of believers. One way to glimpse a view of the church's collective teaching over time is through the various creeds of the church, which emerged from theological reflection on the meaning of scripture and significant debate in the church over specific doctrines. One example of a doctrine based on scriptural images and subsequent theological reflection is the doctrine of the Trinity.

While scripture refers to the Father, Son, and Holy Spirit, specific theological claims about the relationship between these three persons of the Trinity emerged later from critical and constructive reflection on scripture by theologians, including Augustine and Aquinas. Their theological arguments, which have become a part church's tradition, were often formed in situations in which Christians were trying to explain and defend the principles of their faith to others outside of their particular cultural and historic context.

Reason

Among the tasks that theologians undertake is making reasoned arguments to present Christian truth claims in ways understandable to those outside as well as within the Christian community. In those arguments theologians often use cultural metaphors or others systems of contemporary thought. Augustine, for example, used language from Neoplatonic philosophy, which would have been familiar to his contemporaries, to communicate Christian truth.

As a source of theological reflection, reason may refer to the process of logical inquiry, or the content of forms of reasoned inquiry carried out by disciplines other than theology, such as philosophy, psychology, sociology, anthropology, cultural studies, linguistic studies, literary theory, and neuroscience. Using other disciplines in conversation with theological principles is a practice that began long ago in the church. Modern pastoral theology draws primarily on psychological theories, but also on sociology, anthropology, cultural studies, feminist theory, and postcolonial theory, for example.

Experience

We often use the term *experience* in everyday speech to describe something that happened, as in, "I had an awesome experience at the airport! I saw my favorite movie star." Experience can also refer to the sum of events over the course of our lives. As a source of theological reflection our primary interest is in *religious experience*, which may be defined as the various ways that individuals and groups "become aware of things or events that are sacred" or encounter the holy.[33] Religious experience includes cognitive dimensions, or what we believe and know, emotional dimensions, such as feelings of trust or love, and volitional dimensions, reflected in our choices and actions.[34]

Convictions differ about how religious experience occurs. Some people say that religious experience is mediated through everyday events. Perhaps we stop to help a homeless person on the street, rather than passing by as we have before, and come to a new understanding of the incarnation. Others view religious experience as extraordinary or distinctively different from common human experience. Throughout the ages, mystics like Julian of Norwich have written of encounters with God through visions, divine visitations, or a profound sense of God's near presence, often while in prayer. John Wesley wrote of his heart being "strangely warmed" as he heard Luther's preface to Romans being read at a gathering at Aldersgate.[35] Individuals may seek encounter with the holy through spiritual practices, such as prayer or meditation. Communal practices, such as worship and sacraments in the Christian tradition, or religious practices, such as fasting and congregational prayer, are usually intended to facilitate religious experience.

Theological method refers not only to the way we approach the various sources of theological reflection, but also to how we move from theological reflection to pastoral practice.[36] Correlational theological methods look for the connections and mutual influence between Christian tradition and culture. How does culture shape religious practices or traditions? How might religious convictions challenge cultural practice? How might cultural values challenge religious practices? A critical correlational method views both religion and culture as potential sources of divine revelation.[37] Practical and pastoral theologians often use a correlational method to make connections between the Christian tradition and the practice and cultural context of ministry.[38]

Let's consider an example of what a correlational method might look like in practice. The biblical call to love not only those who love us, but also our enemies (Matt. 5:44-48) may challenge cultural tendencies to dehumanize or demonize our opponents, especially in war (e.g., calling a regime an "evil empire"). In this case the Christian narrative calls into question the values and practices of cultural narratives. On the other hand, the ecological crisis and resultant cultural movement have challenged traditional interpretations of humankind's charge in Genesis (1:26 NIV) to "rule" over all the creatures of the earth as a call for care and careful stewardship rather than indiscriminate use of natural resources for human benefit alone. In the second example, the changing cultural contexts and values have influenced our interpretation of the Christian narrative.

Religious and Theological Narratives

Stories play a significant role in most religious traditions. Consequently "stories of or about God or gods" often figure prominently in human stories.[39] Though we may have some passing familiarity with the stories of Krishna (Hinduism) or Muhammad (Islam), our knowledge of these other religious stories will be limited unless we have lived with and lived out these religious stories. The stories of a religious tradition "offer possible worlds, created through narrative and portrayed in stories and symbols, rituals and moral guidelines."[40] Religious narratives, composed of stories and doctrines, provide an interpretive framework, a master narrative, through which we understand who we are, whose we are, from whence we come, and some sense of our final destination and give us guidance about what to do in between.[41]

Master Narratives

The master narrative through which we interpret our own lifestories may be provided by a religious tradition, or it may emerge from a national, cultural, political, or economic narrative, or from a combination of these.[42] Communism and capitalism are both examples of a master narrative in which politics and economics are intertwined. For those who have rejected religious master narratives, another usually takes its place.

For some, science may serve as "an all-inclusive story by which to comprehend the universe and their place within it."[43] When one master narrative no longer makes sense for us, we may find ourselves searching for another.

A number of years ago while teaching in Russia, I met a man who had converted to Christianity not long after the collapse of the Soviet Union. He told me that before the collapse he knew who he was—a Communist, a Soviet. His own identity was formed within the master narrative of a political and national identity, and one that formally excluded a religious narrative. When the Soviet Union dissolved and capitalism began to replace or at least transform the communist economy, the master narrative of which he had been a part ended. He found himself confused about who he was. In the midst of his identity confusion, he was introduced to Christianity and became a devoted and active Christian. He now interprets his life through the lens of a new master narrative.

While master narratives can provide wisdom, they are not without problems and can even be dangerous. Oppression and violence have been justified in the name of various master narratives, including religion.

> To focus on religion specifically, however, the excesses of grand master narratives are eminently documented in the annals of history: the unholy alliances with sexism and racism, and the rancor and violence, the ignorance and arrogance in which such alliances have issued the subjugation of countless lives, not to mention other narratives; and the consequent extinction of untold potential for creativity and love.[44]

Master narratives can exert power on individual stories to conform. They can promote some stories and silence others. We recognize this sentiment in words most often attributed to Winston Churchill: "History is written by the victors."[45]

Postmodern theorists, from a variety of fields including theology and pastoral care, have been suspicious of master narratives and have criticized their tendency to deem certain lifestories as acceptable while silencing and marginalizing others. Various liberation movements, including the civil rights movement in the United States, the women's movement, and other struggles for liberation in places around the world including South Africa, have challenged oppressive master narratives. Postcolonial theologians have pointed to the hegemony that Western Christian master narratives have had over other narratives, including those indigenous to a particular culture.[46]

Because our own lifestories may be so formed by a particular master narrative, we may not be fully aware of its influence. For example, the Protestant missionaries who arrived in Korea in the late 1800s, largely from the United States, brought with them a particular version of the Christian master narrative entwined with a Western cultural narrative. Because of their own religious and cultural master narrative, they viewed Korean cultural practices, such as honoring one's ancestors, through this lens. Deeming it a form of worship and therefore idolatrous, they forbade those converting to Christianity to continue worshipping their ancestors.

Confucianism, however, is more properly understood as philosophy. The practice of honoring the ancestors is connected to other Confucian values regarding

37

communal care and responsibility, and its demonization by missionaries undercut an important social value that held the society together by connecting individuals to each other and to their past. In reaction to this prohibition, some converted Christians in a number of places, including Asia, Africa, and the Caribbean, broke away from the influence of the missionaries and formed religious communities that blended Christian and indigenous religious narratives.[47]

Yet master narratives can also have a positive side, not least that we humans are drawn to some kind of overarching framework through which we make sense of our individual stories and experiences. Master narratives can help us feel a part of something larger, connect us to a history longer and more enduring than our own, and perhaps even provide a sense that as our individual stories are part of a larger one, which will continue into the future beyond our physical lives.[48]

Narrative Environments and Theological Narratives

Over the course of two thousand years of history and across various cultures, a recognizable core of the Christian master narrative persists: God creates, redeems creation when it falls through the incarnation, death, and resurrection of Jesus Christ, and sustains creation through the ongoing presence of the Holy Spirit in the unfolding process of redemption. This grand master narrative, however, has been quite plastic, adapting itself to a variety of historical periods, geographical locations, and cultural contexts, or what might be called "narrative environments."[49]

The narrative environments in which we live include not only the larger settings of our culture, religion, and history, but also particular aspects of these, such as nation, region, community, family, denominations, congregation, and important interpersonal relationships. As we move daily though these narrative environments, we experience a particular version of a master narrative, or what Stephen Crites calls our "sacred story."[50] While sacred stories may be present in any master narrative, my interest here is how they function in the Christian master story.[51] I use the term *theological narrative* to refer to the particular way we tell the story of the Christian faith shaped within a specific narrative environment.

An example might be helpful here. While I identify myself as a Christian (a broad term), I grew up in the more specific context of a United Methodist congregation in California that was predominantly white and middle-class. Though I had attended worship in other Protestant churches, they were all fairly similar to what I knew, as were the churches I later served as a pastor. I was not fully aware of how the narrative environment in which I lived out my Christian faith shaped my theological narrative until I moved to the southern part of the United States and attended a funeral at a Black Baptist church.

I had conducted a good number of funerals by this time, but all of them had been in my own native narrative environment. The funeral was unlike any I had attended before and the Christian story expressed through the funeral, while generally similar in shape to the one I knew, had a quite different accent from what I had encountered before. Women in white suits or dresses, most with hats, were walking up and down the aisle. The coffin was open and people going by to pay their respects were openly weeping, some shouting as the organ played in the background. One woman approached the coffin and began to wail loudly and then move erratically, and appeared to faint. The white-suited women moved toward her and attended to her. Several men in black suits carried her from the sanctuary.

I was not used to seeing such an open and dramatic expression of grief during a funeral. Just as I sometimes had difficulty understanding the accents and expressions of patients from the Appalachian Mountains at the hospital where I served as a chaplain, such as "She thinks he hung the moon," I had some difficulty following the particular accent of the theological narrative being enacted in this funeral.

Our theological narratives may be organized around a primary metaphor that points to what we consider most central within the larger story. For example, liberation theology might be understood as a theological narrative that emphasizes God's salvation as liberation from injustice and oppression. This narrative, which draws significantly on biblical images of God's liberation of the oppressed from captivity and bondage, such as the exodus story, becomes for some the lens through which they view the history of the church and its teachings.

Discerning Theological Narratives

Whether you are fully able to articulate it or not, you have some sort of theological narrative, which you may express primarily in confessional language that reflects your embedded theology. Perhaps a life crisis has led you to question the adequacy of the theological narrative and the embedded theology you have inherited from your family or church, as was the case for Jenna and Jim. Or perhaps you are engaged in some formal theological education and find yourself exposed to what seems like a dizzying array of theological narratives and you find yourself wondering which one is most true for you.

Being able to articulate our own theological narrative and assisting others and a congregation as a whole in this process is crucial to the practice of ministry. Our theological narrative will inform our preaching as well as our pastoral care. Being able to discern the theological narratives of those with whom we minister is equally important, not only for pastoral care, as we have seen in the case of Jenna and Jim, but for our entire ministry. Just as individuals develop theological narrative as a particular way in which to understand the larger Christian story, so, too, do congregations.

A good way to discern a congregation's espoused theological narrative is by going to its website and finding a vision, mission, or purpose statement. Such statements intend to communicate something about the identity of the congregation. Here is one example: "Our Mission is to fulfill the First Commandment of Jesus Christ by loving God and our neighbors with heart, mind, soul, and strength. As a congregation we are devoted to being and helping others become disciples of Jesus Christ."[52]

Theological narratives are expressed through worship and embodied in ritual practices. More than one pastor has run into conflict because he or she was either unaware or dismissive of certain dimensions of the theological narrative of the congregation in which he or she served.

For example, in one church I served, congregants had a long history of participating in the Lord's Supper by kneeling at the altar rail and receiving a small individual cup and a Communion wafer from the pastor. Embedded in this practice was a view of this sacrament as a largely private devotional practice, something that emphasized an individual's relationship to Christ, even though the ritual occurred within corporate worship. When the new pastor wanted to emphasize *communion* between the entire community and God, she instituted a common cup, a single loaf, and intinction (dipping the bread into the cup).

The reaction from the congregation was swift and intense. Members expressed objections to the common cup in the language of health concerns, even though this was a religious practice. All those fingers dipping in the same cup was unsanitary, they said, and might spread illness through the congregation. Opponents tried to enlist the support of one member who happened to be the head of the county health department. Competing stories about the meaning of Communion were embedded in these two practices of this ritual.

We need not endorse the theological narrative of a congregation without critical theological reflection. Part of the task of a pastor is to discern and evaluate the theological narratives of the congregation. Are these narratives faithful to the larger Christian narrative? Does the congregational narrative facilitate growth in love and lead to engagement with the needs of the larger community? Pastors and religious leaders have a particular responsibility to facilitate deliberative theological reflection and assist all believers in this vocation.

So how do we go about the process of discerning theological narratives? Aside from reading the church's mission statement, one way to do this is to identify a guiding image or metaphor that already organizes our narrative. Perhaps we organize it around love, liberation, compassion, or justice. We can then explore how this metaphor shapes the way we interpret the major teachings of our faith tradition.

The examples I give in the following table trace the way in which different organizing metaphors may shape our interpretation of some of the major doctrines (teachings) of the Christian tradition. A similar process can be used to identify the theological or religious narratives of other traditions.

Theological Doctrines and Their Guiding Images
Table 3.1 depicts a number of theological narratives and the way in which these narratives interpret some of the core doctrines that comprise the Christian master narrative. Each category across the top of the table represents a particular theological doctrine, while the far left-hand or first column indicates the guiding image or metaphor that informs that particular theological narrative. The guiding images may be drawn from the biblical witness, the tradition of the church, human experience, or a nontheological discipline. In other words, the guiding images may come from any one of the four sources for theological reflection discussed earlier. The chart presents a small sample of various theological narratives and is not exhaustive. The Christian tradition embraces all of these theological narratives; they are not mutually exclusive.[53] Which of them sound familiar to you?

Table 3.1 Theological Narratives, Doctrines, and Practices

Theological Narrative	Theology (God's nature)	Anthropology (human beings)	Christology (person of Christ, e.g., two natures)	Soteriology (work of Christ, e.g., atonement)	Ecclesiology (church)	Eschatology (reign of God)	Practices of Care
Triune God who is love	Triune God: relations within the Trinity love	Image: created for loving relationship. Sin: broken, unloving relationships.	Focus on triune God of love incarnate. Jesus's loving relationships.	Restoring loving relationships in all of creation.	Communion: Love moves out into world.	Banquet: Welcome table.	Create community, foster just and loving relations.
God the creator	Creation ongoing	Image: human beings as cocreators. Sin: uncreative, destructive activity.	Christ as new creation.	Restoring creativity and human capacity for cocreation.	Stewards of creation.	New heaven and earth.	Creative, aesthetic, ecological practices.
God is *Logos*/ Word	Divine reason	Image: capacity to reason. Sin: irrational behavior.	Christ as the incarnate Word.	Restoration of reason and reordering of the will.	Community rightly and reasonably ordered.	Restoration of divine reason and wisdom.	Focused on correct knowledge of God.
God as monarch	Divine ruler	Image: perfect subjects. Sin: rebel against divine rule.	As the perfect, obedient son of a monarch.	Christ's obedience restores us to right relationship.	Community of obedient followers.	Restoration of right order.	Focused on following God's rules.
God as Spirit	Mystical presence	Image: embodied spirit. Sin: separated from God.	Spirit made flesh, blows where it will.	Restores us to intimate communion (deification).	Mystical or spiritual communion.	God's work brought to perfection through the Spirit.	Focus on spiritual practices.
God as liberator	Liberates the oppressed	Image: liberator, shalom seeker. Sin: oppression, bondage.	Christ as new Moses.	Overthrows oppressive and unjust powers and systems.	Nonhierarchical community committed to liberation and justice.	Justice and mercy rolling down like a river.	Liberative practices, justice seeking.
God as Storyteller	Speaks creation into being through love	Image: narrative beings, storytellers. Sin: refusal to participate in process of authoring.	Embodies God's love story. Jesus is the story.	Deconstructs dysfunctional and oppressive narratives.	Community of storytellers joining in God's love story.	Unfolding of God's future story.	Narrative practices: deconstruct problem narratives, construct life-giving stories.
Your image	Your theological narrative	View of human beings.	Person of Christ.	Work of Christ.	Nature and purpose of the church.	Vision of God's reign.	Practices embodying beliefs.

41

Let's look at a couple of examples in more depth, attending to the way a few doctrines may be interpreted through a particular theological narrative. The first is the theological metaphor of God as *Logos*. The second theological narrative we will examine is shaped by the metaphor of God as liberator. This theological narrative has been well developed in various forms of liberation theology.

God as Logos

Let's begin with the image of God as *Logos* (third row) and the narrative constructed from this image. As used in Greek philosophy during the time at which the Gospel of John was being written, *logos* referred to a rational divine intelligence, the rational principle that governs and develops the universe, or divine reason. Many English translations of John 1:1 render *logos* as "word" and capitalize it as a title.[54] The writer of John's Gospel uses a Greek philosophical concept with strong resonance in Greek philosophy to convey a Christian theological conviction about the nature of the incarnate God to readers who were familiar with this philosophical term. God as *Logos* is divine reason, and the source of all knowledge.

Theological anthropology: If God is the *Logos*, or divine reason (which is a theological claim about God's nature), then to be created in the image of God is to be capable of reason. Rationality then becomes the human quality that reflects God's nature. Christian theologians in the patristic period, such as Augustine, as well as in the medieval period, including Thomas Aquinas, "stressed that the human soul was rational and intellectual" and was the seat of the image of God.[55] A corollary to the belief that rationality reflects God's image is a particular understanding of the ordering of the human soul. Reason is the highest capacity, which influences the will, which in turn shapes the affections.[56] Sin, a consequence of the fall, results in the loss or distortion of the image of God, thus leaving us irrational and unable to will the good or follow God's commands.

Soteriology: How do we understand Jesus Christ in this theological narrative and how are we saved through him? In the narrative we are following, Jesus Christ, "the Word became flesh" (John 1:14), who is perfectly obedient to the Word as the Word, comes to restore in us the capacity to obey God's word. Anselm's atonement theory can be associated with this theological narrative.

Ecclesiology: If Word is the means through which God saves, then the role of the church is to proclaim the Word and the establishment of a new order (God's kingdom) in which God's supreme *Logos* reigns. The image of God as *Logos* or Word has, at times, also been linked to monarchial or kingly images of God, which emphasize God's sovereignty and power. Following the theological narrative through to the practice of ministry may lead us to an emphasis on preaching as the principle practice of the church.

For example, the mission statement of one congregation reads, "Our Mission Is To Be A Word-Centered Ministry. We Proclaim The Providence, Presence,

Purpose And Power Of God, In A God-Glorifying, Christ-Centered, Holy Ghost-Empowered, Word-Based, People-Oriented Local Church To Change The World."[57]

God as Liberator

A theological narrative shaped by the metaphor of liberation begins with the lived experience of those who are marginalized and oppressed. This approach to theological reflection also draws on guiding biblical images, primarily from the story of the exodus in the Hebrew scriptures and the concept of freedom in Christ in the New Testament (Gal 5:1, 13). The image of God as one who liberates the oppressed has been prominent in various forms of liberation theology. The first expressions of liberation theology emerged from the lived experience of the oppressed within Latin American societies.[58] Other forms of liberation theology draw on the experience of other oppressed and marginalized persons and include Black liberation theology, feminist theology, womanist theology, and *mujerista* theology.[59]

Theologian James Cone is one contemporary theologian who has drawn attention to the role of liberation in African American Christianity and has played a key role in the development of Black liberation theology.[60] Prominent Latin American liberation theologians include Gustavo Gutiérrez, Leonardo Boff, and José Míguez Bonino, among others. Feminist theologians such as Mary Daly, Rebecca Chopp, and Elizabeth Johnson applied the principles of liberation theology to analyze women's oppression and second-class status. Womanist ethicists and theologians such as Delores Williams, Kelly Brown Douglass, and Emilie Townes have challenged feminist theology's assumption of the universality of white woman's experience and emphasize instead the experiences of Black women.

Theology: God advocates for the poor and marginalized and liberates the oppressed. For enslaved African Americans before emancipation, liberation meant the release from chattel slavery and all its horrors.[61] Cone states that the justice of God, linked with this worldly liberation, has long been a prominent theme in Black religious thought,[62] as have hope and love.[63] Cone argues that while "theologically God's love is prior to the other themes," this love is made known through "divine righteousness, liberating the poor for a new future."[64]

Theological anthropology: Because all persons are created in the divine image of God, they are sacred beings and children of God. Violating the dignity of any person, through slavery, racism, and other forms of oppression, is a violation of God's great commandment to love as we are loved and is an expression of sin.[65]

Soteriology and eschatology: Jesus Christ can be understood as the new Moses who leads the oppressed to freedom. Soteriology and eschatology are closely linked, in that salvation in the form of liberation is not simply a future but a present hope (referred to as *realized eschatology*). Moreover the church as the body of Christ, here and now, plays a key role in bringing God's vision of justice and liberation to reality. Ecclesiology and pastoral practice are shaped by the conviction that Christians are called to enact God's vision of justice and liberation in concrete ways in this world by caring for the poor, challenging unjust social structures, and opposing all forms of oppression, including racism, sexism, homocentrisim, and ageism. A commitment to justice is evident in the Covenant of Oakhurst Baptist Church, a copy of which hangs in the sanctuary and is posted on their website.

> In this fellowship, "there is no longer Jew or Greek, there is no longer slave or free, there is no longer male and female, for all of us are one in Christ Jesus" (Galatians 3:28) Therefore, we reject any status in this fellowship in terms of church office, possessions, education, race, age, gender, sexual orientation, mental ability, physical ability or other distinctions.[66]

The next chapter explores a theological narrative shaped by the metaphor of love. Subsequent chapters present the model of narrative pastoral care, as well as specific practices and strategies of pastoral care shaped by God's love story.

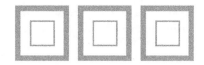

Chapter 4
A Love Story

Dear friends, let's love each other, because love is from God, and everyone who loves is born from God and knows·God.... God is love.

—1 John 4:7-8

Where there is love, there is life.

—Mahatma Gandhi

Not all of us can do great things, but we can all do small things with great love.

—Mother Teresa

In the musical *Fiddler on the Roof*, influences of a changing outside world encroach on the village of Anatevka, undermining the traditions that have ordered life. Tevye is especially baffled by his three oldest daughters' desire to marry for love rather than enter marriages arranged by parental wisdom, as he and his wife Golde did. Trying to sort this out, Teyve asks Golde about love in the duet "Do You Love Me?" Golde is taken aback by the question and at first answers, "Do I what?"[1] After pondering their long years of marriage and shared life, she decides that is what love looks like, so yes, she loves him.

At this point, you might be thinking, "Well, that is a pretty good story, but what does it have to do with pastoral care?" In order to develop a model of narrative pastoral care that fosters growth in love, along with Tevye we need to ponder the nature of love. Is love an emotion, a disposition, a virtue, an action, a pattern of practices, a divine gift, or the nature of God? And where do we turn for answers to these questions?

Popular culture abounds with portrayals of love in music, poetry, literature, television, and film. Love is also a topic of scientific study, both in the social and natural sciences. For example, neuroscientists might locate the origin of love in the structures and chemistry of the brain.[2] Ideas about both divine and human love, and the relationship of these to each other, are found in Judaism, Hinduism, Buddhism, Christianity, and Islam.[3] All of these major religious traditions connect divine and human love and the metaphors they use to speak of divine love are often drawn from loving human relationships, such as those between parents and children or lover and beloved.[4]

Theological Sources for a Narrative of Love

While a variety of religious traditions have rich and complex narratives of love, the focus of this chapter is to develop a specifically Christian theological narrative of love. Let's begin by turning to the four sources of theological reflection. Here I draw significantly on the recent work of Catholic theologian Werner Jeanrond and Protestant theologian Thomas Jay Oord in the construction of a theological narrative of love for narrative pastoral care.[5]

Scripture: Biblical Views of Love

Both the Hebrew scriptures and the New Testament "consider love *a*, if not *the*, primary attribute of God."[6] The scriptures repeatedly affirm divine love as the basis of the relationship between God and God's people. We do not, however, find a concise definition of *love* in either the Hebrew scriptures or the New Testament, and multiple Hebrew and Greek words are translated into the singular English word "love." Though many of the languages, cultures, and religious traditions of the world have a more nuanced and complex vocabulary to describe this human experience, the English language renders it with the singular word "love."[7]

Some of the words (*dod, 'aheb, hesed,* and others) that the Hebrew scriptures use to describe the nature of the relationship between God and God's people depict different nuances of love.[8] The meanings of love contained in the range of words used include "obedience to God's commandments, serving God, showing reverence for God"; a close relationship, which might or might not connote sexual intimacy depending on the particular term and its usage; and a connection between love and forgiveness.[9] The process of the Septuagint translation reduced these broader understandings of God's love and restricted the vocabulary of love to the Greek terms *agape, philia,* and *eros.* We can trace some of the subsequent difficulties in holding together both *agape* and *eros* within divine love in the Christian tradition to a restricted view of love in the Hebrew Bible as a result of the process of translation.[10]

Although differences exist between the views of love in the Hebrew scriptures and the New Testament, both proclaim God as the origin of love. Divine love emerges from God's activity as creator and redeemer of creation.[11] In the Hebrew scriptures, God's love is enacted through covenant and the greatest commandment within the covenant is the commandment to love God with one's whole being (Deut 6:4-6).[12] This love relationship between God and God's people set out in the Sinai covenant is less about intimate affection and more about obedience, reverence, and loyalty to God alone. Despite differences in emphasis, language, and expression, both the Hebrew scriptures and the New Testament agree that among the many attributes of God are faithfulness, mercy, and forgiveness.[13]

The biblical witness is also in agreement that divine love makes human love possible. To accept the divine offer of love is to recognize that God's love is all encompassing and "implies accepting and respecting the creative power of God's love and presence," and loving others and oneself.[14] The New Testament portrays Jesus as clearly holding together the love of God and neighbor, as is evident in his formulation of the double commandment to love God and "your neighbor as yourself" (Matt 22:37-40). In the Synoptic Gospels, God's love is the basis of a loving relationship between humans and God and between human beings. The character of this love calls for deliberate action, or a "praxis of love," rather than merely emotion or legal debate.[15] John's Gospel expands the praxis of love by including the dimensions of communal concord and Jesus' self-giving love.[16] The Apostle Paul names love as the highest spiritual gift (1 Cor 13:13).

Tradition: The Teachings of the Church on Love

Many of the earliest theologians of the church sought a deeper understanding of the biblical command to love God and neighbor and turned to the language and concepts of the culture around them to convey the unique meaning of Christian love to those both within and outside of the church. When speaking of love, the New Testament writers most frequently used the Greek words *philia* and *agape*. *Philia* speaks of human love and describes the mutual affection and regard that exists between friends or those connected by the bond of faith.[17] *Agape* denotes a distinctive theological understanding of the quality of God's love, which is given freely without consideration of the "goodness or lovability" of the one loved or the expectation that the beloved will meet the lover's needs.[18] *Agape* is love for its own sake. Through the long theological history of the church the question of the relationship between human and divine love persists.

Early Church

Theologians of the early church drew on the Greek term *eros* (though it does not appear in the New Testament) to designate a particular form of human love. While we often associate eros with romantic or sexual/erotic love, it more accurately describes love that is motivated by desire and the needs of the lover with the expectation that the beloved will fulfill those desires.[19] Both ancient and more recent theologians have paid significant attention to the relationship between these forms of love. Augustine of Hippo, whose life bridged the fourth and fifth centuries, has been one of the most influential theologians in Christian history, particularly in the Latin or Western tradition. We may, however, be unaware how his thinking has shaped our own on a variety of theological topics, including love. Love plays a central role in Augustine's theology and he wrestles with questions about the nature of God's love and its similarity to or difference from human love. Augustine draws primarily on biblical sources for his theology of love, though he often makes connections to concepts from Neoplatonic philosophy, which was familiar to both Christians and non-Christians of the time.[20]

Love is a central theological category for Augustine. To him, all Christian doctrines, from the Trinity to love of neighbor, involve the concept of love.[21] For Augustine, love of God and love of neighbor are inextricably intertwined. Our love for others is an expression of God's love for us. Augustine used the Latin term *caritas*, which translates into English as "charity," to refer to the particular nature of God's love and Christian love for neighbor.[22] *Charity*, however, does not fully embrace the meaning of the term for Augustine and additional terms, such as *grace, favor, love*, and *benevolence*, are needed to adequately reflect what Augustine meant by it.[23] In Augustine's usage *caritas* love for God and to God is primary, a love made possible by God's love for humankind.[24] *Caritas* is love rightly directed toward God; all other forms of proper love and virtues emerge from it.[25] *Cupiditas*, a consequence of sin, is misdirected love, a self-interested love that seeks fulfillment of its desires in transient things of this world that cannot satisfy our desires and leaves us anxious and empty.[26] In *Enchiridion*, Augustine makes clear this distinction between love that is properly ordered or rightly directed and love that is not: "When one asks whether a human being is good, one does not ask what this person believes or hopes, but what he or she loves. The person who loves in the right way, undoubtedly believes and hopes in the right way."[27]

Augustine identifies four proper objects of love: our selves, our bodies, our neighbors, and God.[28] Augustine believes that love for self and body come naturally to us, while love for God and others require specific commandments. Although love of God is the first commandment, Augustine holds that "love of neighbor comes first in time as a necessary prerequisite."[29] He explains that as we grow in love we become more like God and "aware of God as a radically mysterious other—our eternal and everlasting good."[30] In *The City of God*, Augustine describes an earthly city created by improperly directed self-love that leads to the domination of others, and a heavenly city, created by the love of God, the highest good, and characterized by humble self-giving love to others.[31] While we now dwell in the earthly city, it is not our true home, but rather the "means for our return to God."[32] God's descent to human beings in Christ enables our ascent to God and our return to our true home. Augustine paints a picture of Christians as pilgrims in an alien land, an image that continues to be both influential and sometimes problematic in Western Christianity.[33] But perhaps Augustine's greatest contribution to the tradition is his assertion that the love expressed within the Trinity through the Holy Spirit is "the same love offered to Christians."[34] The human will, reformed by the Holy Spirit, not only receives the gift of freedom but also "enables it to love with divine love."[35]

The Medieval Period

We find few significant contributions to the theology of love in the early Middle Ages. Augustine's influence persisted, but the difficulties of life in feudal Western Europe in the Middle Ages apparently left little room for scholarly reflection on love.[36]

The church's suspicion of eros and its identification with sexuality and disordered love influenced attitudes toward celibacy as the higher moral path, marriage as a necessary though lesser virtuous choice, and procreation as the only justification for sexual relations in marriage.[37] A consequence of attempts to remove eros from sexual relations led to a devaluing of sexuality, the reduction of women to the roles of procreation and "remedy" within marriage for "the flames of passion," and a sense of shame attached to most forms of human love.[38]

A rediscovery of love emerges in the eleventh and twelfth centuries in the writing of the mystics around the same time as notions of courtly love developed.[39] One of the theologians who contributed to new views of love during this period was Peter Abelard (1079–1142). We touched briefly on his contribution to atonement theory in the previous chapter. For Abelard, salvation is the expression of divine love. In contrast to Augustine who believed that love of neighbor was an expression of the love for God, Abelard held that "God's love is discovered and realized in human relations."[40]

One, if not the most, influential theologian of the high Middle Ages was Thomas Aquinas (1225–1274), whose use of Aristotle's philosophy in his theological method significantly influenced the course of scholastic theology.[41] Aquinas discusses the topic of love in both the *Summa Theologica* and a dedicated treatise on the subject entitled *De Caritate* (On Charity.) While Augustine held that God's love made rightly ordered human love (*caritas*) and our return to God possible, Aquinas understood this return as a purification by God's love, one that allows us to rise to God's level. God's love flows downward to humankind, allowing our upward rise to salvation.[42] This metaphor of salvation as ascent medieval art often depicted with a ladder of virtues stretching from earth to heaven.[43] Scholastic thinkers like Aquinas maintained that while we are to love God for God's own sake, we also find "personal happiness, joy, and heavenly reward" by loving God.[44]

The Reformation

A profound shift occurred during the Reformation regarding the role of love in the process of salvation. We will look specifically at Martin Luther's view as the first of the reformers. For Luther, God's love is received through faith alone, and one is solely dependent on God's grace for salvation. One's own actions, such as prayer, fasting, or almsgiving, which might help one ascend the ladder of virtue and demonstrate one's rightly ordered love for God, gain one nothing.[45] Luther rejected Aquinas's notion of striving toward heaven with love focused solely on God, which might also benefit one's neighbor, in favor of the notion of God descending to the human level.[46] Here, all the initiative comes from God. This shift from human ascent to God to God's descent through incarnation had a profound effect on the understanding of neighbor love.[47] This shift in emphasis from human love reaching up toward God to God's love flowing down toward humankind continues to be influential in current Protestant theology.

Reason

We have already seen examples of the use of reason as we skipped through several centuries of the church's teaching on love. Reason can refer to both the process and content of reasoned inquiry on a question. Augustine used familiar concepts of Neoplatonic thought and Aquinas turned to Aristotle's method of philosophical inquiry to engage in theological reflection on love. Although philosophy is still utilized in reasoned theological inquiry, both the social and natural sciences have now joined the conversation. The literature on the psychology of love is quite vast and it would be difficult to summarize. We will focus here primarily on the methods used in the psychological study of love.

The psychology of love, as distinct from a theology or philosophy of love, has a relatively short history, beginning at the end of the nineteenth century and the beginning of the twentieth with the work of figures such as Sigmund Freud and William James.[48] The psychology of love focuses on the human experience of love, particularly as experienced through loving relationships. A variety of approaches are used in the psychological study of love. Research psychologists may conduct large-scale surveys in which respondents are asked about their "thoughts, feelings, and actions toward those they love" and then analyze these findings to identify common qualities of love, such as caring.[49] Such studies depend on accurate self-reports but may also be influenced by the investigators' own assumptions when interpreting the data to find common qualities.[50]

A second approach to the study of love is based on the researcher's or clinician's observations of love from which he or she then develops a theory of love or some kind of classification system.[51] Both Freud and James utilized an observational method to develop theories of love, as have attachment theorists who focus on the way children form bonds of love with their parents or caregivers.

Until very recently, much of the psychology of love focused primarily on the consequences of the problems and failures of love, whether in the parent/child relationship or in romantic relationships.[52] Positive psychology, however, has identified love as a character strength and is interested in love as a positive trait evident in caring relationships.[53] In their study of human love, positive psychologists make a distinction between *interpersonal love*, such as that expressed between parents and children, and altruism or regard for the other, what in theological language we would call *neighbor love*.

Altruism has received increasing attention from both the social and natural sciences. A number of experimental studies have been conducted to determine the conditions under which a bystander will or will not assist a stranger in distress.[54] One of the questions this research tries to answer is about what motivates care for another. Do we care for others only if it benefits us, or are we capable of putting our own self-interest aside to promote the well-being of another? Psychologist C. Daniel Batson asked exactly these questions in his social/psychological research on altruism.[55] Neurologists, geneticists, and evolutionary biologists have also tried to untangle the mystery of love and altruism. Is there something in our brains, our genes, or our evolutionary history that leads us to care for others even when it seems contradictory to our best interests?[56] We can hear in these questions the echo of Augustine's questions about the proper motivation for love.

Experience

Experience can refer both to general human experience as well as to specific personal experience. When it comes to thinking about love, both types of experience might provide helpful resources for our theological reflection. If you have any question that love is important to most people, just ask them! You may find, as the World Values Survey (United States version) did, that 90 percent of Americans report that love is highly valued in social relationships, and particularly in marriage and family relationships.[57] This same survey reports that 95.7 percent of Americans say their loving family relationships are most important to them.[58] Other surveys show that altruism is also highly valued.[59]

When it comes to religious experiences of love, we might turn to our own experiences within religious communities in which we experienced both God's love and neighbor love. We might also turn to the testimonies of religious mystics, who often speak of direct, loving experiences with God. We will look briefly at one example here.

A new form of religious life for laywomen took form in the thirteenth century with the Beguines.[60] Women who joined the Beguines sought to live lives of poverty, chastity, and obedience either alone or in organized houses, but without taking vows or joining established orders.[61] These women were "dedicated to prayer and contemplation for the sake of the knowledge of God through love."[62] In addition to earning a living through selling handmade crafts, they engaged in various acts of charity in the world, teaching girls and attending to the sick, the poor, and the dying.[63] In the midst of the catastrophes of war and plague these laywomen lived out Christ's love.[64] They also had a deep desire for mystical union with God, expressed often in the language of courtly love.[65] Lacking full access to theological education and resources available to monks or some women in established orders, the women of the Beguines relied heavily on personal experience as the "central source for their theological thinking."[66]

Summary

Let's summarize what we have learned from these sources for a theological narrative of love. Our starting point is the biblical affirmation of God as the origin of love. God's nature *is* love. God's love creates a reciprocal bond; God's love makes possible our love of God and one another. Love occurs in a relational context between subjects and intends the flourishing of the other. Any definition of love that shapes our pastoral theology and practice must be grounded in this biblical witness to love, as well as in human experiences of love.

In constructing a theological narrative of love for pastoral care we also draw on theological sources from tradition and from our reasoned reflection to affirm the centrality of God's love, and the possibility of our participation in love also informs our narrative. Scientific studies of love that help us understand the relational and reciprocal nature of love give us deeper insight into the human experience of love as a form of participation in God's love. We also draw insight from our own experiences of love within family relationship and communities of faith, and these experiences provide us with metaphors through which to speak of divine love.

Let's return for a moment to table 3.1 in the last chapter and look at some key doctrines through the lens of love. "God is love" (1 John 4:8) is one of the biblical pronouncements on which claims of this narrative about God's nature are built (*theology*). Theologians of the early church moved from this biblical image about the nature of God to considered arguments on the nature of divine love existing within the Trinity.[67] Human beings are created by God in God's image and are intended to reflect divine love, though on account of sin we often fail to love as God loves (*theological anthropology*). Through God's love revealed in the incarnation, death, and resurrection of Jesus Christ, we come to a deeper apprehension of God's love for us (*Christology*). Through God's love manifested in Christ, we are restored to a loving relationship with God (*justification*) and empowered to grow in our love of God, self, and others (*sanctification*) though the companionship of the Holy Spirit (*pneumatology*). The purpose and mission of the church (*ecclesiology*) as the body of Christ in this world is to proclaim and embody God's saving love (*soteriology*) within and beyond the Christian community, as also the belief that Christ will come again (*eschatology*).[68]

Through this exercise, we have developed an outline of a theological narrative of love, but we do not yet have a fully formed story.

The Relationship Between Divine and Human Love

One of the key questions in a theology of love is the relationship between human and divine love. Are human and divine loves of the same order? Can human love be described in scientific terms without reference to God's love? Does some similarity exist between them? Are they part of the same continuum or are they distinct?

Theologians come down on different sides of the question even while referencing the same scriptural texts. Augustine is on the side of those who argue for some distinction, though not a complete disjunction, between human and divine love. Augustine held that "only God can love or be loved," and that though we are called to love our neighbor as ourselves, loving our neighbor is actually a form of loving God, and a form of God's love.[69] Augustine is primarily concerned with "what God is doing in and through human love" and is less confident about human efforts to love.[70] Augustine's view has been influential for a number of Christian theologians including Martin Luther, Søren Kierkegaard, Anders Nygren, Karl Barth, and Eberhard Jüngel.[71] All of these theologians wanted to make some distinction between natural human love and authentic Christian love.

Theologian Anders Nygren put forward the most forceful argument for the radical distinction between divine and human love in the twentieth century. Although numerous theologians have challenged Nygren, his views still hold considerable influence even in the twenty-first century.[72] Nygren makes a sharp distinction between *eros*, which he identifies as the Platonic concept of love, and *agape*, which represents the Christian view of love.[73] Human love is identified with *eros*, which is "egocentric and desiring love which strives to reach the divine sphere by its own strength" while *agape* "originates from God and therefore requires a human attitude of receptivity and passivity."[74] Nygren seeks to elevate divine love and protect it from distortions of human desire. The radical distinction between human and divine love results in God's being the only subject of love. Human beings become mere conduits of God's love.[75] As Thomas Jay Oord rightly points out, this view poses a significant challenge to our ability to follow the commandment to love God "if only God can love."[76]

In contrast to a theology of love that sees a radical distinction between divine and human love, contemporary Catholic theologian Werner Jeanrond draws on biblical and theological sources to retain some sort of human agency or participation in love. While Oord also draws significantly on biblical views of love, his perspective is significantly influenced by the theology of John Wesley.[77] Wesley's view of grace affirms that love originates in God, who "initiates relationships moment by moment and [to which] creatures freely respond."[78] The concept of prevenient grace allows us to retain the primacy of God's initiative in love while also affirming the free response of creatures. For Wesley, the content of God's grace is love, so we may think of love and grace as synonymous.

Drawing on different sources within the tradition, Jeanrond also rejects the notion that human beings are simply conduits for divine love and that other human beings are primarily a means to express our love for God. Love requires our participation, yet God "wills and respects the freedom of human beings to say yes or no to the invitation to participate in the dynamics of love."[79] How we answer the question of the relationship between divine and human love will have a significant impact on our definition of love, to which we now turn.

Love Defined

While Golde and Tevye are trying to puzzle out the human experience of romantic love, they remind us that love is not only about what we feel but what we do. At the beginning of the chapter, the quotation by Mother Teresa expresses the same sentiment as does Golde in her response to Tevye's question: love is expressed through our actions. In defining love, I employ Oord's definition: "To love is to act intentionally, in sympathetic/empathic response to God and others, to promote overall well-being."[80] Behind both Mother Teresa and Oord's statements we hear the echo of the parable of the good Samaritan (Luke 10:25-37) in which Jesus answers the question of what it means to love one's neighbor and who counts as one. Love, as a way of living, undergirds the theological narrative presented in this chapter. Oord's definition of love is intended to be descriptive of both divine and human love and "to account for all actions we should genuinely call loving."[81] Let's look more carefully at the components of this definition.

Love, both human and divine, that intentionally promotes "overall well-being" is grounded in the common testimony of the Hebrew scriptures and the New Testament, in which "the essence of love is doing good or being a benefit."[82] God, whose nature is love, intends the good of others, and we are to do likewise through our love of others. In explicating the commandment to love God and neighbor, Jesus tells the story of the Samaritan who attends to the man left for dead by the side of the road and takes action to love the man by doing good and restoring his health and well-being. Though the term *well-being* is not a biblical phrase and is more often found in the social sciences, Oord argues that it encompasses a number of biblical terms, such as *blessing*, that refer "to benefitting, helping, and being or doing positive things" or "doing good."[83]

Concern for well-being encompasses not only concern for the physical, emotional, mental, and spiritual well-being of individuals, it also requires justice and attention to the structures of society that promote or thwart communal well-being. Oord's qualifier "overall" denotes that love is more directed to the "common good" (1 Cor 12:7) and includes the stranger, the outcast, and the enemy.[84] Love and justice are connected. The reign of God, proclaimed by Jesus, is also an expression of God's love, which intends the well-being of creation. The well-being of the entirety of creation "requires creaturely contribution," and those who respond to God's love are called to seek and participate in God's reign.[85]

Love occurs in the context of relationship, including the relationships within the Trinity, between the triune God and creation, including humanity, and among human beings. The relational character of love is behind Oord's claim that love occurs in the context of "sympathetic/empathic response to God and others."[86] As we saw in our brief review of scripture and Christian tradition, God is understood as the origin of love. "We love because God first loved us" (1 John 4:19). While love emerges from the context of relationship, love is not to be equated with relationship. Some relationships do not express love, and love may require us to sever relationships that promote evil.[87] Love can occur in a number of different relationships but, given the centrality of love in Christian theology, the church holds a particular responsibility for fostering love. The church, however, should not be blindly equated with love. Even a brief review of the history of the Christian church reveals the danger of assuming that involvement in the church necessarily leads to the expression of Christian love.[88]

Love defined as intentional action is also grounded in biblical accounts, including Jesus's command to the lawyer to "go and do likewise" following his telling of the story of the good Samaritan (Luke 10:37). Intentional action can include cognitive and emotional dimensions that may not result in visible action, as well as specific visible actions.[89] Intention can also motivate a pattern of action or set of practices designed to promote individual and communal well-being. An intention to promote the well-being of another must be deliberate; that is, we must think about what we intend, if only momentarily. Additionally, our motives must intend good, not harm, though we cannot guarantee that our motives will ensure well-being in the other. Love must also be freely given, not coerced, even though our freedom may be limited.[90]

A definition of love as intentional action that is relational and moves toward the promotion of well-being contributes to the construction of a pastoral theology of love by providing a view that is based in the Christian witness of scripture, tradition, reason, and experience. A second contribution of this definition is the conviction that the church has a central role to play in forming persons in love. This definition can allow us to explore the particular role of pastoral care in the process of growth in love.[91] Emotion is included as one element of love, but we might also say it involves a particular way of being in the world, which gives rise to a specific set of practices.

Love as a Practice

As we move toward constructing a theological narrative of love to inform narrative pastoral care of love, we can conceive of love as a form of Christian practice. Both practical and pastoral theologians have paid significant attention to Christian practices and have defined these terms in a number of ways.[92] Elsewhere I have described Christian practices as embodying our beliefs about and understandings of the world and as being one of the ways in which we live out our vision of the church.[93] Both social processes and the divine/human relationship through which we are constituted as persons shape Christian practices. Through Christian practices, we respond to God's grace by attending to human need in light of and through God's transformative love.

How might we envision love as a Christian practice? Theologian Werner Jeanrond proposes the concept of a Christian "praxis of love," which holds together the loving encounter with the other and "ongoing critical and self-critical reflection."[94] Though the terms *practice* and *praxis* are not identical, they share common roots.[95] Jeanrond's use of the term "praxis of love" refers to what I call the Christian practice of love. In the sense that I am using the terms here, both praxis and practice require critical reflection on actual practice, and though technically the meanings are not identical, for the purposes of this discussion I am using them interchangeably.

The starting point in developing this Christian practice of love is the biblical witness, beginning with the Hebrew Bible. New Testament accounts portray Jesus as the one who lives and proclaims God's praxis of love, reaching out to all sorts of people: friends and enemies, neighbors and strangers, and especially those who are weak, sick, marginalized, poor, and powerless.[96] This praxis of love extends God's goodness to all and love gathers "all people around God's creative and reconciling presence."[97] The praxis of love includes the presence of desire, and the encounter of difference. Jeanrond eloquently describes the praxis of love:

Love seeks the other. Love desires to relate to the other, to get to know the other, to admire the other, to experience the other's life, to spend time with the other. Nobody else can love in my place. There is no vicarious love. Love requires a concrete agent, a loving subject.... Hence love always includes emotion, yet it is more than emotion. It has the potential to affect the entire fabric of our human relationship.[98]

A Christian praxis of love asserts that divine love and human love are intertwined, though not identical. Because God is the origin of love, "God's love is and remains divine" while "our love is and remains human."[99] Despite human failures to love, God's self-giving love remains steadfast. Divine love for human beings enables what Jeanrond calls a "process of humanization" in which "God wills and respects the freedom of human beings to say yes or no to the invitation to participate in the dynamics of love."[100] Historically this process has been called *sanctification*, or what I am calling *growth in love*.

Toward a Theological Narrative of Love

Our theological narrative of love begins with the assumption that God's nature *is* love. Human love is made possible by God's love. God's love freely given makes it possible to love the stranger and move beyond our own self-concern. Love does not deny the reality of human sin. It is God's love, through prevenient grace, that illumines our sin and our need to be restored and invites us to participate in "God's creative and reconciling project of love."[101] Saving love makes possible and indeed requires that we participate and grow in love toward God, self, other, and the whole of creation.

Participation in love makes our Christian practice (or praxis) of love possible. Human beings are not passive funnels of divine love but are invited to become active and responsible agents of love.[102] An essential dimension of salvation is "becoming a full and fulfilled subject with others and with God in and through love."[103]

Participation in love requires an ongoing critical assessment of the structures of evil and sin, both individual and corporate, which continue to distort human life and all of creation. Continuing participation and growth in love requires an "acute awareness of the need for confession, conversion, forgiveness, reconciliation and healing."[104] These are not conditions for divine love. Yet participation in love initiates a critical review of the personal, social, political, economic, and cultural contexts in which love occurs.[105]

Love is a relational practice and cannot occur in isolation. One's own experience of love is "always already part of the universal love story initiated by God."[106] Participation in love also requires lifelong support and a sustaining community. A theological narrative of love is lived out in the mission of the church to increase the love of God and neighbor. The communal experience of participating in love may challenge the postmodern tendency to focus on love of the individual and neglect the broader dimensions of love.

In order to promote growth in love, our theological narrative of love must be able to draw an analogy between divine and human love. Oord's definition of love applies both to God and human beings. If no distinction exists between the kind of love expressed by the creator and that expressed by creatures, we can draw an analogy between divine and human love. Only this conviction "makes the possibility of imitating God make sense."[107] Though God and humans may express the same *kind* of love, the *forms* of love (*agape, eros, philea*) each expresses may differ.[108] All of the forms of love promote well-being, but each in its own way. God "intentionally responds to ill-being by promoting overall well-being" through *agape* while divine *eros* "appreciates the value of others" and desires the enhancement of what is valued, and in *philia* God works "cooperatively with creatures to increase the common good."[109] God's love is multidimensional, yet freely given.

The God of love who calls us to participate in love and makes this participation possible is a relational, passible being "affected by those with whom God relates."[110] God is affected by creaturely participation or nonparticipation in love, yet God's "nature as love remains unchanging."[111] It is God's love that makes creaturely response possible, and though these responses to God's love may shape the particular form of love that God expresses, the essential nature of God as love remains. Because God loves freely and does not coerce, God calls each being to love "within the particular circumstances that each creature faces."[112]

Love is God's nature, our human vocation, and a central mission of the church. Created in God's image, we are created by and for love. Critical reflection on love is an important and appropriate starting point for pastoral theology and pastoral care, which, as ecclesial practices, share in the church's mission of forming persons in love and fostering participation in the process of growth in love. Although love is not confined to the church, the church does have a particular role in proclaiming divine love and fostering the formation of and growth in love, as well as healing the consequences of the failures of human love in both individuals and communities.

Love as a practice involves intentional action and is rooted in the context of relationship (human/divine and human/human). As it promotes well-being, it also embraces friends, neighbors, strangers, enemies, all created beings, and the earth itself. Pastoral story companions proclaim and witness to God's love story unfolding in the midst of lifestories.

Part II

Being Story
Companions

Chapter 5

Becoming Story Companions

Their story, yours and mine—it's what we all carry with us on this trip we take, and we owe it to each other to respect our stories and learn from them.

—William Carlos Williams

The pastor who does not listen has forfeited the right to speak.

—Graeme Griffin

To enter into another's lifestory is to enter a holy space. As the poet William Carlos Williams reminds us, stories are all we have, all we are. The practice of narrative pastoral care invites us to become story companions to one another, listening in the midst of suffering, listening as a life unfolds, listening for the presence of God. Story companions give attentive reverence to the other and the other's stories, and such companions open themselves to learn from the other.

The English word *companion* derives from the Latin *com + panis*, which literally means "bread mates."[1] Companions are those with whom we break bread, sharing a substance that sustains our bodies. When we eat together, we talk, sharing events of the day, telling tales of the past and hopes for the future. Story companions share a substance that sustains our lives and our souls: the stories we have been, the stories we are, the stories we hope to become. Pastoral story companions pay particular attention to the story God is weaving through and in an unfolding life narrative, inviting and empowering growth in love. For story companions in the Christian tradition, the image of companions as bread mates has significant resonance in the sacrament of Communion or Eucharist. Together we break bread, "take and eat," remembering, receiving healing, restoring, transforming, sustaining grace.

Pastoral Vignette: "Will You Accompany Me?"

Early in my ministry, while I was the pastor of a small congregation, Susan, one of its members, asked if I would visit her friend Dianne.[2] Though not currently active in a church, Dianne had asked Susan if she thought her minister would come and see her. All I really knew about Dianne was that she was a friend of Susan's and had been diagnosed with cancer.

When I arrived at Dianne's home, her adult son greeted me at the door, ushered me into the living room, gestured toward his mom sitting in a beige recliner, and disappeared. The first thing I noticed was the blue scarf covering Dianne's head, bald from the hair loss that accompanies intense chemotherapy. She did not get up. She looked up at me standing just inside the door and said, "I am glad you are here. I don't know much about dying." Sitting down and collecting myself, I stammered, wondering what I should say.

Reflection

This encounter has stayed with me throughout my ministry, not because I had the perfect response, but because it taught me something essential about pastoral care. What caused me to stammer were the words "I don't know much about dying." I thought I was supposed to be the expert, that I should have answers, and I knew I didn't.

Only upon later reflection did I realize that her first words were "I am glad you are here." Only later did I realize she was inviting me to become a story companion. I don't believe she wanted an expert on death or the psychology of grief; such a person would likely have been available to her through the hospital. Nor do I think she wanted answers. I think she wanted someone willing to hear her questions, to "hear her into speech."[3] She was inviting me to accompany her into unknown territory, to become a story companion who would remind her of the stories of her faith, which proclaims a love stronger than death. I am convinced that Dianne hoped the church had something to say about her journey into "the darkest valley" (Ps 23:4). I believe she hoped that I, as a representative of the church, would bear witness to God's promise to accompany her in death as in life.

From Expert to Story Companion

Your first response as a pastoral caregiver faced with a difficult pastoral situation is likely to be the same one I had when I walked through Diane's door: "What am I supposed to do or say when I provide pastoral care?" Many of the students in my introduction to pastoral care course ask this question upon finding themselves in a hospital room, a parishioner's home, at the Communion rail, beside someone's sickbed, in the state prison, or at a homeless shelter in the first few weeks of their theological education. Our anxiety about our performance often gets in the way of listening deeply and fully to another. We frequently rush into speaking, too often as much to quiet our own pounding hearts as to comfort another.

Narrative pastoral care invites us to become story companions to one another. You need not be an expert with all the answers. No one, in fact, can be an expert on someone else's lifestory. You do not have to be a savior. (Many of us believe that job has been taken!) As pastoral story companions, we listen closely for and bear witness to the presence of God who accompanies both the storyteller and story listener in the process of constructing a faithful, life-giving story that fosters growth in love.

As pastoral caregivers we discover our ability to accompany others is made possible by God's prior companionship with those seeking our companionship and with us. Through the ongoing accompaniment of the Holy Spirit, both storytellers and listeners are empowered to grow in love of God, self, others, and all of creation.

Listening to Lifestories

We not only compose stories, *we are composed by stories*, as we saw in chapter 1. Our ability to know one another depends upon sharing our stories. Through listening, entering into another's world shared with us through speech, embodied action, and other forms of nonverbal communication, we come to know each other, though never fully. Even when we hear a person's lifestory, we rarely hear the full story or all the strands of the story. Our understanding is always partial. Even the storyteller does not fully know himself or herself because lifestories are constantly in the process of being written and revised. Neither storyteller nor listener yet knows all the twist and turns of the plot or the ending to come.

Because stories are a dialogical process, the unfolding of a lifestory is shaped by the context and relationship between storyteller and listener. Because we listen through our own stories, there is always the possibility for misunderstanding, especially in intercultural relationships.[4]

The roles we occupy can also shape the stories we hear. When you are in the role of the pastor or representing church authority, a storyteller may edit or revise his or her story. Whatever stories an individual carries around with him or her about ministers and the church, positive or negative, will impact the stories shared when you, as a listener, are identified with these roles. Some storytellers may edit, revise, or even entirely omit certain stories, judging them not suitable for a pastor's ears or fearing a judgmental religious response. Other storytellers may immediately open up with a confessional story, assuming the confidentiality of the pastoral relationship and surprising you with an immediate intimacy.

As pastoral story companions, we find our purpose in listening is not to give advice, solve another's problem, or assign a diagnosis. These may be legitimate forms of listening in other contexts. If I tell my mechanic about the rattling sound that occurs every time I drive over a bump, I definitely want him to identify the problem and fix it. Human beings, however, are not machines, objects, or commodities. Psychologist Jerome Brunner makes a distinction between two types of knowing that can also shape our listening. The form of knowing characterized by empirical discovery, through our five senses, and logical reasoning is "paradigmatic knowing."[5] It is the form of reasoning we use to comprehend the nature of objects in the world. Paradigmatic knowing is exemplified in the scientific method and expressed through a well-formed argument. It is this kind of knowing I expect my mechanic to use to fix my car.

Paradigmatic knowing employs what I call *factual listening*. Factual listening is what I expect of my mechanic, to garner an accurate description of the problem, to find the proper solution. If you are a student, you probably do quite a bit of this type of listening, especially if you are going to be tested on the topic. When asking for directions, caching the newscast, or listening to a doctor's diagnosis, we listen for information and may ask questions to get the details clear. We do a lot of this type of listening to navigate our daily lives. As important as it is, it is generally far less helpful in pastoral conversation. Factual listening rarely invites storytelling.

Understanding human beings and human experience occurs primarily through "narrative knowing," which is expressed through stories.[6] If I want to tell you about love or describe the pleasure I experience in the beauty of the dogwood trees blossoming outside my office window each spring, I will tell you a story. There are times we need a good argument and other times we need a good story. Each communicates something different to us and serves a distinct purpose. "Arguments convince one of their truth, stories of their lifelikeness."[7] The narrative mode of knowing that pays attention to a story, rather than to an argument, is essential to narrative pastoral care. Narrative listening invites storytelling.

Learning to Listen

Becoming a story companion begins with learning to listen. It is something we think we do all the time. Our ears are full of sounds every day, the honking, rushing sounds of the city, music piped directly into our ears, and the chatter of people around us on the street. Even in the quiet of the countryside our ears take in the sound of birdsong, the lilting sound of a flowing creek, or the rush of the wind.

Hearing, however, is not the same as listening. To hear is to "perceive with the ear the sound made."[8] To listen is to "give one's attention to a sound."[9] To become story companions we must learn to listen with reverent attention, which requires intentionality and practice. Listening deeply can be challenging, given all the sounds assaulting our ears, all the voices calling for our attention, not to mention all the chattering going on inside our own heads. Listening reverently is a spiritual discipline, and a spiritual obligation of those who want to become story companions. Pastoral story companions who fail to listen "forfeit the right to speak."[10] The practice of narrative pastoral care begins with paying attention.

Empathic Listening

Empathy is central to all forms of effective pastoral care and essential to narrative listening. Empathy is "the vicarious affective response to another person."[11] The first part of this definition refers to the cognitive dimension of empathy. The kind of understanding required in empathy is more than an objective analytic assessment of information; it requires creative thinking and imagination as well. We imagine ourselves in the midst of the multiple dimensions of another's experience in order to understand it.

Empathy also has an affective dimension through which we feel what the other person is feeling. We step into the other's shoes, imaginatively connecting his emotional experience to our own. Though we can never know exactly what another person is feeling, empathy allows an emotional resonance through which we make a connection between another's experience and our own.[12]

Empathy, while a relational process, involves both a sense of connection and separateness. Empathy requires acknowledging our difference from the other, being aware of our own distinct feelings and thoughts, and stepping back in order to provide another perspective. Empathic narrative listening requires us to join another's story and become absorbed in it, much the same way as you get absorbed in a good novel, follow the plot, feel what a character feels, and stay attentive to potential difficulties the character might encounter but seems unable to anticipate. At the same time, the other's story does not become my own, but rather I maintain an awareness of the distinction between my own story and the other's story.[13] If this distinction is lost, empathy falters.

Failures of empathy may occur in a number of ways. I might overidentify with the storyteller and lose track of my own story and separateness. I might also assume that so much similarity exists between our stories that I impose my own cultural assumptions and worldview on another's story, resulting in misunderstandings and the disruption of empathy.[14] Failures in empathy also occur when the content or emotion of another's story makes the listener anxious, and he or she then seeks to manage this anxiety through emphasizing the difference between storyteller and listener. Empathizing with another does not necessarily mean approving of or agreeing with another's behavior, but it does imply understanding.

For example, Jason, who has overcome some form of addiction, may feel deep empathy with Rhoda, who is still caught in addiction, while being committed to a life of sobriety and hoping for the same for Rhoda. Empathy creates a bond between persons while maintaining an appreciation for the uniqueness of each person.

Although the terms *empathy* and *sympathy* are sometimes used interchangeably, each has distinct meanings and refers to different phenomena. Empathy is feeling *with* another, while sympathy, in personal relationships, is feeling *for* another. When we are sympathetic, we feel compassion for another, and perhaps even sorrow, but we don't generally feel his or her feelings. You might feel sympathy for a friend whose favorite pet has died, but if you have never had a pet, you may not fully understand either the thoughts or feelings of your friend. If a pet of yours has died, you are more likely to feel empathy, recalling vividly what it felt like, and what you thought at the time of your own loss.

This does not mean we can experience empathy only with those whose experiences are identical to our own. Most of us have experienced some form of relational loss, and if we can access our own feelings and thoughts about that, we can empathically imagine what it might feel like for the other person. We can never assume our experience is identical to another's, but empathy does provide a bridge between our own experience and that of another person.

Both sympathy and empathy can play a role in pastoral care. While empathy may create a deeper bond between persons, the compassion expressed in sympathy is also important.

Why We Listen

Listening may serve multiple purposes in the practice of narrative pastoral care. Pastoral theologian Graeme Griffin names three: (1) listening as an end in itself, (2) listening as a means of giving voice to one who is voiceless, and (3) listening in order to speak.[15] Listening as an end in itself is reflective listening.[16] We provide a sounding board for another to sort through his or her thoughts. A storyteller often figures out a conflict in the story or where the plot might go next simply by telling it to an attentive listener. Often little response is required of us when reflective listening is needed. Reverent attention to another, the experience of feeling truly heard, is a gift. If you have been fortunate enough to experience this kind of listening, you know how empowering it can be simply to tell your story and have it fully received. In the process, the storyteller may come to the clarity she sought or find an answer.

Sometimes muteness freezes the tongue. The storyteller cannot give voice to her experience, either because oppressive forces have silenced her, or because profound suffering has left her speechless. In these pastoral situations, the story companion is called to listen in order help the silenced one find her own voice.

Significant research has shown that one of the things that can increase the severity of trauma is being unable to tell the story.[17] Several factors can impede our ability to construct a coherent narrative out of a traumatic experience. Perhaps the first is our inability to process the event. The way that traumatic memories are encoded in the brain is in episodic fashion, often due to a disassociated state, in which our minds leave the event that is occurring in order to protect us from the terror of it.[18] As a result we are left with bits and pieces, unable to patch them together into a meaningful narrative. As a consequence, we may have difficulty telling the story of what happened.

We may want to disbelieve it ourselves or feel shamed by what occurred (as in the case of sexual violence) and choose to keep silent. Because our story appears incoherent or seems to change as we remember more bits of it, others may have difficulty believing us. When a person who has experienced trauma cannot find someone to hear her story, or his recollection of it is flatly denied, that denial, that not being heard reinforces and magnifies the muteness induced by the trauma.

Finally, we tell stories to make meaning out of events, which can be hard to do in what may feel like meaningless suffering.

Therefore, before becoming an advocate and speaking on behalf of another, the task of a pastoral companion is to help the person who has been silenced to tell her or his story. And the listener must believe the story.

At other times, the pastoral situation may call for us to speak to another or on behalf of another. Yet we cannot know what to say until we have listened fully enough to understand the complexities of the story. We might speak a word of comfort, of support or encouragement, of challenge, or of advocacy. Speaking in the context of a one-to-one pastoral conversation may be only one of the places we speak. We may also be moved to speak on behalf of another in a sermon or a public meeting.

For example, if we have worked with women in the community who have experienced violence from a family member, we might address a difficult biblical text about violence in a sermon or pray for those enduring intimate partner violence in a pastoral prayer. We must be attentive, however, to the confidentiality assumed when someone speaks to us as a pastoral story companion. Likewise, we should never use the personal story of anyone in our congregations as sermon illustrations.

Active Listening and Its Use in Crisis

Many of us have been trained in *active listening*—a set of listening techniques intended to improve communication between speaker and listener. Robert Carkhuff, a proponent of active listening, identifies the purpose of listening as information gathering "related to the problems or goals presented by the helpees."[19] Listeners attend to both the "internal experience" and "external behavior" through listening for both content and affect.[20] Learning the techniques of listening "prepares us to respond empathically to our helpees."[21]

Some of the skills of active listening, which are frequently cited in introductory pastoral care texts, include the following:[22]

1. *Paraphrasing* is using your own words, summarizing what the person has said to you. Paraphrasing allows you to test whether you have heard the concern correctly and it communicates your understanding to the speaker.

2. *Asking open-ended questions* such as "Tell me more" invites the speaker to continue while communicating your willingness to listen. By contrast, closed-ended questions tend to close down a conversation. Such questions are usually about gathering facts or have yes and no answers.

3. *Using clarifying questions* can clarify a person's beliefs, values, actions, or wishes.

4. *Making statements rather than asking questions* (which can be a form of paraphrasing) means saying things like "You sound angry" rather than "Are you angry?"

5. *Summarizing* can be a longer form of paraphrasing. This can come after a longer response or story. Summarizing provides a chance for you to help identify the main points of a story or the main concern.

6. *Listening for feeling as well as content* means attending to tone of voice and rapidity of speech. What emotions are being communicated: fear, anxiety, disappointment, longing, anger, love, joy? Sometimes the verbal content and the communicated emotion or affect do not match and that too requires attention.[23]

7. *Attending to nonverbal communication* means that you are aware of body language, make frequent eye contact (depending on the cultural context), are aware of the way a person inhabits physical space and expresses "interest and hospitality by [his] facial expressions and posture."[24]

8. Active listening skills can be important and may often improve communication in everyday settings by helping us learn to pay closer attention in conversation.

In some pastoral situations, particularly crisis intervention in which the goal is to stabilize a chaotic and potentially dangerous situation, active listening can be very effective. Crisis overwhelms a person's ability to cope with his or her problems in a familiar manner. When one's usual problem-solving skills have proved ineffective, what was initially viewed as a difficult but potentially manageable situation is now seen as a crisis. Crisis experiences are also highly emotionally charged situations often involving an unexpected loss as a consequence of a death, illness, job loss, or the end of a relationship. A crisis often initiates a cascade of challenges and changes in one's life, making it difficult to know where to begin to cope with the problem.

The purpose of listening is to gather information from the "helpee" in order for the "helper" to make an assessment about the nature of his or her problem and come to a solution. In the ABC approach to crisis intervention, the helper uses the techniques of active listening to *achieve* (A) contact with the help seeker, and then assists in *boiling down* the crisis to an identifiable problem (B), in order to *cope* actively with it (C).[25] The intention of active listening is to involve the help seeker in solving his or her problems.

Implicit in active listening skills, however, is the assumption that listening is largely a matter of technique that one can master. One of the difficulties with the language of technique is that it can sound mechanical and less-experienced listeners may apply it rigidly. Anxious with getting the technique right, I may begin to view the other person as an object to be fixed. Not unlike the car mechanic, the helper may find herself leaning more toward paradigmatic ways of knowing with its scientific approach and emphasis on description and control. An unintended consequence is that the listener may expect to become an expert, not only on listening, but also on the other person's life, leading to a power imbalance in the helping relationship.

If such an imbalance occurs, the "helper" may see himself or herself as the expert and active agent while the "helpee" is the passive recipient of help. While helping relationships are asymmetrical, the most effective caregiving relationships are characterized by mutuality in which both caregiver and receiver participate.

Narrative Listening

Narrative listening is informed by a set of attitudes and ways of being in relationship, rather than a set of techniques or skills, as is the case in active listening. Narrative listeners bring an open, curious, respectful, optimistic, and hopeful attitude to the conversation.[26] Following the lead of the storyteller, the narrative listener identifies the multiple story strands that compose a life narrative, noting what is included and what is left out. The relationship between storyteller and listener is a collaborative process between two people.[27] A person is not an object to be studied, diagnosed, and fixed by an expert. Narrative therapists are quite insistent that the form of listening characteristic of narrative therapy is not a set of techniques that can be applied.[28] A narrative listener moves away from the position of expert to one more akin to a curious, interested reader of a novel. Lifestories evolve; the plot may shift, characters come and go, and we don't yet know the ending.

Narrative listening, informed as it is by narrative psychology and therapy, reflects a postmodern view of the self. From a postmodern perspective, one *becomes* a self through the dialogical, relational process of coauthoring lifestories.[29] In contrast, a modern view of the self, which operates in the clinical pastoral paradigm, tends to view the self as a preexistent entity. From a modern perspective, one *has* a self, and although it may develop over time, the primary task of psychological growth is to discover, uncover, accept, or actualize the self.[30] Narrative listening facilitates the process of becoming a self as story companions become coauthors of an unfolding lifestory.

Narrative Pastoral Conversation

I use the term *narrative pastoral conversation* in order to distinguish this form of care from narrative pastoral counseling and therapy.[31] Pastoral conversation denotes a mutual exchange between story companions and challenges assumptions that one-to-one pastoral care is primarily about giving advice or providing therapy.[32] Pastoral conversation emerges in the context of a pastoral relationship, rather than a therapeutic one, and focuses on basic forms of care, such as listening for the soul of another and fostering spiritual growth.[33] Pastoral conversation reclaims pastoral care as a responsibility of the whole church, not only ordained priests, ministers, or other specialists, and is "consistent with the Gospel's command to 'bear one another's burdens' (Gal 6:2)."[34] Informed by the image of being a story companion, pastoral conversation emphasizes mutuality between storyteller and listener, as does narrative therapy. While narrative pastoral conversation may facilitate healing, such healing occurs in the context of the larger purpose of facilitating growth in love of God, self, and other.

Distinctions between Pastoral Conversation and Narrative Therapy

In contrast, narrative therapy utilizes narrative listening to deconstruct dysfunctional narratives in order to "re-author" a more life-giving, hopeful, stories.[35] The person seeking assistance takes the initiative to begin therapy. The focus of therapy is generally a problem story that dominates a person's lifestory. For example, a care seeker—let's call her Sue—might identify herself as an overly anxious person who seeks therapy when anxiety begins to take over her life. The narrative therapist invites the storyteller to identify and name the problem, which Sue might name "worry." Together, the therapist and Sue explore the influence of worry on Sue's life, as well as Sue's influence on worry. In the process of therapy, which generally occurs over a number of sessions, Sue and the therapist create alternative stories that facilitate growth, increase agency, and offer an alternative to the dominant problem story of worry.

Narrative therapists, like most therapists, primarily interact with clients during the therapeutic session and rarely outside of it. Still, narrative therapists may make use of letters or other documents in between sessions to strengthen the alternative story being constructed.[36] Therapeutic conversations foster emotional healing through narrative reconstruction. Those seeking to practice as narrative therapists undergo advanced education, develop professional competencies, and are licensed as therapists after completing a requisite number of supervised clinical hours and passing a licensing exam.[37]

Pastors are often advised to avoid pastoral counseling and refer to professionals those who seek it. The reasons given are good ones based on ethical considerations of appropriate care: pastors often lack the necessary training needed to provide in-depth pastoral counseling. Additionally, increased public attention to clergy sexual misconduct has led many denominations either to limit the number of sessions of pastoral counseling offered by parish pastors or to emphasize referral in almost all cases. The risk factors leading to boundary violations ending in clergy sexual misconduct are readily present in long-term pastoral counseling relationships: a high degree of intimacy, a private relationship, and the potential for abuse of pastoral power. Add to this the frequent sense of isolation of the pastoral role, the high incidence of clergy burnout, and the difficulty in maintaining clear boundaries amidst the multiple relationships of ministry and you have the conditions that often lead to clergy misconduct.

I am in agreement with limits on long-term counseling by parish pastors. An unintended consequence, however, with the emphasis on referral is often a devaluing of pastoral conversation. Confusion about the appropriate role of a pastor in providing care was expressed to me recently in a conversation with a candidate for ordination in my denomination. In a brief coffeehouse encounter he shared his confusion about his role in pastoral care. He reported that the advice he continually receives in the formation process required of candidates is to refer in almost all situations. In response to his comments, I replied, "That probably leaves you feeling like there is little you can do as a pastor." "That's it!" he exclaimed. Clarity about both the process and purpose of pastoral conversation can provide guidance about what kind of pastoral care is appropriate to the pastoral role.

Features of Narrative Pastoral Conversation

Narrative pastoral conversation, like narrative therapy, is a hermeneutical process through which story companions interpret a lifestory, making meaning of the twists, turns, problems, and unexpected events in an unfolding lifestory. Narrative pastoral conversation, however, is less formal, may occur anywhere, and may begin as social conversation but move to pastoral conversation. Social conversations, such as those that occur between friends, engage the stories of everyday life, while pastoral conversations also attend to the intersections of God's stories and our own.[38] The initiative to enter a narrative pastoral conversation may either come from the pastoral story companion or the storyteller. Narrative pastoral conversation generally focuses on difficulties of daily life that temporarily disrupt our lifestories, rather than the more entrenched problem-saturated stories, which are typically the focus of narrative therapy.

Many people manage quite well day to day until an unexpected plot twist due to illness, loss, or a life transition occurs. Some life transitions, such as marriage or the birth of a child, may be positive yet still require revision of our narratives as new characters or new roles are added to our stories. On any given day "people not suffering from a mental disorder" but who "are trying to make sense of the world" represent "more than 80% of the population."[39] Narrative pastoral care has much to offer anyone engaged in the ongoing process of constructing a meaningful and purposeful lifestory.

At times, narrative pastoral conversation may reveal a lifestory that is problem saturated and cripples a person's ability to live fully, requiring additional attention. In some cases, *narrative pastoral consultation* may be in order. *Pastoral consultation* is the term I use to indicate short-term pastoral counseling in which a formal arrangement is made to address a specific problem in no more than five sessions.[40] Consultation indicates a slightly more focused and in-depth process than does conversation but retains a sense of partnership between the story companions.

I reserve the term *pastoral counseling* for longer-term work with a specialist who has received advanced training in narrative therapy or other therapeutic modalities. When consultation is not adequate, referral to a professional therapist is in order. I will discuss guidelines for pastoral consultation and referral in more depth in a subsequent chapter.

In becoming a pastoral story companions, we join the storyteller in the process of coauthoring a lifestory as she seeks to make sense of an experience, overcome a difficulty, incorporate a new experience or relationship, or come to a new self-understanding over the course of life as transitions are faced. Stories are not a source of information in narrative pastoral conversation or "illustrations to make a point" but rather are "the primary means for helping people."[41]

In many ways story creation is more akin to an artistic process than a mechanical one. It is a poetic process, though not in the sense that we convert our life experience into poetic verse. The word *poetic*, first defined by Aristotle, "derives from the ancient

Greek verb *poiein*, which means to 'make or create.'"[42] While *poetic* has been used to refer to a finished creative design, such as a poem, "contemporary usage focuses on activity" or the creative process of making meaning.[43]

As pastoral story companions we join the storyteller in a poetic process, interpreting a life narrative in the context of God's unfolding love story. Pastoral conversation may be understood then as a "therapoetic" process, rather than "therapeutic, which deals with more significant emotional disturbance or psychopathology."[44] As a "therapoetic" process, pastoral conversation facilitates making meaning, deepening our self-understanding, and revising stories that thwart growth in love.

Pastoral conversation can make a significant contribution to developing a richer and more complex lifestory. Through narrative pastoral conversation we may discover "who we are, where we are going in life and how we relate to others, and to the world around us, and to the God who created us."[45]

Table 5.1 provides a brief overview of some of the differences between narrative pastoral conversation, consultation, and narrative therapy.

Table 5.1

Elements	Narrative Pastoral Conversation	Pastoral Consultation	Pastoral Therapy
Number of conversations	Often begins with informal conversation. May involve only one conversation.	Agree to set number of formal consultations.	Usually involves multiple conversations.
Contract	Usually an informal contract but assumes confidentiality and ethical behavior.	May establish a formal contract for short-term narrative consultation (one to five sessions).	Explicit contract for counseling. The length of sessions is determined, while duration of the counseling relationship is open-ended.
Initiative	Initiative for conversation may come from pastor/chaplain or from storyteller.	Comes from storyteller. May be in response to pastoral invitation.	Initiative for counseling comes from counselee.
Entry point	May begin in social conversation and move to an implicit or explicit request for pastoral conversation or arise in the context of general pastoral care.	May follow pastoral conversation when need for deeper exploration of an issue is identified.	Begins with a request for help with a specific difficulty.
Goals	1) Assist in coauthoring lifestory with greater complexity and meaning. 2) Assist in identifying oppressive personal, social, and religious stories. 3) Connect divine and human stories, enabling growth in love. 4) Draw on religious rituals and communities to support new story.	1) Assist in coauthoring lifestory with greater complexity and meaning. 2) Address story deficits due to foreclosure, thin stories. 3) Help create preferred stories. 4) Refer for therapy for more help if needed.	1) Deconstruct problem-saturated story. 2) Name dominant discourses. 3) Reconstruct more hopeful future story. 4) Recruit witnesses/audience to support new story. 5) More likely to aim for and facilitate in-depth psychological and relational healing.

Ethical Responsibilities of the Pastoral Story Companion

To be entrusted with the lifestory of another is to receive a precious gift, which requires ethical behavior on the part of the story companion. The general ethical behavior expected of all Christians—to love God and to love one's neighbor as oneself—are certainly expected of pastoral leaders. The general rules of the Methodist movement, which were originally intended for all members, continue to provide a sound ethical framework for ministry: "Do no harm, do good, attend the ordinances of God."[46] Candidates for ministry in the United Methodist Church are expected to recite these general rules at the time of ordination and subsequently to live by them.

Ordained ministry implies ethical responsibilities, including being trustworthy, having personal integrity, practicing confidentiality, maintaining appropriate boundaries, and attending to the power dynamics inherent in a pastoral relationship, all of which compose an implicit contract for care. In formal therapy, the contract for care is explicit and establishes the length and frequency of sessions, the duration of the counseling relationship (though it may remain open-ended), fees, confidentiality, and expectations about contact between therapist and client outside of the therapy room.

One of the unique features of providing pastoral care in the context of a parish is the possibility of long-term relationships with individuals, and often multiple generations of the family. When a parishioner approaches you to become a story companion, it is very likely that you have a preexisting relationship with that person. If trust has already been established between you and the storyteller, you are often able to move much more quickly into the story. A disadvantage may be that the storyteller assumes you already know parts of the story. This may require you to slow down the storytelling process and ask questions that reveal parts of the story unknown to you.

Preexisting pastoral relationships are not always the case in larger congregations and in many chaplaincy settings. While many hospital chaplains do not have an opportunity to develop longer-term pastoral relationships, chaplains working with incarcerated men and women or with older adults in residential facilities may have the chance to do so.

Confidentiality and Its Limits

Confidentiality should be assumed in all one-to-one pastoral conversations, whether formal or informal. Any form of short-term pastoral consultation or counseling, including premarital counseling, requires confidentiality. Many parishioners assume that any conversation with a pastor is confidential, including news about an illness or upcoming hospital stay. When in doubt about whether such information can be shared with the congregation through a prayer chain or in a pastoral prayer, ask.

Confidentiality in pastoral relationships, however, does have limits. In some cases, a higher ethical value, such as preventing violence and protecting a life,

73

supersedes the ethic to maintain confidentiality. In most states pastors have a legal as well as an ethical responsibility to break confidentiality in cases when someone is at risk of self-harm or harming another. All states have mandatory reporting laws in the case of child abuse in any form and some states have mandatory reporting in cases of elder abuse.[47]

Figuring out how to communicate the limits of confidentiality can be tricky. Careful and empathic listening and pastoral support can often help a storyteller find a way to communicate with the appropriate authorities designated by law.

Multiple Roles

Another distinction of a pastoral relationship from a therapeutic one is the multiple settings in which story companions may interact, such as during worship or committee meetings, at the Communion rail, in Sunday school, at a community event, or at the local grocery store. In addition to interacting with one's pastor in church settings, parishioners may encounter a pastor in the role of parent at the local school, in the role of spouse at a business or community function, or in the role of a friend at a nonchurch-related social event. One of the challenges of the multiple roles a pastor inhabits is that while you may see yourself differently in these various roles, parishioners may see you as the pastor regardless of the setting.

A question that often arises in the classroom when discussing multiple roles and boundaries is "Can I be friends with my church members?" It is difficult to give a simple answer to this question, and there are multiple opinions about it among pastors and in the literature on pastoral care and pastoral ethics. In part, the answer may depend on what one means by *friend*. Friendship often indicates a mutual and symmetrical relationship in which both participants have equal power to influence one another. I have already indicated that mutuality is a feature of narrative pastoral care. Mutual relationships, however, including pastoral relationships, may not be symmetrical.

An asymmetrical relationship is one in which the participants have mutual influence on one another but may play different roles and carry different power within the relationship. A good example of an asymmetrical relationship relevant for the pastoral role is the example of teacher and student. The most effective teaching and learning relationships are those in which both are partners in the learning experience. One of the most rewarding parts of teaching for me is the mutual process of discovery when students and teachers cocreate learning. Yet, as a teacher, I do have different responsibilities from those of the students, and I have a certain degree of power over the students in determining topics, assignments, and grades.

Likewise, the pastoral role has symbolic power and real power, which can complicate our relationships with parishioners as we move among multiple roles. I believe pastors can have friendly, mutual, and meaningful relationships with parishioners, but we must recognize that these relationships are asymmetrical. Anyone in a church leadership position needs to have friends, interests, and connections outside of the church and the ministerial role. This can be difficult to do since church work can feel all-consuming, but having a life outside of ministry is essential not only for one's own mental health, but also for the health of the church. The principle guideline of any pastoral relationship is that the parishioner's needs, not those of the pastor, are the focus.[48]

Power and Boundaries in the Pastoral Relationship

The asymmetrical character of the pastoral relationship is due largely to two factors: the power of the pastoral role, and the specific responsibilities and privileges of the pastoral role, both of which bring expectations of ethical conduct. Ethical use of the power of the pastoral role requires that we recognize its presence and monitor our use of it. Most denominations and religious communities now have specific codes of conduct for clergy and often for volunteers, especially those working with youth.[49] These official codes of pastoral conduct recognize the power of the pastoral role, which is both symbolic and real. In addition to assumed spiritual authority, pastors also have significant executive authority over the resources and people of a congregation. Ministerial codes of conduct may specify expected ethical behavior in a number of areas, including financial responsibilities, when confidentiality is expected and when it is limited, conflicts of interest, and specific prohibitions against potentially exploitive relationships between pastors and parishioners.

Pastoral power. What do I mean by *pastoral power*? First of all, the pastoral role has symbolic power for many people. Pastors are often seen as representatives, not only of the church and its authority, but also of God. The symbolic power assigned to us as pastors often has little to do with us and much more to do with others' perceptions of and experience with the pastoral role. Recognizing and acknowledging this symbolic power is very important in using it ethically. The first-year students in my pastoral care course who are currently serving as chaplains in a state women's prison are often quite surprised what happens when they put on the chaplain's badge. Not only are they referred to as "Chap" rather than by their names, they are also assigned a power and authority they don't feel they have.

Let me give another quick example from my own ministry. After serving two years as an associate pastor and at the age of twenty-eight, I was assigned to be the pastor in charge of a congregation of about 120 members with an average attendance of about sixty members. Not long after I arrived, a new family joined our church. The father in the family was a Marine Corps drill sergeant, in his midforties, career military, and a rather large man—about six feet tall and sturdy. One Sunday morning, as the liturgist he had to read an Old Testament passage with a lot of hard-to-pronounce names. As he practiced reading before the service, I could tell he was having difficulty with the names. Glancing at the passage, I determined he could skip most of the names without affecting the meaning of the passage and told him this.

During the service, when he was reading the passage, he got to the names, stopped, and said, "The pastor said I could skip part of this" and then went on. I stood next to him, a good foot shorter, several years younger, and a fairly new pastor, and realized the power of my role. I apparently had authority over what could and could not be read from the Bible, an authority he would not claim for himself.

In addition to the symbolic power of the pastoral role in which we are seen not only as authorities on the Bible but also as spiritual guides, pastors often have real power over the daily matters of the church. How much power pastors have may depend in part on the polity of the church. In denominations in which pastors are hired by a congregational board, the pastor may feel as if he or she is an employee of the congregation rather than the executive director.

Pastors, however, are expected to be leaders and often have extensive authority over the finances of the church, over which members will serve in leadership positions, as well as over the hiring of staff. Pastors also determine what is preached every Sunday and have significant influence over the direction of the church. In most denominations, pastors are granted authority through ordination and assigned specific duties according to denominational policies.

In the United Methodist Church the ordination of a pastor occurs when the bishop places his or her hand on the head of the candidate and intones the words, "Take authority as an elder in the church to preach the Word of God and to administer the Holy Sacraments" or "Take authority as a deacon in the church to preach the Word of God and serve all God's people in the church."[50] By recognizing the power of the pastoral role, we are much more able to use it ethically and wisely on behalf of individual church members and the congregation as a whole to foster well-being, spiritual growth, and faithful ministry.

It is largely on the basis of the asymmetry of power between pastors and parishioners that dating relationships between clergy and members of their congregations are precluded. A dating relationship requires not only mutuality, but also the capacity for genuine consent, which exists only when power in the relationship is equal.[51] Sexual misconduct by clergy is the most egregious misuse of clergy power and a violation of the boundaries of the pastoral role. Engaging in a sexual relationship with a church member is often grounds for dismissal from a church placement and often results in loss of the privileges of ordination and being barred from engaging in any form of ministry. In many cases, however, clergy sexual misconduct occurs after a long history of boundary violations and less-obvious misuses of pastoral power and privilege.

Boundaries. A boundary is "a point or limit that indicates where two things become different."[52] Boundaries may also define acceptable limits of behavior.[53] Both personal and professional boundaries are relevant in ministry. Personal boundaries are experienced in our everyday interpersonal encounters. Clear personal boundaries allow me to have a sense of where I begin and end and where another person begins and ends. I am aware that my thoughts and feelings may be quite distinct from those of another. While my own experiences and story may allow me to empathize with another person, I maintain clarity about the distinction between our stories.

Maintaining a distinction between oneself and another, which is facilitated by clear personal boundaries, is an essential condition for empathy. Ideally, boundaries are flexible. At times boundaries may become too diffuse or open, leading to *fusion*. Overidentification with a care seeker, or losing ourselves in another's story so that we cannot distinguish our thoughts and feeling from those of the storyteller, is an occurrence of fusion.[54]

At other times, boundaries may be rigid or closed, leading to *disengagement*.[55] In this case, caregivers distance themselves emotionally from the care seekers. This can occur because we become uncomfortable with the topic under discussion, because of the presence of powerful emotion on the part of the care seeker, or because powerful emotions are triggered in us that we want to disavow.[56]

When personal boundaries are too diffuse or open, we may feel ourselves spilling over into another person or vice versa. You may have experienced diffuse boundaries while traveling on an airplane when your seatmate shared details of his or her life that struck you as far too intimate for a stranger's ears. People often do have a different sense of what are appropriate boundaries in personal relationship depending on family background and culture. In United States culture, it is often considered rude and overstepping a boundary to ask an adult his or her age. In another culture in which age confers status, asking another's age may be seen as crucial to determine appropriate behavior and personal boundaries.

Maintaining appropriate pastoral boundaries as trustworthy story companions also requires that we pay attention to our own stories. We need to know our own stories as well as we can to resist fusion or disengagement as both storyteller and listener are engaged in the dialogical, relational processes of coauthoring lifestories.

Becoming Story Companions: Reprise

When people engage us in the important questions of their lives, they are inviting us to become pastoral story companions in the creative act of crafting a lifestory. Often the issues at the heart of the stories shared are themes of love and loss, joy and sorrow, despair and hope, joy and despair, and death and life, all of which are deeply theological themes whether or not explicitly religious language is used. To become a story companion is to accept an invitation to accompany another in the unfolding story of a life and to witness to the interwoven threads of divine love.

Chapter 6

Reading Stories: Narrative Environments and Development

There is no agony like bearing an untold story inside of you.

—Maya Angelou

Narrative pastoral care begins with careful listening, but it doesn't end there. Stories are more than a source of information from which we abstract a solution: the story *is* the means of care and emerges in the relational space between storyteller and listener. As a story unfolds, it takes on a particular shape and meaning in *this* telling to *this* listener. The meaning assigned to stories is crucial in shaping our sense of identity and purpose. How one interprets past events influences expectations of the future and what is imagined as possible.

As story companions we participate in a hermeneutical, or meaning-making, process. To do so well requires increasing our knowledge of narrative. What is a story? What is the plot? Is it believable? Who are the major characters? Is the story complex or thin? Together storyteller and listener come to a deeper understanding of a lifestory, joining in the process of coauthoring good, strong, faithful lifestories.

Narrative Knowing and Narrative Knowledge

Stories are the means through which human beings make sense of the myriad sensory perceptions, events, and experiences that occur in the course of a day, a year, or a life. Stories are understood through *narrative knowing*, a particular way of knowing discussed in chapter 5. Underlying the idea of narrative knowing is a hermeneutical perspective, or the assumption that human beings are interpreting, meaning-making beings. Because stories are the way in which human beings construct identity and assign meaning, narrative knowing is the primary mode or way of knowing we use to understand each other. Narrative knowing fosters a deeper understanding of

79

the particular events that occur in a specific lifestory; they do not necessarily reveal universal truths.[1]

Narrative knowledge is what we learn about stories and the process of story construction. Increasing our narrative knowledge can provide a more complex and nuanced understanding, or way of knowing, of a person's lifestory.[2] The skills we bring to reading written texts, including novels, memoirs, and biblical and theological texts, can assist us in reading the "living human document."[3] Narrative knowledge facilitates our ability to look at how individual lifestories "illuminate the universals of the human condition by revealing the particular."[4]

Pastoral story companions can benefit from a growing body of narrative knowledge from a broad range of fields that provide a deeper understanding of "what narratives are, how they are built," and how they communicate information, shape beliefs, organize life, and assign meaning.[5] As our narrative knowledge increases, we gain a better sense of "what happens when stories are told and listened to" and how this this dialogical process allows both storyteller and listener to grasp a story's meaning.[6]

As a result, we increase our capacity to "read" another's story, to perceive more clearly and appreciate more deeply the joys and challenges another person faces. When we learn to read with curiosity and imagination either a written novel or a lived one, we are able to enter "others' narrative worlds and accept them—at least provisionally—as true."[7] Learning how to "read" well and attend closely to a living story is part of the process of becoming story companions.

Perhaps if I had had greater narrative knowledge when a young man entered my office some years ago and asked to see the pastor, I might have been able to enter into his story more fully. Instead, I initially created a story about him based on my own first impressions and past experience.[8] The story I created had more to do with my story than his. I came to know his story—partially—only when I could move far enough beyond my own story to be curious about his. Although I responded to his specific request to conduct a funeral, I did not have the necessary narrative knowledge at the time to read his story more closely.

Pastoral Vignette Reprised: If I Had Known Then What I Know Now

After hearing the knock at the door of the church office, I opened it to find a young man in his early twenties whom I did not know. He was not a member of the congregation, but he wanted to see the pastor. I immediately found myself tensing up and thinking: "Here we go again. One more request for a handout." This church was not in a prosperous community and we often had folks asking for various kinds of assistance. I had nothing left in our emergency fund and dreaded telling him so. Despite my reluctance, I asked him to come in and sit and tell me how I could help him. Dwayne told me that he and his wife lived next door and had very recently had a baby. He stopped talking for a moment, looked down, then went on, slowly, "Our baby died. We want to have a funeral. Will you do it?" His words stopped me in my tracks and immediately challenged the story I was already beginning to construct about him.

Reflection: An Invitation Missed

Before I realized it, and before he had opened his mouth, I had created a story about Dwayne: who he was, his motivations, what he wanted from me. I had "story-o-typed" him.[9] The story I created had nothing to do with him, since he had not said a word. It was *my* story *about* him, based on my assumptions and past experiences of strangers coming to the church door. I almost missed an opportunity for the church to extend its ministry of care because my story *about* Dwayne almost got in the way of hearing his actual story.

And even though I did ask him for (a piece of) his story, I missed the chance to help him develop it further. I did as he asked and conducted a funeral for the baby. But I did not offer him an invitation to become story companions with me so I could assist him and his wife in revising their lifestory to integrate this unexpected and devastating turn. I wish I had understood then the power of story. I wish I had had the confidence to risk engaging them some more. I wish I had asked the couple before or after the funeral who else they might have liked to have there, had it been possible. I am afraid I may have left them with an untold story.

You might notice that the story about the young man is almost identical to a version in an earlier chapter, with only minor revisions. Yet the interpretation or meaning I have assigned to it is quite different. Any story can be read and interpreted in multiple ways. Because the interpretation happens in the telling, why we tell a story, when, and to whom can make a difference in the meaning we assign it.

I think one of the reasons this story has stayed with me for so many years is because it has multiple meanings for me. On the one hand, I read it as a story of loss, and I do believe the church offered something to this young man and his wife through its familiar rituals, which tell a story of a love stronger than death. In the second version, it is not just Dwayne's story, but mine as well. My story is one of a missed opportunity to become a story companion and enter more deeply into Dwayne's story.

Accepting the Invitation

Invitations to become story companions come our way all the time, yet we miss them if we are not attuned to the power of stories. Religious leaders, chaplains, and all who provide pastoral care are in a unique position to become story companions and join the process of coauthoring meaningful lifestories through pastoral conversation. Opportunities for pastoral companionship and conversation abound in the daily work of ministry, in the general practice of pastoral care of hospital or home visitation, and as we encounter people in age-related life transitions. Stories emerge in preparation for ritual events, such as baptism, confirmation, church membership, weddings, and funerals, in which the church provides a framework of meaning for life transitions. Story creation is always a dialogical, relational process. Will we accept the invitation to become pastoral story companions and assist in shaping stories that are attentive to the intersection of divine and human narratives?

If we choose not to respond to this invitation, someone else will. Many someones are waiting to suggest what a good lifestory looks like. If you walk into a bookstore and find yourself in front of the self-help section, you will find a myriad of experts telling you how to improve your life. All you have to do is conform your lifestory to their version of it. The ministories in television ads often promise us how to find love, be more popular, or succeed in life by having whiter teeth, cleaner breath, or shinier hair, or by drinking the right beverage. "Someone" might be a well-meaning but ill-informed neighbor who says, "Don't worry, you can have another baby," on hearing the news of a couple's miscarriage, unaware of the pair's long struggle with fertility. The consequence is very likely to be the agony of the untold story of which Maya Angelou speaks in the opening quotation.

Many pastoral companions have the advantage of previous and long-standing relationships with storytellers and often have knowledge of the settings, or "narrative environments," of family, and community in which a particular story unfolds.[10] Pastoral story companions not only hear a story being told, they often see it lived out. Increasing narrative knowledge is a prerequisite to effective story companionship. Developing greater narrative knowledge helps us become better readers of lifestories and increases our ability to assist story companions to "write" richer stories in the midst of life's twists and turns.

As pastoral story companions, we continually pay attention to the thread of God's story in a particular lifestory. Becoming pastoral story companions involves a way of being in relationship, and a body of knowledge with a related set of skills. As a way of being in relationship, becoming a story companion can be an act of love. Recall that Oord defines love as "act[ing] intentionally, in sympathetic/empathic response to God and others, to promote overall well-being."[11] Listening to the story of another with our full attention is an intentional, loving action. As a "therapoetic" process, pastoral conversation facilitates making meaning, deepening our self-understanding, and fostering growth in love.[12]

Increasing Narrative Knowledge

Developing narrative knowledge increases the capacity of pastoral story companions to assist editing and revising or "restorying" lifestories over the course of a lifetime.[13] This process becomes increasingly important as time moves on and life situations change. So in what follows I present five elements of narrative knowledge essential for competent pastoral companionship. The first is the connection between storytelling and identity, a topic covered in some depth in chapter 1. Because our brains are wired for story, the relationship between narrative and identity is inseparable. The sense of self we develop is an autobiographical self.[14]

Second, because narrating our lives is a relational process that takes place in a social context, we must learn to read the "narrative environments" that shape a story in both positive and negative ways.[15] A third necessary element is knowledge of narrative development over the course of a life. Research on narrative development illumines the process of story construction from childhood through later life and leads to a fourth element of narrative knowledge. Knowing how narratives usually develop over the life course can help us identify when lifestory development gets off track.

Fourth, improving our skills in reading is essential to our formation as compassionate and knowledgeable story companions. Whether reading a written story or a lived text, we often "underread," missing much of the deeper meaning of a text.[16] As it turns out, the skills that serve us well in reading literature are intimately linked to our ability to read lifestories. Improving our reading ability begins with rediscovering our imagination, which is essential to processes of story creation, empathy, and interpretation.

Fifth, assessing whether a lifestory meets the criteria of a functional or good lifestory is dependent on the skills of close reading, knowing the criteria, and being able to recognize their presence or absence in a lifestory. Having a sense of what makes for a good lifestory also helps us recognize stories that are problem-saturated, too thin, or fixed and rigid.

The remainder of this chapter examines the linked concepts of narrative environments and narrative development. Narrative environments are the contexts—familial, social, and cultural—in which our narratives are formed.[17] "Master narratives" embedded in narrative environments shape assumptions and beliefs about matters such as gender, race, class, sexuality, and religion.[18] We are not always aware of these master narratives, though they influence the stories we tell about others and ourselves. Unexamined master narratives may lead us to "story-o-type" others, creating stories based on what we assume rather than on what is actually there in the living story before us.[19]

In order to assess the impact of narrative environments and master stories, I introduce a method for analyzing narratives and discerning the influence of both on lifestories and identity. Seminary students who have been introduced to social or contextual analysis as an integral part of action/reflection methods of pastoral or practical theology will find the analysis of narrative environments quite similar.

The latter part of this chapter provides an abbreviated overview of narrative development over the life course. Chapter 7 discusses methods for improving our reading skills, beginning with reigniting our imagination and specific skills of close reading. I examine in depth one type of close reading familiar to seminary students and ministers: exegesis. The latter part of that chapter addresses criteria of "good lifestories." Subsequent chapters consider various ways narratives fall short of the criteria of good stories and get off track, and the process of story revision.

Narrative Environments

Narrative environments are the contexts in which we construct our lifestories.[20] The microenvironments of the family, school, religious community, and city or town in which we dwell, as well as the macroenvironments of region, nation, and culture, comprise narrative environments.[21] An additional dimension of a narrative environment is a vast array of written and oral narratives we encounter in our daily lives: news articles, movies, TV shows, novels, Facebook posts, and many others. To some extent, the narrative environment in which we live shapes the stories to which we are exposed. As forms of global media expand, we are bombarded with stories. Like novelists weaving snippets of overheard conversation, literary allusions, or memories of a beloved grandmother into a new story, we draw on images from the various stories available within our narrative environments to compose our lifestories. The multiple narrative environments in which we live influence the way we interpret stories—our own and others'.[22] While I may believe I am writing my own story on a blank page, I am always a coauthor, constructing my story in an array of narrative environments.[23]

Microenvironments

Family is the usually the first narrative environment we enter and one of the most influential. In some ways, the family story has already begun before each of us appears as a new character. We absorb the stories of our families and "a set of unconscious and nonverbal attitudes about self other and world" that comprise the "narrative tone" of a family.[24] An optimistic narrative tone shapes a family's view of a world as a place full of wonder and opportunity in which other people are reliable and trustworthy.[25] A pessimistic narrative tone shapes a view of the world as unpredictable or full of dangers, and others as unreliable or indifferent.[26] A family's narrative tone may fall anywhere in between these poles and is reflected in the stories we hear and learn to tell.

Imagine two families going on summer vacation to a national park. Each car is fully packed with camping gear, two parents, and three kids. An hour away from the park both cars get flat tires; neither car has a spare. While waiting for roadside assistance to fix the tires, one family makes a game of finding unusual rocks, leaves, and other objects by the side of the road. The story they tell of that summer vacation includes a happy memory of the roadside scavenger hunt, reflecting an optimistic tone despite the setback. The other family tells a pessimistic story of the summer vacation that was ruined by the flat tire and the endless wait for a tow truck, leading to a stay-at-home vacation the next year.

From daily stories of school events or the funny thing that happened on our way to the grocery store, and the bigger stories about our places and purposes in the world, we learn "entire strategies for composing and editing the stories of our lives."[27] We also learn which stories are meant to be shared only in the family and which ones we can share outside of it. In short, we learn the implicit rules of which stories are to be shared with others and which are private.[28]

For example, while sitting around the dinner table a family may recall with laughter the story of how Grandma threw a plate at Grandpa's head one Thanksgiving but missed when he bent over to tie his shoe, but the family may prohibit the telling of this tale to anyone outside the family.

We may also inherit different styles of storytelling from each side of our family. One side may have a repertoire of rich, full stories about the extended family, while the other side may share only a bare outline of the family's history. For example, you may know much more about one side of the family, going back several generations, and have only a sketchy outline of family history from the other side. Have you ever asked why?

Macroenvironments and Master Narratives

National cultures as well as regional or ethnic subcultures are all forms of macro-environments.[29] Embedded within these environments are master narratives that significantly shape our beliefs and basic assumptions about topics such as gender, sexuality, politics, and religion.[30] If you have grown up in a religious narrative environment immersed in the master stories of the Jewish or Christian traditions, you may believe that God spoke and the world came into being. As an adult you may choose to leave behind one narrative environment and its stories in favor of another one. Conversion from one religious tradition to another is an example of this kind of movement. A religious narrative environment and its stories may be rejected for an alternative framework for meaning making, such as a scientific one.

Given that we navigate multiple narrative environments, we may draw from several in constructing our worldview, believing for instance that scientific and religious perspectives on how the world came into being are not in conflict but tell different stories for different purposes.

The master narratives of gender and race, which are often communicated through the stories we absorb in the microenvironments of family and school, significantly shape our sense of self and the roles we inhabit.[31] For example, ordained ministry is still not an option for women in some Christian denominations where the notion of gender is based on the interpretation of certain biblical passages and their view of women's roles. Educational institutions may convey the master narratives operating in a culture at a particular time.

For example, embedded in the Dick and Jane children's readers, in use from the 1930s to the 1970s, were master narratives on gender and race. Dick played actively with Spot the dog while Jane generally watched from the sidelines. Dick and Jane were white, as were all the characters in the books. The publisher made some effort to introduce new and diverse characters into the books in the 1960s, but the books fell out of use soon afterward.[32] While the main intent of these stories was to teach reading, they also communicated implicit stories and rules about gender roles and racial identity: boys were active, girls were passive, white was normative, and Black was invisible.

We may assume our own narrative environment is normative until we move into another one. What people talk about and how differs from place to place. A common conversation starter in the United States—"What do you do for a living?"—may be considered too personal a question in another country. In another part of the world, the introductory question may be an inquiry about your family, because in that culture one's connections to others are more important than how one earns a living.

Subcultures within a larger culture also have distinct narrative environments; these may be based on ethnic difference or geographic region. When I moved from San Diego, California, to Nashville, Tennessee, to attend graduate school, I moved northeast (geographically) to live in the South and found a summer job in a bank. Two of my colleagues, both native Tennesseans, taught me "how to eat and talk Southern." I soon learned to say "y'all" instead of "you guys" and found that "talking Southern" was not simply about a particular accent or colloquial expressions but included protocol for how one talked about certain topics. The blunt and direct communication I was used to, as well as the fast pace of my speech, in this different geographic region was considered impolite, even rude. I also discovered that conversations about race were shaped differently in the South, with its own history and stories, from the way they were shaped in the West, with its large population of Asian refugees and immigrants, Hispanics, African Americans, and Pacific Islanders. We often interpret others' stories from the perspective of our own narrative environment, which can result in miscommunication.

Like our own narratives, the narrative environments in which we construct stories continue to change and evolve. For example, master narratives about sexual identity are in significant contention in the United States right now as debates rage in the larger culture and in many Christian denominations about the appropriateness of marriage for same-sex couples or ordination of clergy candidates identifying as lesbian or gay. At any one time we may be navigating a number of narrative environments, such as of family, school, religion, community, nation, ethnic or racial identity, or class. These environments influence us, but we also contribute to changes in these environments.[33]

Each of these environments may have its own rules about what constitutes an acceptable or good story. To participate in a particular environment is, to some extent, to accept those rules as valid.[34] Our lifestories take form and substance within an "intricate, multilayered setting" and contribute to an evolving and changing narrative environment.[35] We both shape and are shaped by the stories in which we dwell.[36]

Why Narrative Environments Matter for Story Companions

It is crucial for story companions to be attentive to the narrative environments that shape stories, for such narrative environments are not neutral; for better or worse they influence how we construct our lifestories. While the influence of some narrative environments may be fleeting, others are enduring, some have a major influence, others a minor one. Some have a positive, creative influence on our sense of self as active agents and worthy human beings, and others can have a constraining or destructive influence.[37]

Some narrative environments are rich and offer us multiple stories through which to imagine ourselves, opening new possibilities for the construction of a self.[38] Debbie Thomas recalls such a rich environment in describing the reading room her mother created for her out of a small closet, with words and pictures cut out of magazines artfully decorating the walls. Thomas recalls spending time with her mother in the reading room.

> Every morning after breakfast, we would sit together at the tiny table, surrounded on all sides by my mother's word-and-picture tapestry. She would point and I would read, matching pictures to letters, symbols to meaning. Kitten, puppy, horse, rainbow. Star, ball, leaf, sun. Our bodies pressed together, her gaze guiding mine, we feasted on words.... By the time I turned four, my mother's project had succeeded; I was both a bookworm and a self-proclaimed writer.[39]

On the other hand, some narrative environments, such as prisons, are impoverished, restricting communication and usually forbidding images or pictures to adorn inmates' walls and restricting reading materials, if a library is available at all. To a large extent, one's story is dominated by the label "inmate" or "convict." In such a sterile and controlled environment few resources to imagine one's story, other than those imposed, are available.[40] Recent research on juvenile correction facilities suggests that these narrative environments unintentionally play an active role in constructing and reinforcing the very narratives of delinquency, dysfunction, and hopelessness in adolescents that one would assume such institutions were designed to deconstruct.[41]

Collusion of Micro- and Macroenvironments in Domestic Violence

The following case vignette illumines the destructive potential of the collusion between micro- and macroenvironments that give rise to various forms of violence and abuse. In this case abuse is in the form of parental neglect as well as sexual and physical abuse.

Case Vignette

Gemma was twelve when she was first offered to her mother's drug dealer in exchange for monetary payment.[42] Shortly after that, Gemma found herself living with the drug dealer who had become her pimp, offering her sexual service to others in exchange for the room and board he provided her, which her mother could no longer do. Gemma quickly learned several things about herself: she was a commodity, her worth was as a sexual object, and she had little control over her own life. The label "prostitute" shaped her lifestory and identity for many years.

Note that the lifestory of a prostitute was not one Gemma initially chose for herself but was imposed upon her in an environment of drug addiction, broken family, and poverty. At some point, it became the story of her life, one she felt powerless to change. Gemma, like "79% of women who completed a rape report," was raped before the age of twenty-five.[43] Male victims also experience rape at a young age; 28 percent are victims before the age of ten.[44] Recent statistics indicate that "nearly one out of two women and one out of five men experienced sexual violence victimization other than rape at some point in their lives."[45]

Various forms of violence affect people from all economic, racial, and ethnic classes, sexual orientations, and religious communities. Master narratives of gender in the larger culture support views of women as primarily sexual objects and violence as an acceptable means of resolving conflict. Women's bodies are objectified and continually used to sell products from cars to whiskey.[46]

Violence in the home continually puts many at risk. Family violence occurs all too frequently in the United States. According to the Centers for Disease Control, twenty people per minute are victims of intimate partner violence in the United States.[47] Unfortunately, by its silence the church has often colluded with other cultural master narratives that uphold domestic or intimate partner violence. Unspoken stories can be as powerful, if not more so, than stories told. When was the last time you heard mention of intimate partner or domestic violence from the pulpit in sermon, a pastoral prayer, or even in an announcement to collect supplies for a domestic-violence shelter?

A counternarrative is possible. Religious communities can tell a different story. The mission of the FaithTrust Institute is to call all religious communities to acknowledge that victims and survivors of various forms of abuse are among its members.[48] Religious communities can take action against violence, hold perpetrators, including clergy and religious leaders, accountable, and stand with victims and survivors. Religious communities can examine the ways in which religious texts and scriptures are interpreted to condone or allow communities to remain silent about family violence.[49]

After many years of suffering and assuming the end of her lifestory was fixed, Gemma was able, with assistance, to construct a counternarrative to those that had shaped her story for much of her life. After numerous arrests and imprisonments for prostitution, Gemma encountered prison chaplains who saw her differently from the way she saw herself, and she could finally begin to imagine another story with a different ending. Only as she allowed herself to imagine a different future was she able to complete a long-term recovery program within a supportive community, which also helped to construct a new narrative and sense of self.

In a very different narrative environment Gemma began to question the beliefs she held about herself that she had absorbed in the narrative environment in which she grew up. Slowly her story changed from one of prostitute to victim of child sex trafficking, to survivor, and finally to spokesperson and activist on behalf of other women with similar stories. A key factor in Gemma's transformation was entering a supportive community that required her to seek treatment for drug addition and attend support groups for survivors of sexual abuse and offered a narrative environment in which she was valued simply for being herself. In this environment she discovered new talents and abilities and was helped to construct a hopeful narrative supported and reinforced by those around her.

Challenging "Story-O-Types"[50]

Lest you are not yet convinced about the subtle power of narrative environments to influence our assumptions about the world, ask yourself if you made any assumptions about Gemma's race as you read her story. Her racial identity is not mentioned, but an environment of poverty and drug addiction is. Many of us who are white and grew up in suburban areas may assume that Gemma is African American and grew up in an impoverished urban area. Constant media images reinforce a stereotype of drug users as poor, Black, urban dwellers. Gemma did grow up in an impoverished community, but it was a rural, predominantly white community. Gemma, her mother, and her pimp are all white.[51] As we read Gemma's story, we might not notice that even though her racial identity or ethnicity is not mentioned, our minds fill in the blanks of the story, often outside our awareness. Before we know it, we have created a story about Gemma influenced by the assumptions and beliefs embedded in the narrative environment in which we grew up.

We all have a tendency to create "story-o-types" of others.[52] It is almost impossible to keep from creating a story of another person from the outside in from what we see.[53] As soon as we meet someone, we try to figure out who this person is and create an outside-in story before we know the inside-out story from the perspective of the other.[54] Even as pastors who desire to listen to the stories of others, we may find ourselves "story-o-typing" before we are aware we have done so.

Our stories of others are significantly influenced by the master narratives of the narrative environments in which we function, which often shape our assumptions and beliefs about the world. When I create a story based on master narratives of age, race, gender, national origin, or any other category, a narrative mismatch is likely between my outside-in story and the individual's inside-out story.[55] When a person's inside-out story is denied, rejected, or ignored, the person feels shut down, disconnected, and invisible.[56]

The stories we draw from our narrative environment can affect our own sense of identity as well. Unless we pay attention to the master narratives and environments that shape our stories, we are likely to take them for granted. We may assume the way we see things is the ways things must be. When we face similar scenarios over and over again, we are apt to sigh and say, "Well, that's the story of my life." We seldom pay much attention to the construction of our lifestories or critique the impact of narrative environments on our self-construction.[57] While we may be somewhat aware that we tell our stories differently as we move from one setting or context to another, we rarely self-consciously examine this process.[58]

Yet we can. We can become aware of this process, interrupt it, and critique the stories we create for others and ourselves. A first step is to become aware of this internal process, acknowledging that we are always interpreting experience and crafting a story. When we find ourselves sizing up someone and creating an outside-in story, we can ask questions of ourselves and challenge our assumptions and interpretations.

For example, when Dwayne entered my office and I found myself thinking, "Here we go again," I might have noted my reaction and wondered about it. Rather than assuming he wanted something simply because he was a stranger to me and not well dressed, or that I knew the reason for his visit based on appearances, I might have asked myself, "I wonder who this young man is. I wonder what brings him to the church office in the middle of the day. What need has led him here? Why do I assume he wants something from me? Where did I learn that?"

Deconstructing Master Narratives

Stories have power: they can heal or wound.[59] One of the basic practices of narrative therapy, a theory developed by Michael White and David Epston, is to recognize and analyze the power of master narratives, which they call "dominant sociocultural discourses."[60] White and Epston draw on the work of philosopher Michel Foucault to analyze, and in many cases, to contest the power of the dominant sociocultural discourses (master narratives) in shaping life narratives. While Foucault's overall analysis of power is quite complex, the particular insight relevant for us is the relationship of knowledge and power.[61] To put it simply, social power is exercised in such a way that some forms of knowledge, and therefore stories, are considered more acceptable or reliable than others. Some stories are pushed aside, "subjugated," marginalized.[62] This process can occur in the larger culture when stories of one group's conflict is seen as more authoritative than that of another.

For example, the rallying cry "Black lives matter" arose following the death of Trayvon Martin in 2012 and gained momentum as subsequent deaths of African American young men in police custody were revealed. We might interpret this phrase as "The stories of Black lives matter." At stake were conflicting stories of the event and the character of the young men involved. After Michael Brown was killed in Ferguson, Missouri, in 2014 he was portrayed as a thug in some media stories and a young man from a troubled community trying to make it to college by others. Who decides which story has more authority? Power is involved in this decision. Underneath these conflicting stories are master narratives of gender, age, and race.

Conflicts can occur in individual narratives if some stories are considered more authentic or more acceptable than others. As a consequence, stories of ourselves that might be more liberating are pushed aside or are forced underground. For example, I remember the Dick and Jane Readers. It has taken me many years to undo what I learned by following Jane's example, which was also reinforced in my family and church: good girls watch from the sidelines and aren't active or aggressive. The goals of narrative therapy include challenging oppressive master narratives and dominating discourses and reclaiming and strengthening alternative stories.[63] While narrative pastoral care is not intended to replicate narrative therapy, both share a common goal: to rediscover and strengthen alternative stories that allow for new, liberating, healing possibilities and ways of being in the world.[64]

Returning to the case vignette of Gemma, we might challenge the master narrative operating in Gemma's primary narrative environments. Imagine that somewhere along the line a seminary chaplain intern asks Gemma, "How did you come to believe your only value as a woman was as a sex object? When did you first learn this? How was it reinforced?" Gemma is likely to begin with stories from her family. Her mother, a powerful figure for any child, first conveyed this message to her. Her pimp and then her "customers" reinforced the message, and then so did the larger culture that labeled her a "prostitute" rather than a "victim of childhood sexual abuse." Gemma's story illumines how self-stories and identity develop over the course of a life as some stories are reinforced and others neglected.

Uncovering the Influence of Narrative Environments

Pastoral companions listen with three ears: two for the storyteller and one for the self. Our third ear is attuned to the internal stories we compose about others and specifically about the storyteller before us. As we listen, we continually challenge the story we are creating about this person. With our two ears, we listen to the storyteller and to the voices of the narrative environment in which stories are composed.

Many pastoral companions have previous and long-standing relationships with storytellers and often have knowledge of the larger narrative environment, or context of family and community, in which a particular story unfolds—though automatically assuming this storyteller's path echoes that of her family can also be misleading.[65] If we are aware of the influence of these environments on story formation, we can help the storyteller become aware as well.

We can assist the storyteller's discovery of the influence of narrative environments by keeping these questions in mind. Preferably, the storyteller will begin to ask these questions of him- or herself. When this does not occur, consider asking these questions in a form appropriate to the story being told.

- Where did you learn this way of thinking, believing, and/or acting?

- What authorities reinforced these beliefs?

- Who modeled this behavior for you?

- What contributed to your believing this story about yourself?

- Have you ever questioned this belief?[66]

As with any skill, the ability to analyze the impact of a narrative environment improves with practice. Asking ourselves some of these questions as we reflect on our own stories is one way to do this.

Educational settings often provide opportunities for practicing these skills of analysis. In-class role-playing based on fictional case studies also provides an opportunity for practicing these skills. The advantage of case studies is that they are often brief and the complexity of details can be controlled. A disadvantage is that a case study can be static or feel contrived.

A third method, and one I utilize in my teaching, is the analysis of a memoir. The advantage of a memoir is that it is a lived text, one based on real experiences. A memoir may cover only one portion of a person's life or cover a specified period of time, while an autobiography typically reflects on an entire life course up to the time it is written. Like all our stories, a memoir is an interpretation of events. Some memoirists, such as Jesmyn Ward, are motivated by a desire to make sense out of a difficult series of events and perhaps reinterpret them.

One disadvantage of a memoir is likewise that it is a lived text. The story is often complicated, with multiple characters and a plot that meanders between present and past. In a memoir, however, we can see the interpretive process; we follow the author as she sifts through memories, linking them in new ways or illumining them with new insights as she seeks to make sense or meaning of a portion of her life. Memoir analysis provides an effective means of discerning the influence of narrative environments on identity and lifestory formation.

Memoir Analysis: Discerning Narrative Environments and Master Narratives

Jesmyn Ward wrote her memoir *Men We Reaped* in 2013 after completing two novels and winning a 2011 National Book Award for her second book.[67] Ward's memoir seeks to make sense of the early deaths of five Black men, including her brother, and to honor their memories. She grew up with these young men who all died violent deaths between 2000 and 2004.[68] In the preface she notes that this is also her story, and the story of her family and community.[69] She writes to learn something about herself, these young men, and the people of her community. She is motivated to tell a different tale from what is often told about why young Black men in the South die young.

While she does not use the language of "master story" or "narrative environments," she does refer to the larger stories of racism and poverty that shaped her story and identity, those of her lost friends, and the possibilities imaginable and those out of reach. She writes in order to understand what happened and how "racism and economic inequality and lapsed personal and public responsibility festered" and infected the lives of her friends and community.[70] By writing the stories of these young men, she hopes to understand why their stories have become hers to tell.

Ward was reluctant to write a memoir, though encouraged by her editor to do so. Her hesitancy, writes Kevin Nance in an article discussing her memoir, was due not to a lack of material, but rather a wariness of being transported back to a place she was reluctant to revisit: the poverty of her youth, her hometown of DeLisle, Mississippi, and the overwhelming grief she felt at the four of her friends and her beloved brother.[71] To go back was to face a "culture that devalued their lives."[72]

In addition to her own emotional reluctance, Ward also wanted to protect the people of her community, comprised primarily of working-class and poor Black families. At the same time, she wanted to be honest about the reality of life in DeLisle shaped by racism, poverty, and economic inequality, which often led its citizens to use recreational drugs as a solace. The risks of this solace, however, were high, including addiction, drug dealing, or other illegal activity to support one's habit, and the potential consequences associated with those behaviors.[73]

Ward's rich depiction of the lives of her friends challenges the "story-o-types" of poor Black men and women who turn to drug use because they are more interested in criminal behavior than work. Her friend Roger turned to drugs out of desperation and the crushing weight of racism and poverty. Only after he died of a drug overdose, the last of the five young men whose lives and death she recalls, did Ward connect her own alcohol use to the drug use rampant in her community and the despair underlying both.[74] Ward knew she "lived in a place where hope and a sense of possibility were as ephemeral as a morning fog," but did not see the connection between the lack of hope and the rampant drug use in her community.[75] In a narrative environment in which despair is the predominant tone, drug use became an expected form of relief.

As Ward reflects on the events that followed Roger's funeral, we see her shifting her focus from the immediate story of her friend's death to the influence of the larger story in which the deaths of all five of her friends occurred. As Ward and others stand in front of Roger's house as his body is being carried away, her ex-boyfriend Brandon says, "They are picking us off one by one."[76] As she drives home, she ponders Brandon's statement and wonders "who *they* were" and were *they* us?[77] Ward wonders what she is not seeing and as she drives home in the darkness, "suddenly *they* seemed as immense as the darkness, as deep, as pressing."[78]

As Ward continues on her way home, she wonders about the identity of the invisible author who seems to be writing the stories of her friends and community.[79] We see Ward beginning to discern the influence of the narrative environment and the master narratives of race and class on shaping her story and those of the young men who died. Though Ward does not formally propose a set of questions like those suggested earlier, she does begin to wonder about the sources of the stories that shaped her own identity and those of her friends so that drug use was one of the few available escapes from despair.

As Ward's memoir unfolds, she reveals what is true for many of us: when we are young, we are not fully aware of the impact of the narrative environment. As children, we take for granted the world in which we grow up. We assume that what we see is the way it has been and always will be. Although Ward was aware of racism in her childhood, it does not appear she reflected on it much in her early life lived largely in the embrace of a close-knit family and predominantly Black community. She became more acutely aware of the powerful but often unspoken master narrative of race as an adolescent due a change of circumstance and developmental changes.

Beginning in junior high school and continuing through high school, she attended a private school in which she was often the only Black student or one of only a few.[80] Ward's education was made possible by some of the clients for whom her mother worked as a maid. The new cognitive capacities of adolescence, which give rise to an increased self-awareness of one's identity and the capacity for critical thinking, are evident in Ward's reflections of this time in her life. In recalling her visits to see her father in New Orleans, she reveals her growing awareness of the unspoken master narrative of racism through her classmates' perceptions of New Orleans as a dangerous place where white people were attacked without provocation.[81] What was left unsaid was that those who committed such crimes were assumed to be Black. Such perceptions conflicted with her experience of New Orleans and the young men she knew, her father's half-brothers.[82] Ward has difficulty reconciling the myth of New Orleans she hears from her classmates with the reality she experiences of playing football with her uncles, enjoying ice-pops melting in the summer heat, and spending time with her father.[83]

Observations about the impact of race and gender on identity run throughout Ward's memoir. As she talks about her younger brother Joshua, she wonders about the impact of the unintended lessons he learned from their father about being a Black male in the South: "unsteady work, one dead-end job after another."[84] Ward notes that what these lessons taught him is how little value his life had.[85]

Ward's mother found ways to create opportunities for her that might have been more accessible to both her and Joshua if their lives "weren't marked by poverty or race."[86] With the advantage of a strong education, Ward went on to college and eventually graduate school. She notes that her brother had fewer role models and opportunities. Her brother focused on survival, while Ward was able to dream about the future.[87]

Ward explores family stories that shaped her and her brother's identities. Jesmyn Ward was the firstborn child but was premature and not expected to live. She was so tiny that her father's "finger was the size of my arm."[88] When she was a teenager, her father told her, "I wanted to tell them you were a fighter."[89] This sense of being a fighter shaped Ward's identity and she saw it reflected in her family.

She recalls the story of her maternal grandmother who raised seven children on her own.[90] After holding a number of low-paying jobs she was hired to work at a pharmaceutical plant.[91] "My grandmother got the factory job after a man saw her lift and carry a full grown hog on her shoulder."[92] Ward observes, "We come from a long line of men and women who have fought hard to live."[93]

While Ward learned to be a fighter, she observes that her brother had to learn how to "be a Black man in the South" and would face different challenges from those she did[94] and "have to fight in ways that I would not."[95] As a Black male he was seen differently and faced what Ward calls "a different kind of racism" from what she faced.[96] While she faced "blatant, overt, individualized racism" at school, her brother faced a more subtle form in which he was seen as "just another young Black male destined to drop out."[97]

As Ward reflects on these experiences, we see again an increasing awareness of the influence of a larger story in which her brother's stories and hers were being written. She realizes that her brother's story and hers were being written against the backdrop of a larger story over which they had little control.[98] Some of the questions that help reveal the influence of a narrative environment implicit in Ward's reflections are, Where did you learn this way of thinking, believing, or acting? What authorities reinforced these beliefs? Who modeled this behavior for you?

In the final chapter of her memoir, Ward explicitly names the larger story in which her story and those of the five young men whose lives and deaths she recounts were authored. She cites statistics about "what it means to be Black and poor in the South."[99] Mississippi, with a Black population of 38 percent of the total, is one of six states in which African Americans account for at least a quarter of the total population.[100] Mississippi has the highest poverty rate in the South, which overall has a poverty rate higher than other regions in the United Sates.[101] Ward interprets the impact of these statistics, which give a picture of the narrative environment in which her own story is formed: "By the numbers, by all the official records, here at the confluence of history, of racism, of poverty, and economic power, this is what our lives are worth: nothing."[102] The power of these larger stories is felt internally, impacting individual lives. "We inherit these things that breed despair and self hatred and tragedy multiplies."[103]

Ward's memoir offers an alternative narrative to the narrative environments and embedded master narratives that shaped her life, her brother's, and the lives of and deaths of the other four men whose stories she shares. She writes, "This story is only a hint of what my brother's life was worth. . . . It is worth more than I can say. . . . All I can do in the end is say."[104] In the closing pages she wrote about the unacknowledged "great darkness" that shadowed her friends lives and hers and proclaimed "*You are nothing*."[105]

Ward's narrative does just that: it names the darkness. She illumines how our small stories are caught in larger ones that we may hardly notice. We may feel the effects of the larger stories but assume we alone are responsible as the authors of our own stories, not recognizing we are at most coauthors. Not all narrative environments are negative, and because we navigate in more than one at a time the positive impact of one environment may mitigate the negative effects of another. Ward illustrates this as well when she speaks of her mother's example and how it gave her courage to tell a difficult story: "My mother had the resilience to cobble together a family from the broken bits of another."[106] From her mother's example Ward learned how her people had survived oppression and the violence of slavery for generations. She learned survival.[107]

In the midst of a cultural narrative environment that would have her believe she was worth nothing, in the environment of her family, under the tutelage of her mother, Ward learned "to have courage, to have strength, to be resilient, to open [my] eyes to what is, and to make something of it."[108]

As pastoral story companions we can learn from Ward and others to open our eyes and to notice the larger environments in which stories unfold. By asking questions of these environments we can discern the positive or negative impact on individual stories. By attending to the multiple environments in which we all live, we may identify alternative stories that challenge the negative impact of some of the master narratives that dominate our stories and shape our identities. Because our lifestories are continually under revision, we have the opportunity, as Ward demonstrates in her memoir, to revisit the stories of the past and to give them new meaning, which often opens up new possibilities for our stories of the future.

Lifestory Development

The stories of our lives do not appear fully formed and beautifully crafted but rather develop over time, within narrative environments.[109] Narrative development begins in infancy and continues throughout our lives. Lifestories evolve, becoming more complex as we interpret and reinterpret events of our lives. The meanings we assign to certain events tend to shift as we look back or forward from new vantage points, as Ward's memoir illustrates.[110] Because storying our lives is an interpretive process, imagination plays a key role. Functional lifestories, however, are not simply made up; to be believable, our stories must be grounded in the world in which we live.[111]

Lifestory Development in Childhood and Adolescence

In childhood, we begin to gather the raw materials for the construction of our lifestories from our own experiences, from our families, and from the cultural contexts in which we are raised. Usually by age two, the emergence of an "autobiographical self" can be observed as toddlers begin to tell "simple little stories" about themselves.[112] By age five, children have gained a sense of "what stories are about," that they contain "motivated, mindful characters acting upon their beliefs and desires," that the actions of one character will be met by reactions from other characters in the story as the plot moves along from beginning to end.[113]

Children learn to expect stories to be structured in a particular way. Try changing the ending of a young child's favorite story and see what reaction you get. You are likely to be met with confusion or correction as a child restores not only the correct content of the story, but also the flow and structure.

Children continue to develop capacities for "autobiographical memory and personal storytelling" throughout childhood and into adolescence within the contexts of family, community, and culture.[114] Parents and other adults who encourage children to shape their experiences into stories provide "verbal and psychological supports" for children as they begin to develop a sense of self.[115] Children encouraged "to reflect and elaborate on their personal experiences" generally develop "richer autobiographical memories" and are able to "tell more detailed stories about themselves."[116] In contrast, children who are not so encouraged may have less-developed self-narratives.[117]

What was your favorite story as a child, the one you asked to hear over and over? Chances are bits of this story are somehow woven into your own story. Think for a moment about the message the story imparted to you. Maybe it was one of being brave, or curious, or independent. Throughout childhood we collect the stuff out of which lifestories will be more consciously constructed beginning in adolescence. Experiences we have, people we meet, and challenges we face shape the themes or tones of the stories we will begin to construct more self-consciously in adolescence.[118]

By the time children begin to transition into adolescence they have learned to narrate their own experiences to conform to social expectations of what good stories are about and how they are structured.[119] The biological, cognitive, and social changes that occur in adolescence set the stage for "the emergence of identity as a new problem."[120] Their developing cognitive capacities allow adolescents to understand the world in abstract terms and to reason from hypotheses leading to the questioning of reality.[121]

Assumptions about self-identity may be challenged as adolescents realize that different people can see them differently.[122] A dawning awareness that *who I am now is not who I was* results in questions of identity: Who am I really?[123] Adolescents become more actively involved in the construction of identity and lifestory, challenging the given ideologies and narratives of childhood and forming their own. Ward's reflections on her experiences in high school illustrate this process.

Lifestory Development in Adulthood and Later Life

While we become more actively involved in the formation of identity and lifestory in adolescence, this ongoing process "remains the central psychosocial task of our adult years."[124] In our early adult years we continue to refine narrative identity, which become our internalized and changing lifestory.[125] Popular conceptions about adulthood often assume that little growth and development occur during our adult years. Theories of adult narrative development are influenced by Erik Erikson's view of lifelong development over a series of eight stages.[126]

Narrative development, however, unfolds as a story does—not always in a straight line—rather than progressing through fixed stages. In some ways, however, we can assess development only retrospectively as we look back to where we have been.[127] Just as the plot of a novel can thicken as we get further into the story and more characters appear and more twists and turns are revealed, so, too, can our lifestories thicken over time.[128]

In some situations, however, our lifestories may become thinner, particularly in late life as we outlive spouses, partners, other family members, and friends.[129] Restrictions on mobility due to advanced age or illness can also narrow our lifestories as less happens to us and thus less requires our narration. At the same time, the meaning of our lifestories may deepen as we look back to past events and assign different meanings to them. Ward's memoir illustrates this point. It was not until some time had passed that Ward was able to reflect on the deaths of her friends as something other than random coincidence, something she names "a great darkness."[130]

The tasks of adult development include ongoing identity formation, which has been previously explored in some depth, and generativity. A term drawn from Erikson, "generativity is an adult's concern for and commitment to promoting the well-being of future generations."[131] Narrative psychologist Dan McAdams argues that generativity serves an evolutionary function by promoting the social good and enhancing group survival.[132] Generativity is about passing on some aspects of ourselves to posterity and can be expressed in numerous ways in contemporary societies.[133] While parenting may be the form of generativity that first comes to mind, we also express our generativity through teaching, volunteer work, mentoring, political activity, leadership, and religious commitment and involvement.[134] Generative adults are motivated to make the world a better place, to help shape a good life and a good society, not only for themselves but for others as well.[135] Erikson viewed generativity as the primary psychological challenge of middle adulthood.[136] Given its focus on promoting well-being, generativity has a moral dimension as well and has much in common with the definition of love given earlier in the book.

Research has revealed some intriguing insights about adults who rate high on self-report scales that measure generativity. Highly generative adults tend to have more extensive friendship networks and feel more connected to their communities than do adults who rate lower in generativity.[137] Adults high in generativity tend to be more involved in community and religious organizations, volunteer more frequently, give more to charity, "attend religious services and engage in religious activities more often," and generally demonstrate "more social responsibility and higher levels of moral development than adults low in generativity."[138] Highly generative adults are often less anxious and depressed and more satisfied with life than those with lower generativity.[139] Research on generativity indicates it "is good for others and good for the self."[140]

In general, lifestories provide "justification and motivation for the lives we have chosen to lead."[141] Dan McAdams has also demonstrated that highly generative adults in the United States tend to tell particular kinds of stories—redemptive stories. The basic arc of the redemptive narrative is that though something bad happens, something good ultimately comes out of that difficulty. Redemptive narratives follow a particular plot line, beginning in special circumstances or with a sense of blessing, progressing to an increasing awareness of the suffering of others.[142] The protagonist then encounters setbacks or challenges but triumphs over the difficulty, often with the help of others, and moves progressively forward, contributing to a better world.[143] McAdams identifies six languages of redemption used in the construction of redemptive narratives in the United States, only one of which uses explicitly religious language.[144]

Running throughout all life narratives are the themes of *agency* and *communion* or *power* and *love*. Agency is "a broad tendency to expand, assert, defend, control or express the self."[145] Agency involves an expression of power and a desire to get ahead.[146] *Communion*, on the other hand, is about connection to others, loving and caring for others.[147] Communion is about belonging and "getting along."[148]

The narratives of highly generative adults in the United States often reveal conflict between strong needs for power, or the expression of agency, and strong needs for communion or love and belonging.[149] Attending to the relative strength of these two themes in lifestories can provide some sense of the direction of adult development. Lifestories with "very high levels of agency to the exclusion of communion can suggest narcissism."[150] Lack of agency, however, "may suggest depression or low self-esteem."[151] In the United States a "healthy dose of agency may be necessary for psychological health and flourishing."[152] The relative balance of agency and communion considered optimum for adult maturity might differ in various cultures and is a factor to be considered in developing criteria for evaluating stories.

Conclusion

Gaining a deeper understanding of how narrative environments function and how stories develop over the life course contributes to the formation of compassionate and competent pastoral story companions. Learning to discern the influence of the constricting or demeaning master narratives embedded in a narrative environment prepares story companions to challenge these with alternative stories from another narrative environment, including a storyteller's religious tradition. Congregational settings may provide pastoral story companions an advantage in observing narrative development over the life span. Religious communities are usually intergenerational communities, while in many other settings functions are age segregated. As our narrative knowledge increases, we may wonder, "What makes one story better than another?" In the next chapter, we turn to specific reading strategies in order to answer this question.

Chapter 7

Reading Lifestories: The Art of Close Reading

Before there were books, we read each other. We still do, every minute of every day.

—Lisa Cron, *Wired for Story*

S ome of us take to reading like a duck to water and develop a love of reading from the moment we are introduced to picture books as a young child. Reading is a skill we generally learn early in life as we associate written symbols with words we know: *a* is for apple, and so forth. For some of us, reading requires effort, which may be true for reading lifestories as well as written ones. Fortunately, we can improve our skills for both kinds of reading because they are linked. Psychologists have discovered that the "same processes of perception and comprehension, of memory and imagination that operate in our experience of daily life" are at work when we read the printed word.[1] What we know about reading literature can be applied to reading lives.[2]

If you have had the experience of getting completely absorbed in the story, you know what it is like to feel your heart pounding when the protagonist is in danger or find tears streaming down your face when she is beside herself with grief. When we get lost in a story, we see the world through another's eyes. When we get caught up in the emotion of a story, we experience what neuroscientists have now confirmed: "Everything we experience is automatically coated in emotion."[3] Turns out that reason and emotion are not polar opposites, as many of us were led to believe, but inseparable.[4] According to one researcher, "If it weren't for our emotions, reason wouldn't exist at all."[5]

In a recent study, subjects were asked to read a short story while researchers observed their brain function through fMRI (functional magnetic resonance imaging) and discovered that the regions of the brain that light up when we engage in an activity also light up when we read about it.[6] We can thank our mirror neurons for "allowing us to feel what others experience almost immediately as if it were happening to us" when we hear a lived story or read one in a book.[7]

Why is this important? It reminds us that when reading a life, our task is not to dissect it as we would a pinned insect to figure out how it functions. Such paradigmatic or scientific knowledge may be helpful in figuring out why fireflies glow in the dark, but it is much less helpful in discerning the meaning in lifestories. When we read a story with significant understanding, "we create a mental simulation of the events described by the story."[8] These mental processes contribute to empathy, allowing us imaginatively to enter another's story. At the same time, we bring our own interpretations or perspective to the story we hear based on our own history and experience. Empathy also requires that we maintain an awareness of our own perspective, which may provide the storyteller with a different view, allowing for a new interpretation or meaning. At the same time, we monitor our emotional reactions and perceptions to avoid constructing a story-o-typed story based on our experience rather than that of the storyteller.

Reading Books and Reading Lives

The link between the skills of reading literature and reading lives is good news: we can practice improving our reading skills on written stories before experimenting on the lived version. While much of the research on reading has been applied to fiction, it is equally applicable to reading memoirs. Memoir is considered a form of creative nonfiction. The nonfiction part, of course, assumes that someone's story, while an interpretation of life events, is based on actual events. The creative part applies strategies of fiction writing to craft a riveting story. Reading memoirs is one way for students in the classroom to learn skills of effective life reading necessary for story companionship. Students can practice these skills in a safe space with relatively little risk before trying them out on each other or on those with whom they work in a ministry setting. We do have to be aware, however, of the temptation of story-o-typing, which can occur in reading memoirs as well as in listening to a lifestory.

A first step toward improving our reading skills is rediscovering our imaginations; a second is developing the skills for the close reading, or analysis of a text. Literary analysis provides strategies for examining how stories function and deepening our careful understanding of a story's component parts: plot, character, time, and the relationship between the narrator and the reader.[9] Before we can interpret a text we need to have a thorough understanding of it. Close reading of a text contributes to narrative competence as we learn to pay close attention, developing the imagination and deepening empathy.[10]

A close reading of a text prepares us for the next step, which may be the most important: interpretation. Reading is an interpretive process in which both storyteller and reader/listener are involved. The meaning of a story is revealed through a careful and close reading. Stories are created, woven out of interpretations of selected events and memories. The process of story creation in our own lives happens so immediately that we are often unaware that a story is an *interpretation* of events and not simply a recounting.

In pastoral care, both storyteller and listener are engaged in this process of interpretation. As story companions, we are not passive participants; we always interpret the story we hear, bringing our own perspective to it while seeking to understand the storyteller's perspective. As we engage in this mutual process of interpretation, both companions shape the meaning assigned to a story or a life narrative. In the role of listeners, we must continually revise the story we have created of the other based on initial impressions in order to come a little closer to knowing another's story and the meaning ascribed to it.[11]

Reading and Imagination

Reading well requires that we rediscover our imaginations. When our imaginations are engaged, reading transports us to strange worlds in which we vicariously experience new adventures. Maybe you were thrilled with Maurice Sendak's *Where the Wild Things Are*, still think of the book *Goodnight Moon* when you look up at the night sky, or recall the adventures of Curious George.[12] Some people seem to be natural-born readers, taking in the printed word in all conceivable forms anywhere words appear—on the printed page, the computer screen, or the back of a cereal box. For others of us, reading becomes a chore when it seems merely to be about gathering information to pass a test or complete an assignment. Many of us were taught to believe imagination and wonder are childish things we put away when we become serious adults. Recovering our imaginations, however, is a courageous act that signals a willingness to go into undiscovered territory and experience new adventures.

Without imagination we would have few, if any, stories. Imagination is essential to great literature that transports us to another world or causes us to weep at the misfortunes of a fallen hero or heroine. Narrative and imagination are also intertwined in the stories we tell about the daily events of our lives.[13] Imagination is essential for considering what is possible and plays a role in the meaning we assign to stories of past events.[14] It is imagination that allows us to "time-travel," to move between the past, present, and future.[15] Imagination allows us to see an open future filled with possibilities; it is the foundation of hope.

Much of our formal education, however, focuses on developing our rational intellect. As a result, we may be left with the false impression that reason and imagination conflict rather than exist as close companions. Narrative psychologist Molly Andrews describes the role of imagination somewhat poetically. It is "not something we dust off and put on for special occasions, a psychological tiara of sorts. Rather, it guides us from our waking hour to when we go to bed at night. It is with us always, sitting side by side with our reason and perception."[16] Andrews goes on to say that imagination can transform our individual lives and communities.[17]

Imagine where we would be as a society without Martin Luther King Jr.'s dream of a better future in which all human beings are treated as equals and children of all colors play happily together.[18] Note that King's dream for the future drew heavily on biblical imagination and faith in a God still creating possibilities. The "I have a dream" section of his speech concludes with a quotation from Isaiah 40:4-5: "The crooked shall be made straight, and the rough places plain: and the glory of the LORD shall be revealed, and all flesh shall see it together" (KJV). We may not have fulfilled King's dream yet, but without the possibility to imagine a different future, we would have little hope. Imagination makes change and hope possible.

Imagination is essential to ministry. Without imagination, preaching can easily become a moralistic lecture rather than an invitation to creative and faithful living. Without imagination, church leadership and administration can easily become about doing what we have always done rather than about reimagining how to live out God's love story in a changing context.

Imagination is also essential to narrative competence and pastoral companionship. Imagination allows us to entertain new interpretations of an often-recited story, to create a hopeful vision of the future, and to believe that the way it has always been is not the way it has to be. Imagination is also essential to empathy, allowing us to enter into another's experience that may be very different from our own.

Close Reading of a Text

A "close read" is a way of analyzing a text based on careful observation, attending to a text with "a level of detail not used in everyday reading."[19] A close read pays careful attention to the form and structure of the text as well as the content. It might be more appropriate to talk about close readings, since multiple readings of a passage are needed for a deeper understanding of it. In the first reading of a text, we can simply ask, "What is going on here and how do I know?"[20] In a second reading, we might pay more attention to the author's language and word choice as well as look for patterns, repetitions, or contradictions.[21] In a third pass, we might ask questions about patterns we noticed and pay attention to our reactions as a reader.[22] And so on. A close reading of a text lays the foundation for a deeper analysis, discerning what the text might mean as well as what it says.

Close Reading and Narrative Medicine

One might expect to find the skills of close reading taught in the humanities; however, English majors are not the only ones who learn the skills of close reading. Medical students are learning them as well. Dr. Rita Charon and advocates of narrative medicine have reenvisioned medical education to include the development of narrative knowledge by teaching medical students the art of a close reading of literary texts.[23] The goal of such training is to increase medical students' empathy, imagination, and ability to enter more fully into the world of patients, thus discerning the narrative of an illness, not just its physiological dimensions.[24] Future physicians are learning that scientific knowledge may not provide a sufficiently complex understanding of an illness.

While the pastoral task is not to diagnose illness, as it is for a physician, both pastors and physicians are practitioners concerned with increasing the health and well-being of those under their care. Advocates of narrative medicine have come to realize that body, mind, and soul cannot be so easily separated and that medicine needs to be about more than physical mechanics. Through the art of a close reading of a literary text, physicians learn to read the embodied stories of illness in the context of the larger story of the person who is suffering. Those of us engaged in ministry generally view our task as caring for the whole person, not a disembodied soul. Narrative medicine has much to teach us about developing the narrative knowledge essential to forming effective pastoral companions.[25]

From Reading Texts to Reading Lives

All of us can become better readers of both written and lived texts, though some people seem to have a natural talent for it. Improving our ability for a close reading of written texts such as novels, short stories, poems, memoirs, as well as biblical or theological texts can improve our ability to read lifestories. If you are a seminary student or graduate you have been (or will be) introduced to the skills of close reading in the course of graduate education. Perhaps you have been asked to do a close reading of a passage from James Cone or Karl Barth in a systematic theology class, or Reinhold Niebuhr or Emilie Townes in an ethics class.

One form of close reading that you will certainly be expected to learn as a part of a seminary education is *exegesis*. We may associate the term *exegesis* exclusively with the analysis of biblical texts, but its meaning is broader than that. The noun translated *exegesis* derives from a Greek verb meaning "to relate in detail or expound."[26] Although we don't generally think of it this way, exegesis is actually something we do in our everyday lives.[27] We engage in exegesis any time we seek to interpret or explain any form of communication, written or oral.[28] In the last chapter we began to employ the skills of close reading, or a form of exegesis, in discerning the presence and influence of narrative environments and masters stories in Jesmyn Ward's memoir.

Until now, you may not have connected the skills of biblical exegesis or reading a biblical text and reading a lifestory. Biblical exegesis has its own unique forms of interpretation that relate to the particular characteristics of biblical texts: they are ancient, written in another language, often in a very different cultural context, composed over a long period of time, and are considered sacred.[29] In the case of biblical exegesis, we are clearly interpreting a written text, and often a small portion of it. The exegetical process can be quite technical and draw on a variety of forms of biblical criticism, including historical, textual, grammatical, form, and literary criticism. Yet many of the interpretive skills required for biblical exegesis are applicable to the reading of the lived texts of lifestories. Literary criticism, which pays attention to authorship, historical and cultural setting, as well as the shape, form, and purpose of the text, is worth particular note.

Literary criticism, which provides methods of reading a wide variety of texts, including fiction, poetry, and biblical texts, is foundational to the formation of narrative knowledge advocated in narrative medicine. Physicians who are trained in narrative medicine practice their interpretive skills on literature before learning to transfer those skills to reading the stories of illness in patients' lives. Many pastoral story companions practice the skills of biblical exegesis regularly in preparation for leading Bible studies or preaching. Once we develop a narrative perspective and understand a life as a lifestory, it is possible to see the transferability of exegetical skills from biblical to lived human texts.

Exegesis: From Preaching to Pastoral Companionship

Perhaps the approach to exegesis that provides the best parallel for pastoral care is found in the exegetical preparation required for preaching, something most ministers do on a regular basis. Preaching and pastoral care do have different purposes. Preachers interpret biblical texts to speak to the lives of the hearers. Pastoral story companions interpret lived texts to discern the meaning assigned to an event or a life. Common to both practices of ministry is bearing witness to the interweaving of God's story and our own. Also common to both is the requirement of a full understanding of the story, in all its dimensions, before offering an interpretation. Exegesis prepares us for interpretation.

Homiletics professor Thomas G. Long proposes five steps of biblical exegesis for preaching: (1) getting the text in view, (2) getting introduced to the text, (3) attending to the text, (4) testing what is heard in the text, and finally, (5) moving toward the sermon.[30] How might we adapt this process of biblical exegesis for preaching to the practice of pastoral companionship?

1. Getting the Text in View

Selecting the text, usually with a particular reason in mind, is the first step for the preacher.[31] In pastoral care, you might say, we are often selected by the text, for while in some cases we may initiate a pastoral conversation, much of the time we pastors respond to a person's request or invitation. Intentionality is involved in both preaching and pastoral care. Just as we make an intentional choice about a preaching text, we must make an intentional choice to recognize the (human) text before us and respond to the invitation to become a pastoral companion.

The following case study will serve as our text as we apply Long's five steps to exegeting a lifestory, beginning with the first step of getting the text in view.

Case Vignette: Three Generations under One Roof

Background:

Mrs. Fran Smith (age seventy) is a regular and active member of a church in which you serve. She lives with and cares for her mother, Mrs. Agnes Russell (ninety-two). Mrs. Russell is in relatively good health for her age but is frail and has arthritis. Mrs. Russell has been active in the church but has not attended for the last three months. She has told you that her arthritis makes it too hard to get in and out of the car or to sit in the hard pews for the entire service. She no longer goes out of the house much, except for her doctors' appointments. Mrs. Russell needs assistance with tasks such as getting in and out of the bathroom and dressing herself.

Sylvia Smith, Mrs. Smith's forty-six-year-old, single daughter, also lives with her mother and grandmother. Sylvia has a history of mental illness (schizophrenia), having been diagnosed at age twenty-two, and has been hospitalized on at least three occasions, including for two weeks shortly after her father died. Sylvia has been fairly stable for the last year or so and is doing well on her current medication. She is generally able to help her mother care for her grandmother.

You have been the pastor at this church and to this family for only about a year, but you have gotten to know them well. You have learned that Mrs. Russell has been a member of the church for about seventy years, since she and her husband were married there. Both Fran and Sylvia Smith have grown up in that church. About six months ago, shortly after your arrival, you conducted the funeral for Fran's husband, Mr. Jack Smith, aged eighty-five. Jack died of a heart attack but was in the early stage of Alzheimer's disease. Sylvia was particularly close to her father and has had a hard time with his death. Fran Smith and Mrs. Russell, more acquainted with loss, seemed to cope somewhat better. You have been visiting the Smith home about once a month or so since the funeral.

Presenting Incident:

When you arrive for your monthly Tuesday visit, Mrs. Fran Smith greets you at the door but is not her normal cheerful self; she seems distracted and overwhelmed. Peering in the door, you notice that Mrs. Russell has her right arm in a sling. When you inquire, Mrs. Smith says, "Well, we have had some trouble lately. Mother got hurt, Sylvia has been upset, and I am exhausted." You were not aware that Fran Smith had been struggling. You recall seeing her at church last Sunday, but she did not stop to chat as she usually does. Mrs. Russell is sleeping in the chair in the living room. Sylvia is somewhat agitated and is pacing in the kitchen.

While Mrs. Smith has invited you in, she seems anxious that you not stay long. She asks if you will just say a short prayer today and come back another time. You respond by saying she does seem to have a lot going on and you are concerned for her. You set a time to come back the next day, during Mrs. Russell's nap time and while Sylvia is attending at a program at the church for adults with chronic mental illness.

Note: I have not specified the ethnicity of the persons in this case. You may do so and you might try more than one (change the names if needed). What difference does the racial and or ethnic identity you assign make to your exegesis of this case?

What is the larger story? To return to the preaching metaphor, once we have selected a preaching text, Long advises preachers to "reconsider where the text begins and ends."[32] His point is that the little piece of scripture assigned or chosen for a particular Sunday is a part of a larger story. We are likely to misinterpret a text if we do not understand the larger picture. Likewise in pastoral care we can easily focus on one piece of the story, or an initial question, and miss the larger narrative. Sometimes the storyteller doles out only a little piece of the story to see how the story listener will react before continuing.

For example, when Dave and Lila, a young couple married for a little over a year, asked to meet with me, their initial question was about the church's position on abortion. I easily could have turned to official church documents and given them an answer, and they might simply have left my office with this information. I told the couple I would give them an answer but that first I would like to understand what prompted their question at this time.

The larger story was complex. Dave had been diagnosed with cancer a few months after their marriage, had undergone several difficult surgeries, and was still adjusting to the consequences of his illness. Lila, who had always opposed abortion, was now two months pregnant. Feeling overwhelmed with all that had happened in their lives in less than a year, neither felt ready to be a parent. If I had not been curious about the larger story behind their initial question, I would have missed the opportunity to accompany them as they sorted out how their story would proceed.

As you review the case I've described, what clues might you find to a larger story in the case of Fran Smith? Some of the observations you make that might be linked to a larger story are the following:

- Your recollection of conducting Jack Smith's funeral six months ago.

- Jack died of a heart attack before further progression of Alzheimer's disease.

- Sylvia was close to her father.

- Jack was in the early stage of Alzheimer's and may still have been able to help Fran with her mother's care.

- Mrs. Smith is usually cheerful but is anxious today.

- She usually welcomes your visit and looks forward to your time together in prayer. Today she asks only for a quick prayer.

We don't yet know what these observations mean. Recognition of today's incident as part of a larger story will provide a deeper appreciation of its meaning.

Establishing a reliable translation assists in you in getting a proper and full view of the text.[33] For the preacher this means either turning to the original language or consulting multiple translations. As Long notes, "Every translation of a biblical text is already an interpretation of that text."[34] The purpose of this step is to make us aware of the implicit meanings assigned to a text simply by choosing one English word over another in translating the text from the original language.[35]

For pastoral companions, this step is about making sure we understand that communication and language do play a role. Unless we are providing pastoral care through a translator, storytellers and companions usually speak the same language. Yet we may assume (incorrectly) that because we speak the same language we mean the same thing. The shared language may not be the first or even second language of the storyteller or the story companion. Even when both story companions are native speakers of the same language, regional differences in speech may obscure meaning. For example, the first time a Southern colleague offered to "carry me to lunch" I was tempted to reply, "I can walk on my own." Fortunately I held my tongue; he was in fact offering to buy me lunch.

When I am unclear whether a word or phrase means the same thing to the teller as it means to me, I need to ask for clarification. This holds true in the pastoral context, too. Mrs. Smith's statement, "We have had some trouble lately," could mean any number of things to her or to you. We don't yet know what "trouble" means to Mrs. Smith. We may have our own assumptions about what trouble means and who and what caused it.

2. Getting Introduced to the Text

Two dimensions of getting introduced to the text for preachers are reading for basic understanding, including looking up words we don't know, and placing the text in a larger context.[36] The dimensions of getting introduced to a lifestory are slightly different. At this point, we continue to deepen our understanding of the story, being aware of the temptation to assign meaning based on our assumptions or experience.

Whether we are dealing with written or lived text, we may need to ask clarifying questions to deepen our grasp of the basic story. In pastoral conversation we can utilize some of the skills of active listening, such as such as paraphrasing, asking clarifying questions, and summarizing, while forming a narrative perspective in our listening. Building on the previous step, we check our understanding of particular terms against those of the storyteller. While in sermon preparation we might be able to turn to a Greek lexicon to gain a more precise understanding of a specific word and how it is used, in pastoral conversations we have no handy reference book, except the storyteller.

Returning to the example, asking Mrs. Smith what "trouble" means to her is appropriate at this point. Once we have determined what "trouble" means to Mrs. Smith, we deepen our understanding of it, and perhaps of her as well, by inquiring about when and where "trouble" appears and what may trigger its appearance. At this point, we are not quite ready to interpret the meaning of "trouble," but we are getting a better picture of how it operates.

Since our goal at this stage is clarification, monitoring our tendency to story-o-type another person based on our observations or assumptions is a critical part of this step. Even when we know someone fairly well, we may be inclined to create a story-o-type based on implicit cultural assumptions. For example, if we know little about schizophrenia, we might start constructing a story in which Sylvia became violent and harmed Mrs. Russell. This story-o-type might be influenced by media representations of persons suffering with schizophrenia being prone to violence.[37] Most people suffering from schizophrenia, however, are not violent and commit very few violent crimes.[38] In our minds we have linked schizophrenia and violence in an emerging interpretation of "trouble" before we have the full story.

Another element of getting introduced to the text in view is placing it in larger context. For a written text, this step can be an extension of seeing where the text begins and ends but also includes having a sense of where this story fits in the larger flow of the biblical book in which the story appears. Another way to approach this is to consider where this story fits into the flow of the overall story. In terms of Mrs. Smith's story, we already know that today's "passage" (i.e., the events that occurred) is part of a larger story that includes Mr. Smith's death, which brought about a change in the family structure. We also realize we have several intertwining story strands of the three women. This "passage" may appear in a slightly differently form or place in Sylvia's story or Mrs. Russell's than it would in Mrs. Smith's. The same skills we use to pay attention to how one parable is told slightly differently or placed at a different point in the narrative flow of the Gospel of Matthew compared to Mark can be applied in our reading of lifestories.

3. Attending to the Text

The third step in the exegetical process includes "listening attentively to the text."[39] Attending to a person is, of course, a different process from attending to a written text. The text is not looking back. What this means is that some of the skills of active listening can be helpful in narrative conversation, particularly in terms of attending to physical and nonverbal dimensions of person-to-person conversation, including awareness of body language, use of space, tone of voice, volume and pace of speech, and eye contact or lack of it. Pastoral story companions attend to their own nonverbal communication as well as that of the storyteller.

We now begin to ask different kinds of questions from those we asked in previous steps. Our purpose now is to engage in more substantial and curious conversation with the texts as both preachers and story companions.[40] Thomas Long gives an example of the questions the preacher might ask of Amos 5:21-24: "What in the world does God have against festivals and songs?"[41] We know the palmist calls for God to be praised in music and song, so why this prohibition now? The underlying question for the preacher is, "What is really going on here?"

The preacher's purpose of questioning the text is to challenge "our assumptions about the text so we can speak to it anew."[42] The pastoral companion asks the same kinds of question: "What's going on here?" In both settings, it is a form of *hermeneutical suspicion*, which does not mean that we don't believe the teller or the tale, but that we retain a sense that more is going on than the storyteller or listener may initially see or admit. We also continue monitoring our own assumptions as we read lifestories.

Moving beyond questions for information or clarification, we now ask imaginative, creative, and even playful questions with genuine curiosity in order to open up the story in new ways and generate new possibilities of meaning through the dialogue of the storyteller and companion. If we preach regularly, we continually need to find new readings of a biblical text authentic to the text. It is one of the challenges of sermons on Christmas and Easter: How do we tell a familiar story in a way that allows a new hearing, a new perspective?

One of the ways we get stuck in our lifestories is by telling the same old story over and over again. Even though we have new experiences, we read them through a familiar lens or use a label we have come to believe defines us, such as "I am a procrastinator" or "I am an anxious person." As a result we tend to see the problem as internal. Rather than having a problem, *I* am a problem. Such a belief can lead to frustration and a sense of despair.[43]

How can we tell a story in a different way, especially one in which difficulty or "trouble" plays a key part? One way to do this is to separate the person from the problem by naming the problem and telling its story. This process is referred to as "externalization" in narrative therapy.[44] Externalization is less of a technique and more of a "philosophy that refuses to locate the problem inside of people."[45] Michael White stated this philosophy simply: "The person is not the problem, the problem is the problem."[46]

Externalization can be adapted for use in narrative pastoral care and conversation. It is important to note, however, that externalization is not the same thing as blaming the problem on someone else, nor is it shirking our responsibility for our part in continuing our relationship with the problem. By naming the problem as something outside of ourselves, a character in our story, and asking questions about how it influences our lives and how we can influence the problem, we can create a different relationship with the problem and tell a new story about it and ourselves. Changing our relationship with the problem actually increases our sense of agency and enables us to reduce the effects of the problem in our lives and those close to us.[47]

Returning to our case, we note that Mrs. Smith tells us, "Well, we have had some trouble lately. Mother got hurt, Sylvia has been upset, and I am exhausted." We don't yet know how Mrs. Smith sees the problem. If she internalizes the problem, she may feel she is the problem and unable to provide adequate care for Sylvia and her mother. She could blame Sylvia or her mother for her exhaustion. Imagine we have returned the next day at the appointed time, and after some brief social conversation we ask Mrs. Smith the following questions:

Pastoral Story Companion: Mrs. Smith, I noticed yesterday you said you were having some trouble lately. Can you tell me a little more about "trouble"? What does it look like? When does it come into your house? [At this point, you are using "trouble" as the name of the problem, but we don't yet know if Mrs. Smith agrees with this name.]

Mrs. Smith: Well, trouble seems to come when I get too tired and I can't handle both Mother and Sylvia.

PSC: Is "trouble" a good name for what you and your family are dealing with right now, or is "exhaustion" a better name? Or would you call it something else?

Mrs. Smith: I am not sure. I get frustrated and short-tempered when I get tired and feel I can't take care of everybody's needs.

PSC: I can understand feeling cranky when you are tired—it happens to me, too [empathic response]. I am curious, though, where you learned to feel you are responsible for taking care of everybody's needs. [We are asking about the narrative environment and master narratives that shape her self-expectations.]

Mrs. Smith: You know, I have always just assumed that was my job. I took care of the children while Jack worked, so I see Sylvia as my responsibility. My mother took care of her mother, so that's what I know. Jack was much better with Sylvia after she was diagnosed; it has been harder since he has been gone. He was my rock. He was the strong one. [She begins to share stories giving clues about beliefs about her role and introduces another character in the story, Jack, who is no longer there to help her.]

At this point, we could jump in and offer help from the church in caring for Sylvia or Mrs. Russell. But new elements of Mrs. Smith's story worth investigating have been revealed. Mrs. Smith feels responsible for the care of Sylvia and her mother but does not appear to see herself as strong enough for the task. In this assessment, she is the problem. Although she is aware that Jack is no longer there to help her, she has not named the problem as being "not having enough help." We also see that hints of master narratives about gender and family roles have shaped her expectations of herself as a caretaker.

Our curiosity and genuine interest about how she sees her role as caretaker might help her revise her story of what it means to be a caretaker and her ability to do so. At some point in this conversation or in a follow-up, we might ask about times when she does feel competent, looking for an alternative story. As long she is living out a story line in which she is solely responsible, and accepting help is a further sign of her being weak or not being as strong as Jack, she may well reject any help offered. If, however, we can help her construct a story in which she can see her competency and accept help as a gift from others, rather than a sign of her weakness, she may find a new way to live into her story.

The kinds of questions we ask can open up new ways of reading the story for both teller and listener. The approach to questions developed for narrative therapy can be adapted for use in narrative pastoral conversation, though the form and purpose of each is distinct, as noted in chapter 5.

Mrs. Smith did not approach her pastor requesting counseling, but rather in the midst of an ongoing pastoral relationship "trouble" appeared. Mrs. Smith does ask the pastor to come back, indicating her openness to further conversation. Pastoral story companions often have the advantage of an established pastoral relationship that make it possible to offer an invitation to move from social to pastoral conversation. While not intending to be therapeutic in the clinical sense, story companions can ask questions that open up the possibility of new, more functional stories.

In a workshop on narrative questions David Epston, a cofounder of narrative therapy, made a comment that has stayed with me. My recollection of what Epston said about the kind of questions narrative caregivers ask are questions that are just out of the other person's reach, but not beyond their imagination.[48]

4. Testing What Is Heard in the Text

For the preacher, this step involves checking our understanding of the text gained from the questions we have posed against those of other scholars and by consulting biblical commentaries.[49] This includes gaining a better understanding of the historical, literary, and theological dimensions of the text.[50] This task is a bit more challenging for the story companion, since the only authority on the "text" before us is the person who is living it. We do need continually to ask directly or indirectly if our understanding of the story is consistent with the storyteller's view. Most people want to be heard, and if we are committed to listening storytellers will usually let us know if we did not quite get it right and give us another chance.

We began to test our understanding in this case example when we asked Mrs. Smith if she would name the problem "trouble," or something else. Pastoral story companions can gain a deeper understanding of the text as we move toward interpretation by attending to the historical, literary, and theological dimensions of a lifestory. As we saw in the previous chapter, narrative environments can have a significant effect on the way an individual story is told. Knowing something about narrative development and common human experiences such as grief and loss also deepens our ability to understand a specific story, such as our case story here.

Pastoral story companions can benefit from literary theory as it is applied to a wide range of texts, in addition to biblical texts. Forms of analysis applied to novels can be helpful in a close read of a lifestory, as long as we are mindful of the difference between a written text and an open-ended, evolving lifestory. Some of the questions from literary analyses that can be applied to reading a lifestory are the following:[51]

- What is the basic plot of this story? What happens in this story?

- How does the story move through time? All stories have a beginning, middle, and end, but not all move in a straight chronological line. Lifestories are still in progress, and while the end of a chapter may be known, the end of the story has yet to occur.

- Who are the main characters in the story? Are the characters richly drawn or are they stereotypical or stock characters? Who seems to be missing from the story?

- All good stories have some sort of trouble or conflict. What is the nature of the trouble or conflict here, and how does the narrator name it?

- What is the relationship between the narrator and the other characters? Is it close, conflicted, or distant?

- What form does the story resemble? Is this a short story, a chapter, of a longer work? Is it a tragedy, comedy, or something else?

Whether we are reading a poem, a novel, a biblical text, or a person's lifestory, the reader is actively involved in the creation and interpretation of the text. Entering a text requires a "boldness of imagination [that] is the courage to relinquish one's own coherent experience of the world for another's unexplored, unplumbed, potentially volatile viewpoint."[52] This willingness to see the world from another's vantage point and vicariously to share this experience is what we gain from learning how to read a text closely.

The ability to enter the world of a story or the story of a life is essential for pastoral companions. We can foster our pastoral imaginations and narrative knowledge by including novels and poetry and other forms of literature in the repertoire of texts we consider essential for ministerial formation. Learning how to read written texts closely and with imagination, curiosity, and wonder contributes to narrative competence.

In biblical exegesis in the service of preaching we also look for theological meanings in the text.[53] What is God saying to the people? What does this text tell us about how God acts in the world, and the relationship between human beings and God? Or perhaps the text tells us something about who we are as those created in God's image and what this means for how we are to treat each other. The pastoral story companion also looks for theological themes in the lifestories heard. The storyteller may or may not use theological language to address themes such as loss, grace, forgiveness, guilt, hope, or love, all of which have theological dimensions. What are some of the theological themes you notice in Mrs. Smith's story?

Most storytellers don't want pat theological answers. Storytellers who seek out pastors as story companions want to understand their stories in the context of God's story. A central vocational responsibility of pastoral story companions is helping someone to discover and witness the presence of God in a lifestory.

5. Moving toward the Sermon/Interpretation

The final step in biblical exegesis for the preacher is moving toward the sermon. In this step the preacher considers the claim of the text upon the hearers. For the pastoral companion, the final step in the exegetical process is the move toward interpretation as part of the process of storying or restorying our lives. Changes, transitions in life, and new experiences require us to add to our stories, to make sense out of these experiences. After the birth of a child, how do I understand myself as a parent?

My own story may contain many characters, each with her own role: sister, daughter, wife, and mother. How will these characters relate to each other? Will there be conflict between them? How will I hold together these multiple characters or dimensions of myself in the sense of *me*?

A desire to restory may also occur in the face of change, but most often it arises when the story I am living no longer works, or when the story I am telling no longer has resonance with my experience. Restorying is also needed when I feel I am living the same story over and over again, as in the film *Groundhog Day*, or when my story of an imagined future radically changes.[54] In some situations in which restorying is needed, pastoral conversation is not adequate and pastoral consultation, or what is often called *short-term pastoral counseling*, may be required.

In discussing the claim of the text on the hearers, Long draws a parallel between getting to know a text and a person.[55] He draws similar parallels between coming to know a written text or a lived text through the process of biblical exegesis that I have sought to demonstrate. Long reminds us that the process of coming to understand a text, in whatever form it presents itself, requires something of us.

> It takes time and energy to get to know someone else well. We must be with them long enough, and attend to them carefully enough to know not only who they are at the moment but also who they have been in the past and the vision toward which they are moving. We must ask questions and tell of our own life, but we must not do all the talking.... If we look at them and see only our own reflection, we do not know them. If we look at them and see only an "other," an object of scrutiny, we do not know them. Only when we know who they are with us can we claim to really know them.[56]

Exegesis, the process through which we come to a deeper understanding of a text in order to interpret its meaning, is a daily process of ministry. We engage in exegesis when we are reading Scripture, denominational policy, the unfolding story of a congregation, or the lifestory of a parishioner. To do so with imagination, creativity, and courage is our calling as pastoral story companions.

My aim in drawing parallels between exegeting a text and exegeting a lifestory is to draw attention to the skills pastoral story companions *have already acquired* through education for ministry. While we can learn much from other forms of narrative care, pastoral story companions bring to the reading of lifestories their existing skills of close reading learned through biblical exegesis. In biblical exegesis and reading lives, a dialogue is occurring and meaning emerges from the coauthored conversation of storyteller and listener. Both the preacher and the pastoral companion share a common purpose: to uncover good news in the text, and to discern God's living word in the present, the foundation of hope for the future.

How to Recognize a Good Story

Once we have a deeper understanding of a text through a careful analysis utilizing skills of exegesis or other forms of close reading, we can ask the question, How might a pastoral story companion recognize a functional or "good" lifestory? We now have some idea of factors that contribute to or thwart the development of a good story. Narrative environments can constrain storytelling through master narratives, creating outside-in stories that dictate what are or can be social norms. On the other hand, supportive and resource-rich narrative environments yield richer, thicker stories. We also know adolescence is a key period in narrative development, but that we continue to develop over a lifetime, with a varying balance between the themes of agency and communion. By midlife, our stories "should ideally move in the direction of increasingly good narrative form," meaning they have an author or narrator, complex characters, and a fairly well-defined plot that unfolds over time.[57]

Two attitudes or perspectives on reading, which are part of a narrative orienta-tion, contribute to the ability to recognize a good story. The first is *critical awareness*, which is similar to critical thinking, another skill emphasized in seminary educa-tion.[58] Critical awareness facilitates attending to the form and content of a story at the same time. Applied to reading lifestories, critical awareness enables us to observe the formation of the story as it unfolds.[59] Critical awareness notes the influence of narrative environments and allows us to question assumptions of "that's the way it has always been."

The second attitude, *ironic orientation*, recognizes that both the chapters and the fuller narratives of our lifestories are open to multiple interpretations.[60] Irony, in this sense, is not cynicism or sarcasm, but rather the possibility that what seems to be the case may be its opposite or something yet unimagined. As a consequence, we realize that the meaning assigned to an episode in our lifestory may change in a different telling or over time.[61]

The criteria of good lifestories under discussion here are *coherence, openness and vitality, credibility, differentiation, reconciliation, generative imagination*, and *truth value*.[62] Life narratives that rank high on each of these standards "suggest consider-able maturity in the search for unity and purpose in life."[63] A *coherent* story "makes sense on its own terms."[64] The characters' motivations and actions conform to the way we expect people to act. The plot unfolds in a logical manner without significant internal conflict between parts of the story. An incoherent story is confusing, leaving us wondering how the protagonist got from here to there. Good lifestories need not be perfectly coherent, with everything neatly in place, but they should show a sense of identity, purpose, and meaning.

A good lifestory also allows change; it requires some degree of *openness* and *vitality*. Openness tolerates ambiguity and allows multiple possibilities for the future development of a story; it allows characters to grow and change thinking and behavior.[65] A vital lifestory is energetic; it goes somewhere and it is resilient, open to continual revision, rather than becoming fixed or rigid.[66] While flexibility is a mark of a good lifestory, however, too much openness may reflect a "lack of commitment and resolve."[67]

Good lifestories are also *credible*; they are believable because they have some correspondence to what can be known and verified.[68] Our lifestories must have reso-nance with the known realities of our lives. Perhaps you have known someone who seemed to be living in a fantasy world or had an unrealistic assessment of current life circumstances or future possibilities. If you have ever watched the popular television series *American Idol*, you may wonder about the credibility of a contestant's anecdotes about his singing abilities given the sounds he actually produces.

Good lifestories are also complex, "rich in characterization, plot, and theme."[69] A good story pulls us into an intricate plot, with intriguing fully developed characters, and a tension or problem that is resolved is "richly *differentiated*" (emphasis mine).[70] As experiences accumulate over a lifetime, our identities and lifestories become more multistranded, more complex. Increasing differentiation can lead to a need for "*rec-*

onciliation between and among conflicting forces in the story, harmony and resolution amidst the multiplicity of self" (emphasis mine).[71]

The criterion of "generative imagination" emerged from McAdams's research on lifestories of generative adults.[72] We express generative imagination when we engage in new ways of caring for the next generation, and when we expand our concern beyond our immediate circle of family and friends or even the human community.[73] So while generativity can be expressed in a number of ways, generative imagination is expressed in loving acts that promote the overall well-being of the entire created order.

The criterion of the "truth value" of a story is similar to the notion of credibility.[74] Beyond the need for lifestories to have some correspondence to reality, William Randall suggests that we also "look to stories for something of enduring significance, for a message, an insight, a truth of some sort."[75] We don't generally look to stories for historical or scientific truth, but "we want to get something out of it, some nugget of wisdom to enrich our souls."[76]

For example, we don't turn to the book of Job looking for historical truth but for some word about God's presence in the midst of human suffering. In a similar way, we expect good lifestories to reveal some truth of the human condition. Many of us often understand the human condition through the framework of larger religious narratives. Those who seek out pastoral companions often do so in order to interpret their lifestories within the framework of the religious stories to which they are committed.

As storytelling, interpretive beings we are always in the process of reading and writing our own lifestories. As pastoral story companions, we commit ourselves to improving our ability to read a lifestory closely, to exegete it, in order to assist a storyteller in authoring an interpretation that is life-giving. Having criteria for good lifestories in mind helps us identify when lifestories get off track in some way and guides us in the process of restorying, a topic to which we turn in the next chapter. We are ever mindful as pastoral story companions that our own stories shape how we read others' stories and we are committed to witnessing interwoven threads of God's story in the lifestories of those we companion.

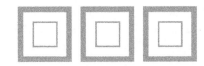

Chapter 8

Restorying in Transition and Trouble

Those who do not have power over the story that dominates their lives, the power to retell it, rethink it, deconstruct it, joke about it, and change it as times change, truly are powerless, because they cannot think new thoughts.

—Salman Rushdie

Writing a lifestory can't be done while seated behind a desk gazing at a computer screen. A memoir may be written this way, but a memoir is a backward reflection on and an interpretation of one part of a larger lifestory. We are always in the thick of our lives, storying our lives as they are lived. Such lifestory development is a lifelong, ongoing, forward-moving, and active process, as our stories are continually taking form. Through storying our lives we communicate "who we are, where we have come from, and where we are headed."[1] Our sense of self, the meaning we assign to events, and our lives as a whole are formed through stories. We *story* our lives as we incorporate new events or experiences and interpret them. We also *restory* our lives when we revise stories, assigning them new interpretations.[2]

We are engaged in both storying and restorying throughout our lives.[3] Much of the time, however, we may not be fully aware that we are actively constructing and revising our stories. We may have some sense that our lifestory changes over time, but because it is the lens through which we make sense of the world we may not attend closely to our role in this process.[4] We are, however, actively engaged in writing and reading our lifestories while simultaneously processing both the storying and restorying.[5] Yet it is not the events of our lives we revise, but rather our memory of them and the meanings that others and we ourselves have assigned to them.

Restorying and Narrative Foreclosure

Restorying may be "gradual or dramatic, natural or intentional."[6] Many of the revisions of our lifestories occur in response to anticipated life transitions, accumulated experiences, and the gradual changes associated with aging. On occasion, some events or experiences don't fit neatly into the plotline we have developed. Significant life changes, transitions, or life-altering losses may challenge the stories we have created thus far, particularly as we project these stories into the future. Such situations may prompt more self-conscious lifestory revision, leading to a reinterpretation of past events and a reimagined future.

A move from a familiar to an unfamiliar narrative environment as a result of geographical relocation, or entry into a new institutional setting, such as a college, a retirement home, or prison, can precipitate restorying. Unexpected transitions related to job loss, unanticipated career transitions, or a change in familiar roles may call our self-identity into question and prompt restorying. Various forms of loss, illness, or the death of a loved one push us toward restorying as we try to make sense out of crises and incorporate them into our lifestories.

Congregations and communities, as well as individuals, are also involved in the process of storying and restorying their communal lives. Congregations that face significant transitions, losses, or other challenges need to revise their stories in order to survive. This chapter examines situations in which pastoral story companions assist in the process of restorying as well as interrupting this process through "narrative foreclosure."[7]

Restorying

Unlike therapists, who wait in their offices until sought out, trained and attentive pastoral story companions have many opportunities in the course of ministry to invite others into the restorying process, and to function as coeditors and coauthors in the ongoing process of restorying with individuals and communities. Although many people are able to revise lifestories simply with the assistance of family or friends as a result of unexpected life events or transitions, those closest to them are usually characters in their lifestories and may not be able to offer a different reading of the story. Pastoral story companions can often provide a different angle of vision, a different way of reading and revising stories, and one that attends to the intersections of God's story with our own.

Those who seek out pastoral story companions as potential coauthors often do so because they wish to make meaning of their lifestories in the context of faith. By virtue of their training, skills, perspectives, roles in the faith community, and commitment to God's love story, those called to become pastoral story companions are privileged to participate in the ongoing process of restorying through pastoral conversation. In some cases, pastoral conversation with individuals may provide an entry to short-term pastoral consultation, or an opportunity for referral to a trained therapist when more in-depth story revision is needed.

More significant and intentional story repair, such as that offered through therapy, may be needed when a lifestory becomes dominated by a problem story.[8] The primary intent of narrative therapy is to deconstruct problem-saturated lifestories and construct healthier, more functional, and preferred stories.[9] When a problem dominates, we read our story through the problem. Because we *are* our stories, we see ourselves as the problem, rather than seeing it as one piece of a larger story. The processes of naming and externalizing the problem, used in narrative therapy and explored briefly in the last chapter, are key to separating the person and the problem.

Much of the focus of narrative therapy is on mapping the influence of the problem on the person and the influence of the person on the problem. A primary goal of narrative therapy is "undermining the life support system of the problem" and strengthening alternative and underdeveloped stories.[10] Some dimensions of narrative therapy, such as externalization and challenging the influence of social/cultural contexts and narratives on personal narratives, can be adapted for use in pastoral conversations or short-term pastoral counseling.[11] Narrative therapy, however, should be reserved for trained and licensed narrative therapists who have undergone advanced education and extensive supervised clinical training.

An effective referral can be a significant act of pastoral care. Referral is most effective if it follows some conversation to determine the best fit and whether the referral is to a professional you know well and trust. Our pastoral obligation to provide ongoing spiritual care is not concluded by referral. When the more intensive story repair of therapy is not needed, pastoral story companionship can be effective. When a lifestory becomes closed down or foreclosed while life goes on, restorying is needed.

Narrative Foreclosure

Occasionally we close a book and say, "That's all, folks," as Porky Pig did at the end of a Looney Tunes cartoon. In a prematurely foreclosed lifestory, the storyteller believes there is nothing left to tell. Refusal or failure to restory one's life in the face of significant loss or other life changes may lead to story foreclosure. Story or "narrative foreclosure" is "the conviction that no new experiences, interpretations, and commitments are possible that can substantially change one's life-story and the meaning of one's life as it is now told."[12] When caught in a foreclosed narrative, we believe our story is essentially over, no new edits or chapters are possible, the ending of the story is known, and no new or alternative endings are considered possible even though life continues.[13] In narrative foreclosure, which can affect both past and future stories, the meaning assigned to a story/life becomes rigid and fixed and lifestory development is static.[14]

Narrative foreclosure is problematic because it reveals an inability to reflect on life and "attribute meaning to it."[15] A foreclosed narrative fails to meet several of the criteria of a good lifestory. It lacks openness and vitality and suffers from too much coherence. A foreclosed story may not seem credible because it fails to incorporate change as a part of life. A foreclosed story is generally simple rather than well differentiated or complex and may be unable to reconcile conflicting forces in the story.

Foreclosed stories also do not meet the criterion of generative imagination, since the storyteller has nothing new to contribute to his or her own stories or to others'.

Narrative foreclosure should be distinguished from normal coherence or "stability and continuity" of a lifestory.[16] Individuals and communities may go through periods of relatively stability in their lifestories as well as times of significant story revision, but in both cases some "process of interpretation and meaning making" is going on.[17] When these processes cease, narrative foreclosure takes hold, and hope gives way to despair.[18]

Story foreclosure can occur at any age but is often observed in older adults.[19] Story foreclosure is present in the lifestories of older adults who feel as if the remainders of their lives are simply a matter of passing time until death.[20] Unfortunately, cultural story-o-types of old age, such as its being a period of unmitigated decline without further growth or development, encourage narrative foreclosure. Given that story development and identity are linked, story foreclosure results in a stagnant, rigid self-identity. The tragedy of narrative foreclosure in aging is that "life and story are torn quietly asunder."[21]

A loss of an important role and changes in narrative environments also play a significant role in story foreclosure. For example, if one's identity is tied to a role, such as CEO of a company, or a professor in a university, the loss of that role and the narrative environment in which that role was lived can feel like the end of one's story. As a result, one lives in the past, without openness to the development of a new chapter or lifestory. Pastoral story companions attentive to the potential for narrative foreclosure, particularly in older adults, may be able to initiate an intentional process of life review leading to restorying.

At some point in our lifestories, loss will play a part, often redirecting the plot in unanticipated ways. Though loss is an inevitable part of life, it often seems to take us by surprise. Death is a particularly unwelcome character in a lifestory. Narrative foreclosure is often related to the end or interruption of an anticipated future as a consequence of loss.[22] For example, if our future story included traveling the world with our life companion following retirement, this story might be interrupted by the death of our companion, physical illness of one or both partners, or financial loss.

Many people are able to make the painful journey through grief and incorporate the loss into a revised story that meets the criteria of a good, strong story. The presence or absence of story companions willing to listen and participate in the restorying process can make a significant difference in a person's adjustment or maladjustment to a significant loss.[23] Both individuals and communities can suffer story foreclosure and an invitation to intentional restorying may be needed.[24] Pastoral story companions are likely to encounter people on a regular basis who have experienced loss and are in the grip of grief. Because of this, they are also positioned to make a positive contribution to the restorying process and potentially forestall narrative foreclosure.

Restorying in Loss and Grief

One loss can turn our world upside down, and multiple losses can be devastating. Whatever we may have considered "normal" disappears and we may find ourselves stumbling along trying to cope with the pain. Loss, and the grief that accompanies it, disrupts our lifestories. Depending on the nature of the loss, this disruption may be minor and one we quickly overcome. In some cases, however, the loss may shatter a lifestory, triggering a crisis of meaning that requires considerable restorying. We can view Jesmyn Ward's memoir as her effort to reinterpret the deaths of her five friends and restory her life in the aftermath. While not all of us will write a memoir, anyone who encounters loss will need to revise his or her story.

Understanding Loss

Because stories of loss are usually complex and multilayered, understanding types of loss can be very helpful in a close reading of these stories. Loss comes in many forms, including loss of a relationship, physical function, material goods or objects, an important role, one's place in a system, and symbolic loss of a dream, a self-image, or anticipated future.[25] What all losses have in common is the disappearance from our lives of something or someone important to us.[26] Some losses may be temporary, such as the loss of physical function for a week or two from a virus from which one recovers, or a loss of income while between jobs. Other losses are permanent, such as the loss of a body part through illness or injury, or the loss of a loved one through death.

Relational loss. The most profound form of relational loss is death. The possibilities for ongoing physical and emotional interaction have ceased. We now need to find a new way to relate to this person whose life has ceased, but who still is a part of our story. Other forms of separation also lead to relational loss. Divorce can be a complicated form of relationship loss for although the intimate relationship has ended, if children are involved some form of ongoing relationship is typically required.

Material loss usually refers to something external to us, such as a beloved item, physical locations such as a home or favorite place, or income. Though we may lose any number of items throughout our lives or move multiple times, material loss is most profound when the lost item or place has some significant meaning attached to it.[27]

Functional loss involves some loss of physical function usually due to illness, disability, or age-related psychical changes, such as changes in acuity of eyesight or hearing.

Role loss occurs when we lose an important role central to our sense of identity such as through retirement or the death of a life partner. Role loss can also occur when changing roles, even when the change is voluntary, such as leaving behind a professional identity to take up the role of student.

Systemic loss results from change of the systems, communities, or networks of which we are a part. *Symbolic loss* of a dream, self-image, or anticipated future is often

123

concurrent with the other losses. We assign symbolic meaning to the persons, places, things, communities, and physical abilities important to us; the stories we have constructed about these are disrupted when loss occurs.[28] Any experience of loss may involve multiple forms of loss, and while any loss may trigger narrative foreclosure, it is often associated with symbolic loss.

Grief and Mourning

At the heart of many stories that grab us is some sort of trouble. In many cases, this trouble is related to loss. Often the power of a novel comes not only from the loss itself, which propels the plot in new directions, but also from the way in which the characters respond to bereavement (the reality of loss through death), grief (the response to loss), and mourning (coming to terms with loss.)[29] Elizabeth Berg's five-page story, "Departure from Normal," is a poignant account of the way in which grief and loss can derail a lifestory. As the story opens, Alice is sitting at her kitchen table reading the newspaper, "amazed at what she has been missing," and after she finishes the paper, she lines the bottom of Lucky's birdcage with it.[30]

Having seen the scar on her chest after her breast was removed, she is now fascinated by the tumor under Lucky's wing. Early after the diagnosis, she laments, "I don't get this. I can't make sense of this. I don't know what to do."[31] Alice survives breast cancer, a functional loss, but her story of herself no longer makes sense. She has retreated into herself.

Today she has decided the one thing she will do is to let Lucky go free rather than find him dead at the bottom of his cage.[32] Alice has imagined the scene many times: Lucky immediately flies away and she is strong and doesn't cry.[33] Only Lucky does not fly away. At first, he sits in a tree nearby and when she tries to walk away, he lands on her shoulder. When she tires to shoo him away, he climbs on top of her head. Lucky doesn't follow the script of the story she has created. And at the end of the story, as she takes Lucky back home, we begin to see Alice entertaining a new chapter in the face of her loss that had threatened to foreclose her story.

Revised Theories of Grief

A significant revision in theoretical understandings of grief has emerged over the last two decades or so.[34] Much of the early research on grief reflected a "medical viewpoint" or was influenced by psychoanalytic theories of loss.[35] An unintended consequence of these approaches was a tendency to pathologize grief, seeing it always as a problem that needed treatment. Now it is more typical to view grief as "a painful experience from which most people will recover with minimal help."[36] Some people may need additional help coping with grief, and "the right help, given at the right time, for the right problem" may facilitate better resolution and reduce the potential for lasting difficulties.[37]

One of the limitations of standard models of grief is prescriptive use of descriptions of the grief process, such as suggested lengths of grieving, or stages/phases of grief. Contemporary theories might identify common processes of grief but recognize varied expression of these processes influenced by personal history, relationships and social connections, and culture, all of which fit under the category of narrative environments we discussed earlier.

A second difficulty with standard theories of grief is the assumption that "mourning serves to restore a person to a pre-loss status or functioning, rather than to transform a person in some way."[38] Many grief theorists now acknowledge the significant impact loss may have on our lives, an impact that can "transform us in fundamental and ongoing ways."[39] This newer perspective is consistent with the narrative perspective on pastoral care, presented in previous chapters, in which a primary purpose of pastoral care is to foster growth in love.

Significant Contributions of Contemporary Grief Research

Three important discoveries of recent grief research will be discussed in more detail.

1. Dual Model Process of Coping

One of the more significant developments in recent grief theory is the "dual process model" of coping with bereavement, which identifies "two distinct but interacting psychological processes that follow all bereavements."[40] These two processes are a "loss orientation" and a "restoration orientation."[41] Some of the task and stressors following bereavement are loss oriented, having to do with the loss itself, such as continued reflection on the circumstances of the death and "yearning for the person who has died."[42] Traditionally, grief work focused primarily on this process of coping with the loss of a significant person. Following a death, however, a bereaved individual often has to "take on new roles and responsibilities," some of which may have been fulfilled by the deceased.[43]

Restoration-oriented tasks and stressors also include beginning new relationships and engaging in new activities.[44] For example, the death of one's partner and the subsequent financial losses may require a partner who has retired or stayed at home to care for children to return to work after a number of years of not working. It is important to remember that these two orientations are present simultaneously and that one may move back and forth between them.[45] Foreclosed stories that follow loss may have more to do with difficulties in the restoration orientation than with coping with the loss.

2. A Continuing Bond

A second significant development in contemporary grief theory is recognition of the importance of some kind of ongoing attachment with the deceased. Drawing on attachment theory, grief researchers now acknowledge the role of an ongoing relationship with the deceased as a significant factor in successful adjustment to bereavement.[46] In contrast to earlier theories of grief, in which the tasks of grief included "withdrawing psychic energy from the lost loved one" in order to reinvest it in new relationships and commitments, more recent theories emphasize some form of continuing bond with the deceased.[47] While the bereaved person must acknowledge the loss of the physical relationship with the deceased, this does not mean the emotional attachment to the deceased must be given up, though it may need to be revised.[48] The bereaved must engage memory and imagination to construct a symbolic connection with the lost loved one.[49]

As the new symbolic relationship is formed, the bereaved may identify with the "values and beliefs" of the one who has died as a source of "inspiration and guidance" in constructing a new life.[50] As the bereaved internalizes a revised relationship with the deceased, a "sense of felt security lost as the result of the death," may be reestablished.[51]

3. Meaning Making Following Loss

Any form of loss is likely to disrupt the lifestories we have lived with so far.[52] Death of a loved one (relational loss) is generally the most significant loss we experience and affects multiple elements of our stories. We may feel as if the plot was suddenly interrupted or took a wild, unexpected turn. A major character in our story is gone and the coherence and continuity of our stores may be threatened.[53]

Contemporary grief theory identifies the "affirmation and/or reconstruction of meaning as 'the central process' in the experience of grief."[54] Grief researchers and practitioners now recognize bereavement as a potential trigger of a crisis of meaning.[55] The unexpected death of someone close to us challenges our assumptions about the world.

Meaning refers to the core beliefs and frameworks through which we make sense of things, understand the world, shape our sense of purpose, and assign significance to life and suffering.[56] Because stories, and the meaning they mediate, provide a sense of order, purpose, and coherence to the multitude of events and experiences that might other wise seem random and chaotic, the significant disruption of a lifestory by loss initiates a search for meaning on multiple levels. The world that once seemed firm and solid may now seem less reliable. Bereaved individuals may question the details of how the death occurred, as well as deep existential and theological convictions about self-identity, the purpose of life, and God.[57]

We see the disruption of meaning reflected in Berg's story when Alice says, "I can't make sense of this. I don't know what to do."[58] Alice can't look in the mirror at her scar and cringes when her husband tries to kiss it. She eventually stops speaking and withdraws from everyone, including her husband through divorce. In a sense she instigates relational loss, perhaps to feel more in control of other anticipated losses.

Alice's story no longer has meaning and she wants to let go of it, of everything, even her beloved avian companion, Lucky. A once-meaningful lifestory has given way to one devoid of meaning and she moves toward emptiness and isolation. Her story becomes foreclosed.

But Lucky refuses to follow Alice's script of a bleak future. His refusal to fly away opens the possibility of a new chapter in her story, even though she is still facing illness. After returning home from the park where she intended to set Lucky free, Alice lies down on the bed, and dials a number. "Her voice says she wants to come home. His voice says he will come and get her. It will be easy to pack. One cage, holding everything, and lined with a weather report that, despite what it pretends, knows nothing for sure."[59]

Although most bereaved individuals will make some revisions to lifestory and identity in the absence of a significant person who was an important character in their narrative, loss doesn't always shatter a lifestory or lead to narrative foreclosure.[60] A variety of factors may influence the impact of a death and the degree of life revision required, including the circumstances of the death, the age of the deceased, the relationship between the deceased and bereaved, and the presence or absence of consoling beliefs and practices, which may be spiritual or religious.[61]

The death of a ninety-eight-year-old woman, lucid until the end, who dies in her sleep after having celebrated her birthday surrounded by family and friends, may be more easily integrated into an ongoing lifestory, requiring a less-intense search for meaning and leading to a more positive grief outcome.[62] The death of a child in a preventable auto accident or of a youth through violence is much more disruptive to a lifestory and requires a more intense search for meaning. The five men in Ward's memoir all died violently at a young age, making it difficult for her to incorporate so much tragedy and loss into her story. Writing her memoir may have been therapeutic for Ward, but it was also an act of resistance. She wants to resist those who might dismiss the deaths of her brother and friends as the anticipated ends of inconsequential lives. She writes in order to understand why her brother died while she still lives.[63]

Restorying after Loss: What Story Companions Can Do

A narrative approach to grief emphasizes the uniqueness of each person's grief experience. While we may identify some common themes or processes in grief, there are no universally applicable stages of phases of grief. It seems more helpful to embrace a complex, multilayered story of grief "fashioned out of innumerable and varied aspects of one's life, such as one's history of losses, one's ways of making meaning, one's experience of the Divine," as well as one's connection to family, community, religious tradition, and culture.[64]

Advanced therapeutic training is not needed to offer understanding, acceptance, and consistent care in the difficult process of lifestory construction following a significant loss. These are compassionate, human responses that any story companion, pastor, or friend may extend to another in the midst of suffering.[65] By offering oneself as a story companion, a pastor may help facilitate a healthy restorying process, particularly in loss-oriented tasks in which meaning is reconstructed and the loss is integrated into a revised lifestory, forestalling a foreclosed narrative.

If grief appears to be complicated in some way, referral for more intentional grief work with a professional may be needed. Congregational support of a bereaved person may prove quite helpful as he or she reorients herself to new roles and responsibilities. For example, while still experiencing the raw pain of loss, a recent widow, widower, or bereaved life partner may now face home upkeep or financial tasks previously performed by the spouse. Volunteers from the congregation may provide that person some initial assistance in gaining competency in newly required skills as she or he reorients to new roles and responsibilities.

Pastoral story companions are often in a position to initiate the restorying process following a death. The process of funeral planning can provide an opportunity to begin this process by inviting the sharing of stories about the one who has died. Many of the stories shared will not, and perhaps even should not, make it into a eulogy or funeral sermon. Laughter and tears are to be expected. Anger, regret, relief, and a whole host of emotions may begin to emerge. A funeral has its own theological narrative and integrity, which ought to be observed, but at this point, soon after the death and before the funeral, story companions can create an open and welcoming space for storytelling.[66]

Strategies for Meaning Making Following Loss

Making meaning is central to the restorying process. Four strategies for meaning reconstruction following loss will be discussed, three of which are adapted from those proposed by pastoral theologian Melissa M. Kelley.[67] The fourth strategy addresses the need for a continuing bond after death, utilizing the idea of "saying hello again" presented by narrative therapist David Denborough drawing on the work of Michael White.[68]

1. Expand or Thicken the Plot[69]

Following loss, our narratives can become thin or shrink. We see this in the story of Alice, whose life is reduced to herself and her bird following her cancer diagnosis and surgery. Cheryl Strayed's memoir, *Wild: From Lost to Found on the Pacific Crest Trail,* depicts the narrowing and disintegration of her narrative following her mother's death.[70] Only when she initiates a radically new plot direction does she begin to reconstruct her story.

With little prior knowledge of or experience in hiking, Strayed decided to hike the Pacific Crest trail, which runs through California, Oregon, and Washington from the Mexican to the Canadian border, following the spine of the Sierra Nevada Mountains for a good portion of the trail. New plot material may stir up a story that has become frozen or stuck with little room for an open or expanding future story.[71] A plot shift that allows for expanding and thickening the plot may open up "new possibilities for oneself and one's future."[72]

2. Develop a New or Revised Interpretation of a Loss[73]

Not only are there two or more sides to any story, there are also multiple interpretations. As Ward reflects on the death of Roger, we see her struggling with such multiple interpretations. In one, he is a tenth-grade dropout and drug addict; in another, he is a young man caught in the grip of relentless poverty who has few options for a hopeful future, and so he turns to drugs for escape.[74] As Ward gains a sense of the larger stories of racism and poverty affecting all their lives, she comes to a new self-understanding, which leads to a reinterpretation of Roger's death.

Religious beliefs, practices, and communities are a primary source of meaning making for many and, we assume, for those active in religious traditions.[75] Some of the religious beliefs we have held may not prove adequate for the challenge of grief, so revising our theology may be part of the task of reconstructing meaning following loss.

Jenna and Jim, whose child died during delivery (chapter 2), struggled with critical theological questions about God's will and God's presence or absence in the midst of suffering and tragedy. Some restorying of their religious beliefs was required to make sense of their suffering. Jenna and Jim had not realized that a view of God drawn from biblical passages in which the righteous are rewarded and the unfaithful punished played a role in their theology until they faced a devastating loss and wondered whether God was punishing them. Participating in ongoing religious practices of worship, prayer, and theological conversation supported Jenna and Jim as they revised their story of God and God's role in their lives. The social support of their church community also played a significant role in their recovery.[76]

3. Attend to the Impact of Narrative Environments on Interpretation and Meaning Making

As we have see in previous discussions, storytelling is a relational and contextual process. Narrative environments can provide rich resources for storytelling or impose rigid and destructive stories, as illustrated in Ward's memoir. We have also seen how stories can be healing, and how they can be harmful when story-o-types determine who we are or can be to others.

About six months after Sheryl's father died at age eighty, Sheryl asked her seventy-year-old mother whether she wanted her to renew the subscription to *Reader's Digest*, which her parents had received for a number of years. Her mother replied, "No, I don't think so. That was your father's magazine. I read it, but I am not that fond of it." Having assented to a particular gender-based role of what it meant to be a wife, she was now finding the freedom to express her own interests and preferences. Exegeting the narrative environments in which stories of loss are constructed or reconstructed can open up space for fuller, more meaningful stories and identity development.

4. Affirm and Support a Reconfigured Continuing Bond with the Deceased

This process can take some time but is facilitated by opportunities to continue to talk about the deceased. Some caregivers harbor the incorrect notion that asking about the deceased will be painful for the bereaved when the opposite is usually the case. Pastoral story companions can facilitate the bereaved person's continued bond with the deceased by asking about the deceased and by remembering the deceased at important markers such as birthdays or holidays. Religious rituals that honor the memory of the deceased and theological narratives, such as the communion of saints, provide a sense of the loved one's continuity not only in the memory of the bereaved, but also in the memory of the religious community, and in the heart of God.

An intriguing strategy for fostering a continuing bond is the idea of saying "hello again" rather than good-bye.[77] Many of us were raised with ideas about grief shaped by earlier theories and attitudes in which the grief task involved saying good-bye and letting go of the lost loved one to get on with one's life. Saying good-bye may be a necessary part of the loss orientation following bereavement. Saying "hello again" relates to the restoration orientation after death by acknowledging the changes in one's identity initiated by grief and the need for an ongoing, but different connection to the loved one. At the heart of this strategy is assisting the bereaved to see herself or himself through the loving eyes of the one who has died.[78] Following the general practice of narrative therapy, the story companion asks a number of questions to stimulate the imagination of the bereaved and open up the story.

The questions Denborough proposes include the following:

- "What did [_____] see when she looked at you through her loving eyes?"

- "How did she know these things about you?"

- "If she could be with you today, what would she say to you about the efforts" you are making in your life? What words of encouragement would she offer?

- "What difference would it make to your relationships with others if you carried this knowledge with you in your daily life?"[79]

Saying "hello again" works best in relationships that were experienced as mostly positive and may be more complicated if the relationship was ambivalent.[80]

Many people will be able to move through the processes of grief with the support of family, friends, and religious leaders and "report resilience or even personal growth after loss."[81] Difficulties or complications with grief are likely to arise when one or both of the dual processes of grief are not fully engaged, when the bond with the deceased is not revised or is ambivalent, and when the meaning-making process is inadequate. The ability to make meaning out of loss appears to be an important indicator of positive outcomes in bereavement.[82] Coping with some forms of loss, such as suicide, the loss of a child, or a violent death, may be more challenging and require additional professional assistance.

Restorying a Change in Narrative Environments

Just as the process of constructing lifestories occurs within narrative environments, so does restorying. We are constantly in conversation with coauthors who influence our lifestories, including friends, families, our religious communities, and the larger culture. One of the situations that prompt restorying may be a change in narrative environments, such as moving to or visiting a new city, state, or country. When telling of a life-changing experience of traveling or living in another country, we are often describing the process of having our lifestories and view of the world challenged or broadened by a very different narrative environment.

While a change in narrative environments may be largely voluntary, it is nevertheless disruptive and disorienting, in part because we tend to take our narrative environments for granted, and in part because losses may be incurred. In the case of an involuntary change in narrative environments due to incarceration or institutionalization, the lifestory disruption may be more severe. In the case that follows, both Mr. Jin Woo Lee and Mrs. Leon experience largely voluntary changes in the narrative environments that have shaped their lifestories for some time.

Case Vignette: Jin Woo Lee and Mrs. Leon

Jin Woo Lee, aged thirty, a first-year seminarian from South Korea attending school in the southern part of the United States, serves as a student chaplain four hours a week in a retirement home concurrent with his enrollment in an introductory pastoral care course. It is his turn to reflect with his site supervisor and classmates in his small group on a pastoral conversation. He shares his confusion about how to care for Mrs. Ruth Leon. If he were visiting a church member back home in Korea with his pastor, he would know what to do: read Scripture, say a prayer, and perhaps sing a hymn. He is not sure how to minister in a culture very different from his own. Although he studied English for eight years, he is much more comfortable with reading and writing and has found speaking in English much more difficult than he anticipated. Mrs. Leon's strong Southern accent only makes it harder for him to follow her. He is ashamed that he can't understand much of what Mrs. Leon says. He often has to repeat himself because she has a hard time with his accent, though she is patient with him.

Jin Woo reports on his conversation with Mrs. Ruth Leon, a white, eighty-year-old retired high school teacher who moved into the Cloisters, a retirement home, about a month ago. She shared that while she decided to move, it was not an easy decision. Though a nearby church sends a van, allowing her to attend church, it is not the congregation she has been a part of for much of her life. Jin Woo notes that she often describes her home of fifty years and how much she misses it. Mrs. Leon's husband died when she was sixty, so she has been on her own for some time. It was the first time she had lived alone, having lived with her parents until she married at age twenty-two. She came to love her independence, but when she moved she gave her car to her oldest grandchild, who just graduated from college. Giving up driving has left her feeling less independent. The Cloisters has a van to take residents shopping, but she can no longer just go when or where she wants. Jin Woo does not understand why Mrs. Leon is not living with her daughter's family, who live only an hour away, nor why they visit only once a month, though he has not asked her about this directly: it would be impolite to ask this of an elder. He believes that elders are to be respected and children and grandchildren are responsible for caring for them in their later years. In his culture it would be shameful for family members to treat their elders in this way.

Observations/Reflection

Jin Woo Lee finds himself in a new culture in which the attitudes about aging and the elderly seem strange to him. He has begun to realize that how elders are perceived and treated in the United States culture conflicts with how one relates to elders in Korean culture. When he visits at the Cloisters, he is very aware of his minority Korean status. He finds himself torn between wanting to befriend as many students native to the United States as he can and feeling drawn to the other Korean students for a sense of familiarity and a break from the difficult task of speaking English. In addition to this, Jin Woo Lee is navigating a new educational environment with different expectations about learning and ministry. He is used to lectures, but being engaged in ministry while also in class and the action/reflection model of learning are unfamiliar to him, as is the amount of discussion in class.

Mrs. Leon is also navigating a new narrative environment at the Cloisters. She now resides only with older adults, while a range of ages and family configurations were present in her neighborhood. She especially misses the presence of children. She lives in a smaller physical space and before moving had to give away many of her possessions. Though she fixes her own breakfast in her apartment, her communal lunch and dinner times are determined for her. Nor can she go shopping whenever she wants. She has had a harder time accepting the loss of independence than she thought she would.

Pastoral Conversation

While Jin Woo Lee is in the role of chaplain, any conversation, including pastoral conversation, affects both storyteller and listener. Let's begin exploring the story revision that might occur as Jin Woo Lee is in conversation with his supervisor and reflection group, and then turn to how he might help Mrs. Leon with the story revision she is facing as a result of her move.

Pastoral Conversation: Jin Woo Lee and His Reflection Group

Jin Woo Lee's contextual (field) education site supervisor and his fellow students are in a position to help him construct this portion of his lifestory as he operates within narrative environments quite different from those most familiar to him. Whether or not he receives this assistance, his lifestory is undergoing revision as he makes sense out of the new and navigates unfamiliar narrative environments.

The reflection group is a perfect setting to help Jin Woo Lee engage in a close reading of his own lifestory in order to become aware of how it influences his reading of Mrs. Leon's lifestory. Members of the group can join Jin Woo Lee in developing a *critical awareness* of the influence of narrative environments on the writing and reading of stories, both others' and our own. As an attitude of *ironic awareness* is cultivated in the group, Jin Woo Lee may realize that just as biblical stories may be open to more than one interpretation, so, too, are his story and Mrs. Leon's.[83]

As Jin Woo Lee and his reflection group engage in exegeting Mrs. Leon's story, they keep in view the pericope (section of text) of Mrs. Leon's move from her home of fifty years to the Cloisters in light of the larger "text" of her lifestory. Getting a sense of what home has meant to her, a home where she shared her life with her husband and raised their daughter, will give him a sense of the larger story. Through continuing conversation, he will have a deeper sense of Mrs. Leon's particular lifestory. His reflection group can help him understand the context of her story within the narrative environments of the southern United States. As he gains a deeper understanding of the influence of narrative environments on a lifestory, Jin Woo may come to a greater appreciation of how Confucian values have shaped his attitude and behavior toward his elders. Coming from a communal culture, he may need help in imagining what independence means to Mrs. Leon. Doing so will require him to interrogate the master narratives of gender and aging in the United States.

As his classmates accompany him in this process, they may also became aware of their own unexamined story-o-types about older adults in general and older women in particular shaped by their own narrative environments. Together the students may also become aware of how one narrative environment and its attendant master narratives, such as a national culture, shape the reading of another, such as Christianity.

Pastoral Conversation: Jin Woo Lee and Mrs. Ruth Leon

As Jin Woo continues his exegesis of Mrs. Leon's story and attends more deeply to its "text," he may begin to ask questions for a deeper understanding. The advantage of a living text is that it can talk back. Jin Woo Lee might ask Mrs. Leon about what her home has meant to her over the years and how she came to the decision to leave it. He might ask what has been difficult about the move and what has been positive. He will pay attention to how she tells the story, keeping in mind that it could be told in any number of ways.

As Jin Woo Lee tests what he has heard, he might consider as a plot twist the factors that lead to Mrs. Leon's move. Was the move anticipated or is there something behind the plot twist that has not made its way in to her story? He might ask more about the main characters in her story, especially her husband, her daughter and family, and her church community. Knowing that she has been a Christian all her life, he might ask about God's role in her lifestory. What kind of character is God? He may also note themes of loss in her story and note any theological meaning she assigns to these experiences.

Both Jin Woo Lee and Mrs. Leon may come to revise their stories as they engage in pastoral conversation with each other. Mrs. Leon is not a passive recipient of Mr. Lee's care. Both are active agents in constructing lifestories. Mrs. Leon, a teacher, may well bring this part of identity into her conversations with Jin Woo Lee, wanting to assist him in his cultural and educational transition. She may ask him questions about his own lifestory, background, and educational goals. Through their shared conversation and Jin Woo Lee's genuine curiosity about her lifestory, Mrs. Leon will have a story companion in restorying her move, acknowledging the losses, but also possibly in beginning a new chapter in her life in a new community.

Both Jin Woo Lee and Mrs. Ruth Leon are experiencing multiple forms of loss. Both have moved from familiar to unfamiliar places of residence resulting in a material loss. Jin Woo Lee left full-time employment and income in Korea to attend school in the United States, while Mrs. Leon had to give away many of her prized possessions to move into a smaller space.

Jin Woo and Mrs. Leo are also both experiencing the loss of immediate access to important relationships and their places in a familiar community, resulting in relational and systemic loss. These losses change the shape of their self-identity and future stories. Mrs. Leon may have anticipated living in her home until her death and must now construct a story about her future in a new location and community. Before coming to the United States, Jin Woo had not experienced himself as a minority or foreigner and is struggling with an identity assigned to him as a consequence of the change in narrative environments.

As Jin Woo and Mrs. Leon become story companions to one another, both have the opportunity to assist each other in restorying their lives in the face of significant changes and the opportunity to construct good, strong stories with coherence, complexity, credibility, openness, differentiation, reconciliation, generative imagination, and truth value, while attending to God's intertwining story.

Restorying in the Face of Violence, Abuse, and Trauma

Unfortunately, far too many children in the world are like Gemma, whom we met in chapter 6, whose experience of violence and abuse began in childhood but continues into adulthood. Abuse simply became part of Gemma's story; it is what she expected from others and eventually unleashed on herself. In many ways her story was foreclosed early in her life with the result that she had no vision of a better future. Through intentional effort on her part, a two-year treatment, and a supportive community of others in recovery, she successfully overcame her addiction and faced the trauma of her history of abuse.

Violence and abuse are forms of trauma that shape one's lifestory and identity. Many survivors of childhood abuse arrive in adulthood having developed patterns of self-destructive and self-abusive behavior.[84] These behaviors are often the consequence of internalized meanings of abuse that convey the belief that one is worth nothing.[85] This negative sense of self is clearly conveyed by Dean, a male survivor of childhood sexual abuse, in this interview with Tim Harker.[86] "When Dean first came to see me he talked about himself as he thought others were seeing him: 'Tim...I just think they see a lowlife, a person going nowhere.'"[87] The experience of sexual abuse often leaves victims with a "sense of inferiority to others" as well as profound feelings of shame and often guilt, of "being responsible for the terrible wrongdoing" committed against them.[88]

Those who have experienced trauma from sexual abuse, war, intimate partner violence, or other life-threatening events often need long-term care. While it is important for pastoral story companions to know something about trauma, restorying usually requires long-term therapeutic intervention. Pastoral story companions can support survivors of trauma and victims of intimate partner violence in a number of ways: First, believe the story you are told. Second, identify resources in your community for survivors of sexual abuse, as well as veterans suffering from PTSD (post-traumatic stress disorder). Third, continue to offer pastoral support and be willing to listen and address the theological and spiritual issues raised by trauma.

If you are working with a person currently experiencing violence, do not deal with this situation on your own or confront the abuser. You are likely to put yourself and the person experiencing violence in danger. Partner with professionals in your community who have experience working with both victims and perpetrators of abuse. Educate yourself about the signs of intimate partner violence so you can recognize the clues when you see them.[89] Make resources, like hotline numbers, available in safe places for women in your religious community who may be experiencing abuse.[90]

Perhaps one of the most important things religious leaders can do is to challenge the religious master narratives used to justify violence in families and in the larger society. We need to tackle difficult scriptural passages that seem to condone violence and be attentive to the religious stories we tell in preaching and worship and those we

135

choose to omit. The religious narrative environments of which we are a part do shape us, but we have the power and responsibility to shape them as well.

Congregational Restorying

Just as individuals tell stories to convey a sense of identity and purpose and to give meaning to experiences and events, so, too, do communities, congregations, and institutions. If you want to get a quick understanding of a religious community's self-identity, look at its mission statement. If you visit Westview Baptist Church on a Sunday morning, you will see the motto "We are not here by chance" on a banner hanging in the sanctuary next to another banner with the church's mission statement. In the midst of white flight in response to school integration in the Southern urban area in which the church was located, the congregation voted not to move to the suburbs as many other predominantly white congregations were doing at that time. The decision did not come easily and followed a long process of discernment. Demographic changes in the community meant the church was likely to face a very different story of the future from what it had anticipated. Rather than face continued growth, it would likely face decline as many of its members moved and left the church. Westview decided it would need to revise its identity and story to stay in relationship with both those remaining in the immediate community and those moving out of it. Though the restorying process resulted in some conflict in the congregation, the members of Westview eventually developed a narrative as a church open to all.[91]

Religious communities can also suffer under the influence of narrative environments, as do individuals. Right now, the prevailing story of the mainline Protestant church is one of decline. With massive membership losses in many denominations, this story of decline may be accurate.[92] It is also possible, however, that the identity and meaning of Christianity are changing. Membership losses are occurring primarily in the United States and Europe. Christianity is growing in many other parts of the world.[93] We may very well be in the midst of restorying what it means to be a Christian, both in the United States and in the global church.

Perhaps you have been a part of a congregation struggling with narrative foreclosure. Let's consider an imaginary church we will call New Hope Community Church. The stories of the church are about its past, when the sanctuary was full. Now a handful of older adults, mostly white, drive past many other churches to attend the one they have called home for years. A few older African American women who live near the church attend regularly.

Though the neighborhood is changing around them, the members of New Hope either don't know how, or perhaps are unwilling to revise their story to open up the plot to new development or an alternate future. They have had countless retreats and strategic planning sessions to set priorities, but nothing seems to change. New Hope Community Church just hired Lisa Hernandez, age thirty-five, a recent seminary graduate, formerly in pharmaceutical sales, as their new minister, hoping she will attract some of the younger neighbors moving into their community.

When Rev. Hernandez came to interview, many of the members story-o-typed her, assuming she was of European descent, though she is of mixed ethnicity. Her mother, originally from the Philippines, immigrated to Texas to work as a nurse and her husband was born and grew up in Texas, though he has extended family members in Mexico.

Many of the members have decided the church is dying but have decided to remain loyal until the end. Some hope that Rev. Hernandez's business background will help them figure out how to "sell" the church to the residents moving into the community.

If we understand this situation as one of narrative foreclosure, we might ask what has led to the foreclosure and how the narrative might be opened up. Doing so does not guarantee that the church will survive in the form it has taken or in the building it has occupied for many years. Rev. Hernandez has been studying narrative pastoral care and narrative leadership in seminary and is anxious to try some of these strategies in her new congregation.[94]

Her first step is to help the congregation to name and acknowledge the many losses it has faced. The congregation may have no future story because its interpretation of the past is foreclosed. In some ways the church is skipping the task related to a loss orientation, denying their losses by holding on to a mythic past. Rev. Hernandez realizes it will be difficult to construct a new story with the church members if they are stuck in an old one. She sits down with a few of the key leaders and conducts an inventory of losses. This might seem depressing, but the congregation may not realize it is grieving and in need of story revision.

Those who participate in this process find it quite freeing to name the losses and resultant struggles and together they produce the following list:

Material loss: The original church built in 1898 is still standing but is in need of significant and costly repairs. The budget has dwindled with the membership. The membership is reluctant to abandon its building but can't keep it up.

Functional loss: In the last three years, two key leaders have had to drop out because of illness.

Role loss: Once the leading church in the community where "anybody who was anybody went," the public profile of the church has declined due to demographic and political changes in the community.

Relational loss: Although the church had been struggling for some time, the decline has been more rapid in the last two years under the leadership of a part-time interim pastor, following the retirement of a beloved pastor who had served the church for twenty years.

Systemic loss: People who have served in key leadership roles have left and the church system is unstable.

Symbolic loss: New Hope remembers itself as a prosperous, thriving church and struggles with the image of decline. Only by identifying and acknowledging the losses can the congregation consider alternate interpretations of the meanings of these losses.

Let's imagine how Rev. Hernandez might apply the four strategies for meaning making after loss in the congregational setting at New Hope. What might it mean for this congregation to *expand or thicken the plot?* Right now, the plotline of the church does not seem to be going anywhere. As the members of New Hope review the church's history, they discover that German immigrants settled in what was then a farming community and founded the church. Many of the new residents moving into the neighborhood are immigrants from various West African and Southeast Asian countries. Rev. Hernandez wonders whether she can tap into the immigrant story of the congregation, as well as the knowledge of her mother's and her paternal grandparents' immigrant stories to help the congregation see a connection between their story and new residents in the community. Rev. Hernandez creates a sermon series around biblical stories of pilgrimage and migration to introduce a new plotline into the congregation's story, one of pilgrimage from the past to a new future.

Keeping in mind the role and symbolic losses of the church's status and leadership position in the community, Rev. Hernandez asks Mrs. Jackson, a longtime leader in the community and unofficial church historian, to help her facilitate a community conversation in which participants discuss the losses identified through the loss inventory and try to name the resources and strengths the church and its members have used to cope with these losses. Her goal is to prompt a *new or revised interpretation of loss.* At the end of the evening, in addition to a list of losses the congregation has a list of resources and strengths gained from coping with loss.

Rev. Hernandez discovers that the church had hired a consultant to conduct a community survey the year before she came, but no one knew what to do with the information. Looking through the information collected on changing neighborhood demographics and income levels, Rev. Hernandez identifies the impact of changes in the *narrative environments* on the church's interpretation of its story. She is still working on the best way to communicate these to the congregation and decides to begin with a conversation with the governing council on her reading of the survey data.

As All Saints' Day approaches, Rev. Hernandez considers some ways to *affirm and support a reconfigured but continuing bond with the deceased.* She has in mind not only church members who are no longer living, but the foreclosed story of the congregation. In her sermon she remembers the church saints who have died and recalls a church she visited in England, built on the ruins of an even older church. Though she is not yet sure what the future of New Hope will be, she invites the congregation to join her to imagine building on the past while walking in faith toward an unknown future accompanied by each other and the Holy Spirit.

Becoming Pastoral Story Companions: Reprise

Those of us like Rev. Hernandez and Jin Woo Lee who provide narrative pastoral care are invited to become story companions with individuals and communities in the coauthoring of lifestories. Pastoral story companions can develop a range of practices and skills to accompany others in growing in love, skills such as learning how to listen to and fully hear the stories of others, learning to recognize the multiple ways in which God's story can be told, attending to narrative environments, engaging in a close reading or exegesis of a lifestory, recognizing narrative foreclosure, being willing to hear stories of grief, and inviting others into a restorying when needed. We, as well as those for whom we care, are called to shape lifestories that are not only good stories, but also faithful stories that foster growth in love.

Afterword

Telling stories is an integral part of who we are as humans. We discover who we are through stories. We come to know others through stories. And through the stories of our religious tradition we come to know something about God. In the book of Genesis God spins a story and brings the world into being. There it is in third line: "God said..." (Gen 1:3). And light and darkness come into being, earth and water, and all manner of living beings, including us. For those of us who are Christians, these words of Genesis are echoed in the first words of John's Gospel: "In the beginning was the Word" (John 1:1). An invitation to enter a lifestory is an invitation to a holy space, a space where not only the two in conversation dwell, but where God awaits. So there it is. Stories are worth our time, as are the people who tell them.

It is important to remember, however, that while we perceive the world through stories, not all stories are told in words. Babies communicate fairly effectively without words for the first year or so of life, stories of hunger, yearning, fear, love. Parents learn to attend to the stories by attending to the body, a reach of the hand, a grunt, or the timbre of a cry. Language gives us something and takes something away. Once we have words, we think we have the means to understand each other fully and we may pay less attention to nonverbal forms of relationship and communication, which are an important part of the stories we are.[1] Remembering how to read embodied stories is important in pastoral care when words fail through illness, such as Alzheimer's disease, or are simply inadequate, as in the case of trauma.

Responsibilities of Story Companions

Taking the metaphor of story companionship seriously requires recognition of its mutual character. None of us are the sole authors of our own lifestories. Our story companions are also coauthoring our stories, including the story of who we are in the role of pastoral story companion. Mutuality carries with it certain responsibilities. Accepting the role of coauthor implies an ethical accountability for our influence on another's lifestory. While language of companionship implies mutuality, it does not necessarily imply equality in power or influence on another's story, or symmetry of roles. Our parents and families of our origin generally have more influence over our lifestories than other coauthors. Leadership roles, including that of pastor, convey power and require ethical use of that power. While story companionship is a mutual process, when we step into the role of *pastoral* story companion, we must be aware of inherent asymmetry in power and influence attendant to that role. Pastoral story companions are not the only coauthor of another's lifestory but the power of our role may increase our influence on another's story.

Becoming a *pastoral* story companion is an intentional act of, and a commitment to, spiritual formation and growth in love, both for those for whom we care and for ourselves. Growth in love is made possible by God's love and is a response to God's generous grace. Various religious traditions may describe this process differently, yet most have some vision of spiritual growth to which all are called. In the Christian story, baptism is a symbol and celebration of our induction into a story that both invites and empowers us to grow in love as we craft a good, strong, faithful, loving lifestories. Ordination provides no shortcut, nor exemption from these lifelong processes. Each of us is responsible for attending to our own growth in love and the shape of our lifestory. Those of us in the roles of church leadership who step into the role of *pastoral* story companions have an ethical responsibility to attend to our own growth in love.

A narrative approach to pastoral care frames spiritual growth as growth in love. Spiritual growth, as I understand it, also includes psychological growth and maturity. Narrative psychology is in agreement with other psychological views in asserting that much of the process of identity formation happens outside of our awareness. Spiritual growth and psychological maturity include becoming more aware, more involved, and responsible for our becoming a self through the construction of a lifestory. Spiritual growth is an individual response to divine love and the vocation of the Christian community. The love at the heart of the church is God's self-giving love in which mercy and justice are held together. Pastoral care promotes growth in love through intentional acts of care, including healing, guiding, sustaining, reconciling, nurturing, empowering agency, and liberation.[2] For those of us in ministry, whether lay or ordained, we encounter people in the midst of living their lives and constructing their stories. We have daily opportunities, and the privilege of pastoral initiative to become story companions, to be coauthors of lifestories that are good, strong, life-giving, and faithful. Becoming a pastoral story companion is an important and vital ministry in the name of the one who spoke creation into being.

Multiple potential story companions, however, vie for the role of coauthor. Not all coauthors are intent on promoting individual or communal well-being, spiritual growth, or a just society. For example, consumerism is a powerful master narrative in our culture and many voices promote a story of having more means being more: beautiful, important, influential or . . . (fill in the blank). Other potential coauthors support the cultural myth of individualism, in which success or failure is construed as an individual achievement or responsibility, ignoring our creation in God's image as relational, communal beings. An overemphasis on personal agency downplays our need of communion with each other. Paradoxically, an individualistic focus can also diminish our sense of agency by obscuring the constraining power of narrative environments, leaving us feeling powerless to revise our lifestories or challenge the story-o-types embedded in certain environments.

Because our minds think in stories, it possible that creating a story about another may be an automatic process, largely outside of our awareness. If this is the case, then some degree of "story-o-typing" is inevitable. Story-o-types become problematic when we fail to recognize the way in which these unexamined stories reduce others to caricatures or contribute to an oppressive narrative environment. An ethical responsibility of pastoral story companions is to challenge the "story-o-types" in our own minds, as well as in the larger culture, which marginalize or diminish others. Pastoral story companions are committed to life-giving story interpretations that recognizes God as both an actor in and primary coauthor of lifestories.

Do the ethical responsibilities of pastoral story companionship require us to be transparent about our role as coauthors? Religious leaders do have a responsibility to communicate our understanding of ministry through teaching and preaching, as well as pastoral care. Ministry is not simply a practical matter of strategies; our practices communicate our convictions about human nature, the nature and purpose of the church, and our theology.

A NET model of ministry and pastoral care articulates these convictions in a specific way: we are narrative beings, the church is called to be a community of love, and God's story is a love story. From a narrative perspective, part of our responsibility is to help those with whom we work to become more aware of the process of reading and writing one's lifestory. However, I need not announce my approach in the midst of a pastoral conversation in an obvious way.

A NET model of pastoral care takes seriously the conviction that each of us is created in God's image as a relational being called to love God, self, and others with all our mind, heart, and very being. Also implicit in a NET model of pastoral care is a vision of the church as a community extending love to the world. While this volume has focused on religious leaders as pastoral story companions, opportunities to become story companions abound in life and not just in professional ministry. Whether or not we are in the role of pastor, we will likely find ourselves as a coauthor of another's story. Pastoral story companionship is not the province of the pastor alone. The qualifier "pastoral" points to the motivation of pastoral care as a response to God's love by extending the love we have received to others, not just those we know well but to the stranger and our enemies as well.

Imagine what it might be like to have a community of story companions: each one accompanying another in crafting a lifestory shaped by love, fostering mutual growth in love.

Exercises and Questions for Discussion

Chapter 1

Exercises/Discussion Starters
1. Narrative Introductions

Participants pair off, preferably choosing a partner not well-known. Each person takes a few minutes to think of a story that reflects something about his or her personality and character. It may be a story from any period of one's life. The story may be based on a personal memory of oneself, or a story told by a family member about the person, which has become a signature story even though the protagonist may have little direct memory of it.

For example, one of my signature stories is about the time my mother called my father at work to tell him a rare plant in his garden that bloomed only once a year was now in full flower. Meanwhile, I was outside eating it. According to the story, I was between eighteen months and two years old. I don't remember it. I claim it as a story about curiosity and being drawn to beauty. My parents may have interpreted it differently.

After each person has had a few minutes to think of a story, the partners share their stories with each other. Each partner listens fully, asking clarifying questions only at the end of the story. The point is not to remember all the details in order to report it back verbatim, but to listen to what the story tells of the person's identity.

Each partner then introduces the other person to the entire group. The goal is not to repeat the story but to share what each person has learned about the other through the story. For example, "I learned that Anne is adventurous and likes to meet new people" or "I learned that Joe likes to observe before jumping into new situations, but then does so fully."

Allow five to seven minutes for students to reflect and think of a story and at least ten minutes, preferably more, for sharing between partners. Each partner then introduces the other to the rest of the group.

I find these introductions go fairly quickly as people tell about the qualities that reflect another's identity rather than reciting facts. I also find this helps build community. Participants often learn they have something in common with people who at first appeared different from themselves. I often use this exercise at the beginning of a class or retreat.

2. Tree of Life Exercise

The Tree of Life exercise was originally developed by David Denborough of the Dulwich Centre Foundation and Ncazelo Ncube, who works with traumatized children, particularly those living with HIV/AIDS, in South Africa. While originally developed for children, it has since been used widely with people of all ages. The Tree of Life provides a way to develop what narrative therapists call a "preferred story," one that accentuates our positive characteristics, values, gifts, and relationships, as opposed to one that emphasizes our difficulties, struggles, or deficiencies. Instructions for drawing and sharing the Tree of Life can be found in David Denborough's book, *Retelling the Stories of Our Lives: Everyday Narrative Therapy to Draw Inspiration and Transform Experience.*[1]

I often use this exercise either near the beginning of a course or when discussing preferred versus problem narratives (chapter 8). I provide large sheets of paper, crayons, markers, and colored pencils. The Tree of Life takes some time to draw, and it is important to plan accordingly. While the drawing can be assigned as an out-of-class assignment, I find the sharing is more spontaneous if it comes immediately after drawing when the sense of discovery is still fresh. Also, the process of drawing the tree can stir up powerful, and sometimes painful feelings, so I find it preferable to provide a structured and supervised environment for the exercise. Those who wish to share reflections on their drawing or the process of drawing are invited to do so, though no one is required to share.

Questions for Discussion

1. Narrative theories claim that identity shapes story and stories shape our identity. What are some examples that might support or contradict this claim?

2. Dan McAdams argues that agency and communion are two key themes in people's stories. What are some films or novels that demonstrate the dominance of one theme over the other or a conflict between these themes?

146

3. From a narrative perspective, all people are capable of developing new, empowering stories that include new senses of the self. What might be some of the theological consequences of this claim?

4. According to narrative gerontologists, we are continually writing and revising our lifestories. Is this assumption of ongoing growth throughout life supported by cultural attitudes of aging? Give examples of cultural practices and beliefs that support or deny this claim. If the assumption of ongoing story revision is correct, how might it affect our ministry with older adults?

5. What are the criteria for good lifestories? Can you think examples of (1) someone whose story fits some, but not all, of these criteria; (2) someone whose lifestory seems to fit all of the criteria? What do you notice when you contrast these lifestories?

Chapter 2

Exercises/Discussion Starters
  1. The Church as a Community of Love—or Not?

Either in pairs or in small groups of three or four, share experiences you have had in your church or religious community in which love was acted out in some way. (See the story of Lucy and Ed as an example.) You may have been the recipient of this love or you may have been part of a group expressing it to someone else in the community. It may have been a onetime experience or have occurred in an ongoing relationship of visitation, mentoring, community involvement, or the like. Often the first examples that come to mind are situations in which a church or religious community failed to be loving or compassionate. These stories may be shared as well. In this case, it can be helpful to reflect on what might have been done differently.

  2. A Church's Story

A church's mission or vision statement often contains a microstory and communicates something about a church's identity, self-understanding, and sense of mission. Find the mission or vision statement of your church, religious community, or denomination. What does it say about the church's implicit ecclesiology? Compare this with vision/mission statements from other churches or religious communities. These are easily found on organizations' websites. What different views of the mission of the church (or religious community) do you find in these statements?

Questions for Discussion

1. Discuss some of your own understandings of the nature and purpose of the church. What are the sources of these understandings—biblical images, church teachings, or experiences in a church community?

2. How would you define *growth in love*? What is your understanding of grace? What are the sources of your understanding—biblical images, church teachings, or experiences in a church community?

3. Discuss your understanding of justification, regeneration, and sanctification. How does your tradition understand the relationship between these? If your tradition emphasizes one over the other, what has prompted this?

4. What are some of the similarities and differences between psychological notions of growth and maturity and theological ideas of growth?

Chapter 3

Exercises/Discussion Starters

1. From Embedded to Deliberative Theology

Think of a phrase you have often heard in your religious community or tradition and which you have affirmed or found helpful that might be considered a first-order religious statement or an expression of embedded theology. Examples: "God doesn't give us more than we can bear" or "God finds a way out of no way." What are the embedded theological assumptions in this phrase? If you reflect deliberatively on this phrase, what might be some of its strengths or limitations? How might this phrase be helpful or not in a pastoral care situation? (This exercise can also be given as a written assignment.)

2. Identifying/Building Your Own Theology

Examine table 3.1 "Theological Doctrines and Their Guiding Images" on page 41. Which of these images or metaphors appeals the most to you? As you think about your theology at this point, do you see yourself moving across one of the rows, or jumping from cell to cell in different rows and columns? How would you fill out the last row, in which the far left-hand, or first column reads, "Your image or metaphor"? You can draw on some of the descriptions in various columns or bring in additional ideas and resources. What biblical texts reflect your theological view? Briefly describe your theology, as you would portray it on the chart. (This exercise can also be given as a written assignment.)

Questions for Discussion

1. What are some of the biblical images or metaphors for God informing your theology? (Cite the texts that inform your view.)

2. How might experiences of suffering challenge the adequacy of a theological narrative? Have you had such an experience? (Share only if you are comfortable doing so.) Have you known someone who gave up on faith or God because the theological narrative he or she inherited was inadequate?

3. What are some examples of master narratives from your culture? What are some of the master narratives from your religious tradition? Are these narratives in agreement, complementary, conflicting, or a mixture of all three?

Chapter 4

Exercises/Discussion Starters

1. Consider Oord's definition of love. Do you agree with his definition? How does this reflect a biblical or theological perspective on love? What are some of the strengths or limitations of his definition?

2. What are some of the ways love is portrayed in popular culture in the United States? Do you know how other cultures portray love?

3. How do these cultural portrayals of love fit or conflict with biblical views of love or those from church history as presented in the chapter?

4. Can you think of some examples of what the praxis of love might look like?

5. An example of how one might build a theological narrative around the narrative of love drawing on the theological sources of scripture, tradition, reason, and experience is outlined in chapter 4. Based on this example, how might you begin to fill out the theological narrative you began to sketch in chapter 3 (see table 3.1)?

Chapter 5

Exercises/Discussion Starters

    1. Listening Exercise: Active Listening (in triads)

In rotation, each participant takes one of three roles: storyteller, listener, or observer. The storyteller shares some event or concern that she or he is comfortable sharing in a short conversation. Example: worry over an upcoming test (nothing too personal or traumatic). After listening for some time, the listener responds using active listening skills and responses (paraphrase, and so on) and after five to ten minutes brings the conversation to a close. The observer then comments on what skills and responses the listener used predominantly. The storyteller then reflects on his or her experience of being listened to, giving feedback to the listener.

    Switch roles. Ideally each person has a turn in each role.

    2. Listening Exercise: Narrative Listening

Repeat the previous exercise with all three roles. Engage an attitude of narrative listening. The listener tries to help the storyteller name the problem. If the presenting issue is worry about a test, the problem might be named *worry, perfectionism, self-doubt,* or any number of things. Remember it is up to the storyteller to name the problem. The listener can suggest something, but the final decision of naming the problem is up to the storyteller. The listener can practice asking questions that help the storyteller begin to externalize the issue or problem.

    3. Compare Types of Listening

If both exercises are completed, compare the two types of listening and your experience as listener, storyteller, and observer with each type of listening.

For additional practice in asking narrative questions, see David Burrell Dinkins, *Narrative Pastoral Counseling.*[2]

Questions for Discussion

    1. Discuss the image/metaphor of story companion. What is your response to this metaphor? What are the strengths or limits of this metaphor compared to the more traditional image of a pastor as shepherd of the flock? Are these images compatible? Why or why not?

2. What are some of the differences between hearing and listening? Have you had an experience of being heard, but not really listened to? What gets in the way of paying attention and really listening rather than just hearing words?

3. Discuss the difference between paradigmatic knowing and narrative knowing. Can you give an example of each? What are some situations in which each kind of knowing is most appropriate?

4. What are some of the dimensions of empathy or empathic listening? What has been your experience of being listened to with empathy? What has been your experience of or listening to another with empathy?

5. What behaviors or attitudes can lead to failures of empathy? Can you think of a time when you felt as if your listener failed to be empathic? How did you feel or respond?

6. What is the difference between empathy and sympathy? Can you think of situations in which each would be appropriate responses? How do you feel when you receive sympathy but would prefer empathy?

7. What are three purposes of listening? What are some examples of situations in which each form might be employed?

8. What is the purpose of active listening? Name and describe at least two of the skills of active listening.

9. What are some of the differences between active listening and narrative listening?

10. Discuss some of the distinctions between narrative pastoral conversation, consultation, and pastoral therapy (see table 5.1, p. 72).

11. The most serious expression of ethical violation in professional or pastoral relationship is the violation of appropriate sexual boundaries. What are some more subtle forms of ethical or boundary violations? What are some of the ways we can attend to and monitor appropriate pastoral and professional boundaries?

Chapter 6

Questions/Discussion Starters

1. What are two ways the narrative environments can be understood?

2. How do interpretive communities shape us?

3. How do families function as a "culture of embededness?"

4. What are some of the multiple narrative environments in which we live? Give an example of two different narrative environments and some of their distinct features.

5. What is one of your favorite childhood books, stories, or films? How does the book or story reflect/not reflect the narrative environment(s) in which you were raised? What master narratives are embedded there? What does the book/story/film communicate about narratives of gender, race, ethnicity, or other dimensions of identity?

6. Now consider a current popular film, television show, or bestselling novel. How does it reflect assumptions of the larger culture and narrative environment of which it is a part? What master narratives are communicated in it? Do you see any differences between the master narratives from your childhood stories and those communicated in contemporary stories?

7. Reflect on a memoir you have read recently. How does the narrative environment shape the memoirist's identity? Does she or he accept it, question it, or resist it?

8. Various forms of social media (such as FaceBook, Twitter, or similar formats) limit storytelling to brief forms. How might these forms of social media impact the way we tell our lifestories? What overall impact might such forms of social media have on contemporary narrative environments?

9. Name an experience of being story-o-typed by another person. How did this feel? How did you choose to respond? Have you caught yourself story-o-typing someone else? Did you realize this during the encounter or only afterward? What led to your awareness? How did you respond to your awareness?

10. When have you felt caught between conflicting master narrative or narrative environments—perhaps the environment of family versus culture, church versus culture, family versus church or school, or between cultures or subcultures? How did you negotiate these conflicts?

11. Can you name a story your church has told you about a certain group of human beings that you think plays into a dominant discourse? Alternatively, can you talk about an effort to challenge a master narrative spearheaded by one of your faith communities?

12. With a partner, share a bit about a narrative environment in which you were shaped and the implicit master narrative. Taking turns, ask each other some of the questions on page 91 designed to illumine the impact of these master narratives.

13. Why is it important for pastoral story companions to be able to identify and analyze the impact of narrative environments?

14. What are three features of narrative development? What are some of the activities of narrative development?

15. Narrative development theory suggests that we become more consciously engaged in authoring our own stories during adolescence. Based on your own experience as an adolescent or your work with adolescents, what are some of the positive and negative ways youth engage in this process? If we take this claim seriously, how might it shape our ministry with youth?

Chapter 7

Exercises/Discussion Starters

1. Imagination is not just for kids; it is essential to our lives and ministry. What is imagination? Why is it important for reading lives and for ministry in general? Recall some examples of imaginative and unimaginative ministry that you've experienced. What are some ways to foster imagination?

2. Read Billy Collins's poem "Introduction to Poetry." It can be found at http://www.poetryfoundation.org/poem/176056. How does Collins invite the reader to use imagination to enter the poem? How is

imagination stifled? When have you had experiences like this in reading poetry? What would happen if you did "drop a mouse into a poem" as Collins suggests?

3. Criteria for good stories: Select a story from a newspaper, magazine, novel, or one told to you recently by a friend, relative, or someone you have encountered in ministry. If you choose an oral story, sketch a brief outline or verbatim of the story so you remember as much as possible. Identify the presence or absence of the criteria of good stories in the piece or conversation you have chosen.

4. Many voices clamor to be the coauthors of our stories. How might we use the criteria for good stories to help us discern the potential impact, positive or negative, of a particular coauthor?

5. Practice exegeting a life narrative. Working in small groups, use the steps of the exegetical process, summarized in the outline below to provide a close reading of a portion of a lifestory. The story under examination may be drawn from a case study provided by the instructor or generated by the the students. Alternative sources for a story include a short excerpt of a memoir (such as Jesmyn Ward's *Men We Reaped*, used in chapter 6) or a fictional short story (such as Elizaberg Berg's "Departure from Normal" used in chapter 8).

Summary of Five Steps of Lifestory Exegesis

I. Getting the text in view

Select/identify the text.

Who are the main characters?

What is the plot?

What are the main themes?

What is the larger story?

A reliable translation: do you understand the "text" fully?

II. Getting introduced to the text

Ask questions of clarification.

Does it meet the six criteria of a good story: coherent, credible, open and vibrant, differentiated, contains reconciliation, generative imagination?

Watch out for story-o-types.

Place the text in a larger context.

III. Attending to the text

Attend to verbal and nonverbal communication.

Ask playful, curious questions that open the story up in new ways.

Name and externalize the issue or problem.

IV. Testing what is heard in the text

Check back with the storyteller to make sure your understanding is accurate.

How do narrative environments shape what is told and what we hear?

Consider plot, character, time, and conflict.

Does the story take a particular form?

What are the theological themes or issues in the text?

V. Moving toward interpretation

In lifestory exegesis, interpretation is always a dialogical process. It is not our (the listener's) interpretation of the story that matters, but that of the storyteller. The previous steps, which are also dialogical, prepare listener and storyteller for deeper and perhaps new interpretations to emerge.

Chapter 8

Exercises/Discussion Starters

1. What advantages or perspectives might pastoral story companions bring to the process of assisting others in the process of restorying?

2. Define *narrative foreclosure*. What might lead to narrative foreclosure? What are the consequences of a prematurely foreclosed story?

3. Identify types of loss. Go back to the case of "Three Generations under One Roof " in chapter 7. What types of loss are present in this case?

4. Read and discuss Elizabeth Berg's story "Departure from Normal" in *Ordinary Life: Stories.*[3] Identify the types of loss here. Is Alice's story foreclosed? If so, how does it get opened up again? (These questions can

be applied to any novel, film, memoir, or short story dealing with loss and grief.)

5. Discuss the dual-model process of coping with grief. What are some of the ways that pastoral care providers and religious communities might assist a grieving person or family dealing with both loss and restoration?

6. What are some pastoral care and liturgical practices that might support the ongoing bond between the deceased person and the bereaved person?

7. Review the four strategies for meaning making after loss. How might you apply these steps in Alice's case ("Departure from Normal") or to another story dealing with grief and loss? Some memoirs that work well for this exercise are *Wild* by Cheryl Strayed, Jesmyn Ward's *Men We Reaped*, and Jeanette Walls's *Glass Castle*.

8. A number of films also depict grief and loss and provide an opportunity to examine the ways characters do or do not make meaning after a loss that leads to growth. A few examples are *The Bucket List, Ponette, Extremely Loud & Incredibly Close, The Kite Runner, Up, Wit, Lorenzo's Oil, We Bought a Zoo.*

9. In the midst of loss, we may sometimes feel God's absence more keenly than God's presence. What biblical images, stories, psalms, or passages might speak to this experience of suffering?

10. Discuss the case of Jin Woo Lee and Mrs. Ruth Leon. How do the changes in narrative environments for each of them require restorying? What has been your experience of having to revise your lifestory as you moved from one narrative environment to another?

11. Have you witnessed a congregation who has faced the need to revise its communal narrative? Was the congregation able to successfully revise its narratives in the face of changes challenging the community or not? What led to success or narrative foreclosure?

Notes

1. Telling the Stories of Our Lives

Epigraph: Dan P. McAdams, *The Stories We Live By: Personal Myths and the Making of the Self* (New York: Guilford Press, 1993), 11.

1. William A. Randall and A. Elizabeth McKim, *Reading Our Lives: The Poetics of Growing Old* (New York: Oxford University Press, 2008), 5.

2. Ibid.

3. Ibid., 8.

4. Ibid.

5. See Dan P. McAdams, *The Person: A New Introduction to Personality Psychology*, 4th ed. (Hoboken, NJ: John Wiley and Sons, 2006), 390–93, for a further discussion of these developments. McAdams cites a number of authors, including Jerome Brunner, John Polkinghorne, Alasdair MacIntyre, Anthony Giddens, and B. J. Cohler, who uphold the viewpoint that human beings are, by nature, storytellers.

6. Ibid., 390.

7. Michelle L. Crossley, *Introducing Narrative Psychology* (Philadelphia: Open University Press, 2000), 46. See also Jerome Brunner, *Acts of Meaning* (Cambridge, MA: Harvard University Press, 1990).

8. Paul Ricoeur, *Time and Narrative*, vol. 1 (Chicago: The University of Chicago Press, 1984), quoted in Steven Madigan, *Narrative Therapy* (Washington, DC: American Psychological Association, 2010), 37.

9. McAdams, *The Person*, 391.

10. Antonio Damasio, *The Feeling of What Happens: Body and Emotion in the Making of Consciousness* (Orlando, FL: Harcourt, 1999), 17.

11. Dan P. McAdams, *The Redemptive Self: Stories Americans Live By*, rev. ed. (New York: Oxford University Press, 2013), 55.

12. Anthony Giddens, *Modernity and Self-Identity: Self and Society in the Late Modern Age* (Stanford, CA: Stanford University Press, 1991), cited in McAdams, *The Person*, 389.

13. McAdams, *The Stories We Live By.*

14. William L. Randall, *The Stories We Are: An Essay in Self Creation,* 2nd ed. (Toronto: University of Toronto Press, 2014), 235–36. See also Randall and McKim, *Reading Our Lives*, 5–6.

15. Randall and McKim, *Reading Our Lives*, 103.

16. McAdams, *The Redemptive Self*, 55.

17. Lisa Cron, *Wired for Story: The Writer's Guide to Using Brain Science to Hook Readers from the Very First Sentence* (Berkeley, CA: Ten Speed Press, 2012), 2.

18. Randall, *The Stories We Are,* 84.

19. Ibid., 85.

20. Ibid., 86.

21. Ibid., 86–87.

22. Paul Cobley, *Narrative* (London: Routledge Press, 2001), 6, quoted in Randall and McKim, *Reading Our Lives*, 7.

23. Randall, *The Stories We Are,* 87.

24. Paul Ricoeur, "Narrative Time," in *On Narrative,* ed. W. J. T. Mitchell (Chicago: University of Chicago Press, 1980), 165–66, cited in Randall, *The Stories We Are,* 87.

25. Randall and McKim, *Reading Our Lives*, 27.

26. McAdams, *The Stories We Live By*, 30.

27. Ibid.; see also Randall and McKim, *Reading Our Lives,* 20.

28. Randall and McKim, *Reading Our Lives*, 20.

29. McAdams, *The Person,* 389.

30. See McAdams, *The Redemptive Self.* See also Madigan, *Narrative Therapy.* Both narrative psychology and narrative therapy theory argue for a central role of culture in shaping the stories we tell about others and ourselves.

31. See Herbert Anderson and Edward Foley, *Mighty Stories, Dangerous Ritual: Weaving Together the Human and Divine* (San Francisco, CA: Jossey-Bass, 2001).

32. Bruner, *Acts of Meaning.*

33. Ibid. See also McAdams, *The Redemptive Self*, 56–57, for a discussion of Bruner's theory.

34. See McAdams, *The Redemptive Self*, 61, for a further discussion of the communication of motivation through story.

35. McAdams, *The Stories We Live By*, 5.

36. Ibid.

37. McAdams, *The Redemptive Self*, 62.

38. Ibid., 62.

39. Ibid.

40. Ibid.

41. Ibid.

42. Ibid.

43. Ibid, 63.

44. Ibid, 66.

45. Ibid, 68.

46. Ibid.

47. Ibid.

48. Ibid.

49. Ibid.

50. Ibid., 69.

51. Ibid., 70.

52. McAdams, *The Person*, 423.

53. Ibid.

54. Ibid.

55. Ibid. See also Randall and McKim, *Reading Our Lives*, 104–5.

56. McAdams, *The Person*, 423. See also Randall and McKim, *Reading Our Lives*, 105.

57. McAdams, *The Person*, 423. See also Randall and McKim, *Reading Our Lives*, 105.

58. McAdams, *The Person*, 423. See also Randall and McKim, *Reading Our Lives*, 106.

59. McAdams, *The Person*, 423. See also Randall and McKim, *Reading Our Lives*, 107–8.

60. McAdams, *The Person*, 663–64. See also Randall and McKim, *Reading Our Lives*, 109.

61. See Randall and McKim, *Reading Our Lives*, 109, for a further discussion.

62. Ibid.

63. Ibid., 110.

64. For more information about the development and practice of narrative therapy, see the Dulwich Centre website: www.dulwichcentre.com.au/.

65. Michael White and David Epston, *Narrative Means to Therapeutic Ends* (New York: W. W. Norton and Company, 1990), 14–16.

66. Ibid., 16.

67. See Madigan, *Narrative Therapy*, 163, 165, for a definition of alternative story and deconstruction.

68. See White and Epston, *Narrative Means*, 38–76, for an extended discussion of externalization.

69. See John Winslade and Lorraine Smith, "Countering Alcoholic Narratives," in *Narrative Therapy in Practice: The Archaeology of Hope*, ed. Gerald Monk, John Winslade, Kathie Crocket, and David Epston (San Francisco: Jossey-Bass, 1997), 158–92, for an extended case study in which "Al" is the name assigned to the problem of alcohol.

70. American Psychiatric Association. Diagnostic and Statistical Manual of Mental Disorders: DSM-5. (Arlington, VA: American Psychiatric Association, 2013).

71. White and Epston, *Narrative Means*, 19–27.

72. Gary M. Kenyon and William Randall, *Restorying our Lives: Personal Growth through Autobiographical Reflection* (Westport, CT: Praeger, 1997), 1.

73. Randall, *The Stories We Are*, xiv.

74. Randall and McKim, *Reading Our Lives*, 4.

75. Ibid.

76. Karen Scheib, *Challenging Invisibility: Practices of Care with Older Women* (St. Louis, MO: Chalice Press, 2004), 142–45.

77. See, for example, Kenyon and Randall, *Restorying Our Lives,* 34–36; they use the terms *inside stories* and *outside stories.*

78. William L. Randall, "The Importance of Being Ironic: Narrative Openness and Personal Resilience in Later Life," *The Gerontologist* 53, no. 1 (2013): 9–16.

79. Edward P. Wimberley, *African American Pastoral Care,* rev. ed. (Nashville, TN: Abingdon Press, 2008).

80. See, for example, Christie Cozad Neuger, *Counseling Women: A Narrative Pastoral Approach* (Philadelphia: Fortress Press, 2001); Andrew Lester, *Hope in Pastoral Care and Counseling* (Louisville, KY: Westminster John Knox Press, 1995); Burrell David Dinkins, *Narrative Pastoral Care and Counseling* (Maitland, FL: Xulon Press, 2005); Suzanne Coyle, *Uncovering Spiritual Narratives: Using Story in Pastoral Care and Ministry* (Philadelphia: Fortress Press, 2014); Carrie Doehring, *The Practice of Pastoral Care: A Postmodern Approach*, rev. ed. (Louisville, KY: Westminster John Knox Press, 2015).

81. In *Pastoral Care in Context: An Introduction to Pastoral Care* (Louisville, KY: Westminster John Knox, 1993), 4–6, John Patton proposed three models of care: classical, clinical pastoral, and communal contextual. Carrie Doehring, in *The Practice of Pastoral Care*, (Louisville: Westminster John Knox Press, 2006), 2–6; describes premodern, modern, and postmodern perspectives on care, which correspond to Patton's categories. Doehring argues that all three perspectives can operate simultaneously in pastoral care, while Patton suggests each model emerged historically and replaced the previous model. I agree with Doehring that all three models or perspectives can be operating simultaneously in a congregation and in pastoral care practice.

82. E. Brooks Holifield makes this argument in his study of the development of pastoral care in the US context: *Pastoral Care in Historical Perspective: From Salvation to Self-Realization* (Nashville: Abingdon Press, 1983).

83. John Patton, *Pastoral Care in Context: An Introduction to Pastoral Care* (Louisville, KY: Westminster John Knox, 1993), 5.

84. Ibid, 4.

85. Ibid, 5.

2. The Church's Story

Epigraph: Nadia Bolz-Weber, *Pastrix: The Cranky, Beautiful Faith of a Sinner & Saint* (New York: Jericho Books, 2013), 54.

1. Ibid.

2. Avery Dulles, *Models of the Church: Expanded Edition* (New York: Image Books Doubleday, 1987), 76, 89.

3. Ibid., 76, 89.

4. Ibid., 206.

5. Ibid.

6. Dennis Doyle, *Communion Ecclesiology* (Maryknoll, NY: Orbis Press, 2000), 12.

7. Ibid.

8. Ibid., 13. For a full exposition of various approaches, see also T. Best and G. Gassman, *On the Way to Fuller Koinonia: Faith and Order Paper No. 166* (Geneva: WCC Publications, 1994); J. M. R. Tillard, *Church of Churches: The Ecclesiology of Communion* (Collegeville: The Liturgical Press, 1987); M. Volf, *After Our Likeness: The Church as the Image of the Trinity* (Grand Rapids: Eerdmans, 1998); J. Zizioulas, *Being as Communion: Studies in Personhood and the Church* (Crestwood, NY: St. Vladimir's Seminary Press, 1985).

9. Ibid.

10. Ibid., 14.

11. Peter C. Hodgson and Robert C. Williams, "The Church," in *Christian Theology: An Introduction to Its Traditions and Tasks,* ed. Peter C. Hodgson and Robert H. King (Minneapolis: Fortress Press, 1994), 249–73.

12. Ibid.

13. Martin E. Marty, "Grace," in *The New and Enlarged Handbook of Christian Theology,* ed. Donald W. Musser and Joseph L. Price (Nashville, TN: Abingdon Press, 2003), 225.

14. Craig Dykstra, *Growing in the Life of Faith: Education and Christian Practice* (Louisville, KY: Geneva Press, 1999), 38.

15. Ibid.

16. Ibid.

17. Thomas Jay Oord and Michael Lodhal, *Relational Holiness: Responding to the Call of Love* (Kansas City: Beacon Hill Press, 2005), 73.

18. Norman Russell, *The Doctrine of Deification in the Greek Patristic Tradition* (New York: Oxford University Press, 2006), 1–2.

19. Dykstra, *Growing in the Life,* 34.

20. John Calvin, *Institutes of the Christian Religion,* ed. John T. McNeil, trans. Ford Lewis Battles, The Library of Christian Classics, vol. 20 (Philadelphia: The Westminster Press, 1960), 3.3.9.

21. Randy Maddox, *Responsible Grace: John Wesley's Practical Theology* (Nashville: Kingswood Books, 1994), 32.

22. Theodore Runyon, *The New Creation: John Wesley's Theology Today* (Nashville: Abingdon Press, 1998), 82.

23. Ibid., 30.

24. Ibid., 31.

25. John Wesley, "Preface," 2.9–14, in *The Works of John Wesley*, ed. Thomas Jackson, 3rd ed., 14 vols. (London: Wesleyan Methodist Book Room, 1872; reprint ed., Grand Rapids, MI: Baker, 1979), 14:202–5 quoted in Maddox, *Responsible Grace*, 180.

26. Ibid., 106.

27. Randy Maddox, "Reclaiming the Eccentric Parent," in *Inward and Outward Health: John Wesley's Holistic Concept of Medical Sciences, The Environment, and Holy Living*, ed. Deborah Madden (London: Epworth Press, 2008), 17.

28. Ibid.

29. E. Brooks Holifield, *Health and Medicine in the Methodist Tradition: Journey Toward Wholeness* (New York: Crossroad, 1986), 20.

30. Freud does not use this exact phrase but a similar idea is expressed in "Civilization and Its Discontents" (1930) in which he wrote, "The communal life of human beings had, therefore, a two-fold foundation: the compulsion to work, which was created by external necessity, and the power of love...." ("Frequently Asked Questions," The Freud Museum, accessed October 10, 2015, http://www.freud.org.uk/about/faq/).

31. Clyde Hendrick and Susan SA. Hendrick, "Love," in *The Oxford Handbook of Positive Psychology*, ed. Shane J. Lopez and C. R. Snyder, 2nd ed. (Oxford, UK: Oxford University Press, 2009), 447.

32. William C. Compton and Edward Hoffman, *Positive Psychology: The Science of Happiness and Flourishing*, 2nd ed. (Belmont, CA: Wadsworth, Cenage Learning, 2013), 101.

33. Ibid.,102.

34. Ibid.,104.

35. Ellen Bernscheid, "Some Comments on Love's Anatomy: Or, Whatever Happened to Lust?" in *The Psychology of Love*, ed. Robert J. Sternberg and Michael L. Barnes (New Haven: Yale University Press, 1988), 362.

36. Ibid.

37. Donald Wertlieb, "Affective Development," in *The Concise Corsini Encyclopedia of Psychology and Behavioral Science*, ed. W. Craighead & C. Nemeroff (Hoboken, NJ: Wiley, 2004).

38. McAdams, *The Stories We Live By*, 5.

39. Ibid.

40. McAdams, *The Person*, 423.

41. Randall and McKim, *Reading Our Lives*, 110.

42. Thomas Jay Oord and Michael Lodhal, *Relational Holiness: Responding to the Call of Love* (Kansas City: Beacon Hill Press, 2005), 73.

43. Michael White and David Epston, *Narrative Means to Therapeutic Ends* (New York: W. W. Norton & Company, 1990), 16–24.

44. See for example William Randall and Gary Kenyon, *Ordinary Wisdom: Biographical Aging and the Journey Of Life* (Westport, CT: Praeger, 2001).

45. Rita Charon, *Narrative Medicine: Honoring the Stories of Illness* (New York: Oxford University Press, 2006), 90–103.

46. Ibid.

47. Ibid.

48. John McLeod, "The Significance of Narrative and Storytelling in Postpsychological Counseling and Psychotherapy," in *Healing Plots: The Narrative Basis of Psychotherapy*, ed. Amia Lieblich, Dan P. McAdams, and Ruthellen Josselson (Washington, DC: The American Psychological Association, 2004) 15.

49. Ibid.

50. Ibid.

51. Ibid.

52. Ibid., 12.

53. Ibid., 21.

54. Ibid.

55. Ibid.

56. Ibid., 11.

57. Ibid.

58. Ibid.

59. E. Brooks Holifield, *A History of Pastoral Care in America: From Salvation to Self-Realization* (Nashville: Abingdon Press, 1983), for a discussion about the emergence of psychological forms of counseling from religious practices of soul care.

60. Thomas Jay Oord, *The Nature of Love: A Theology* (St. Louis, MO: Chalice Press, 2010), 17.

61. *Jenna* and *Jim* are fictional names. This is a composite case based on cases from my experience in ministry.

62. Karen D. Scheib, "Make Love Your Aim: Ecclesial Practices of Care at the End of Life," in *Living Well and Dying Faithfully: Christian Practices for End of Life Care*, ed. John Swinton and Richard Payne (Grand Rapids, MI: Wm. B. Eerdmans Publishing Company, 2009), 30–31.

63. Ibid.

64. McAdams, *The Person*, 423.

3. Stories about God

Epigraph: Howard W. Stone and James O. Duke, *How to Think Theologically*, 2nd ed. (Minneapolis: Fortress Press, 2006), 2.

1. Karl Barth reportedly gave this answer at a lecture at the University of Chicago in 1962. For more see Roger E. Olson, "Did Karl Barth Really Say 'Jesus Loves Me, This I Know....'?'" *Patheos,* January 24, 2013, http://www.patheos.com/blogs/rogereolson/2013/01/did-karl-barth-really-say-jesus-loves-me-this-i-know/.

2. While I am placing myself in the larger frame of narrative theology, more specifically I place myself within the strand identified most closely with David Tracy and the Chicago school rather than the Yale school of George Lindbeck and Stanley Hauerwas. While I believe the church has a particular responsibility for the Christian narrative, this narrative holds the church rather than the other way around. For a discussion of these schools see Scott Holland, *How Do Stories Save Us: An Essay on the Question with the Theological Hermeneutics of David Tracy in View* (Louvain; Dudley, MA: Peters, 2006).

3. Stone and Duke, *How to Think Theologically*, 2.

4. Ibid., 3.

5. See *Christian Words* (London: Oxford University Press, 1868), 112. https://books.google.com.ph/books?id=WvQDAAAAQAA/ Google e-book. The original poem was published in 1860 by Anna Barlett Warner while the hymn based on the poem was created by William Batchelder Bradbury in 1862.

6. Stone and Duke, *How to Think Theologically*, 5.

7. T. W. Jennings Jr., "Pastoral Theological Methodology," in *Dictionary of Pastoral Care and Counseling*, ed. Rodney J. Hunter (Nashville: Abingdon Press, 1990), 862.

8. This practice is known as *Tong Song Kido*.

9. Despite the popular belief that this is a quotation from the Bible, it is not.

10. Stone and Duke, *How to Think Theologically*, 18.

11. Ibid. See also Jennings Jr., "Pastoral Theological Methodology," 862.

12. David Guralnik, ed., *Webster's New World Dictionary of the American Language*, 2nd college ed. (New York: Simon and Schuster, 1980).

13. Patrick D. Miller, "Biblical Theology," in *The New and Enlarged Handbook of Christian Theology*, ed. Donald W. Musser and Joseph L. Price (Nashville, TN: Abingdon Press, 2003), 68.

14. Robert L. Wilken, "Historical Theology," in Musser and Price, *New and Enlarged Handbook*, 237.

15. Leonard J. Biallas, "Dogmatic Theology," in Musser and Price, *New and Enlarged Handbook*, 133.

16. "The Nicene Creed," in *United Methodist Hymnal* (Nashville, TN: The United Methodist Publishing House, 1989), #880.

17. Daniel L. Migliore, *Faith Seeking Understanding: An Introduction to Christian Theology* (Grand Rapids: Wm. B. Eerdmans, 1991), 9.

18. Joerg Rieger, "Constructive Theology," in *Encyclopedia of Sciences and Religion*, ed. Anne L. C. Runehov and Lluis Oviedo (Dordrecht: Springer, 2013), 483–86.

19. Ibid.

20. Mark Lewis Taylor, "Anthropology," in Musser and Price, *New and Enlarged Handbook*, 29.

21. Ibid.

22. Monika Hellwig, "Christology," in Musser and Price, *New and Enlarged Handbook*, 94.

23. Joseph F. Kelley, *The Ecumenical Councils of the Catholic Church: A History* (Collegeville, MN: Michael Glazier, 2009), 44.

24. Irenaeus, *Against Heresies* in *The Ante-Nicene Fathers: Translations of the Writings of the Fathers down to A.D. 325*, vol. 1, ed. Alexander Roberts, James Donaldson, and A. Cleveland Coxe (Buffalo: Christian Literature Company, 1895).

25. Eugene Teselle, "Atonement," in Musser and Price, *New and Enlarged Handbook*, 45.

26. Anselm, Why *God Became Man = Cur Deus Homo*, trans. Jasper Hopkins and Herbert Richardson (Lewiston, NY: Edwin Mellen Press, 1974).

27. Teselle "Atonement," in Musser and Price, *New and Enlarged Handbook*, 45.

28. Ibid.

29. The Apostles' Creed, Traditional Version, *The United Methodist Hymnal* (Nashville, TN: United Methodist Publishing House, 1989), 881.

30. Albert Outler used the term *Wesleyan quadrilateral* in *John Wesley* (New York: Oxford University Press, 1964), his edited collection of Wesley's works, to refer to Wesley's sources of theological reflection. These four sources are widely used in the Christian tradition and are not distinctive to Wesley.

31. Entire texts are devoted to this topic. See, for example, Charles J. Scalise, *Bridging the Gap: Connecting What You Learned in Seminary with What You Find in the Congregation* (Nashville: Abingdon Press, 2003).

32. Some Christian denominations include the Apocrypha within the canon of scripture while others do not.

33. Lonnie D. Kliever, "Experience-Religious," in Musser and Price, *New and Enlarged Handbook*, 190.

34. Ibid., 191.

35. John Wesley, *Journal and Diaries,* ed. W. Reginald Ward and Richard P. Heitzenrater, The Bicentennial Edition of the Works of John Wesley (Nashville: Abingdon Press, 1988), 18:249–50.

36. Since a good number of books have been written specifically on this subject, I will focus primarily on the methods used in this volume. See Scalise, *Bridging the Gap* for more information.

37. John Clayton, "Correlation," in Musser and Price, *New and Enlarged Handbook*, 108.

38. The following works have been influential in shaping method in practical and pastoral theology: David Tracy, *Blessed Rage for Order: The New Pluralism in Theology* (New York: Seabury Press, 1997); Don S. Browning, *A Fundamental Practical Theology: Descriptive and Strategic Proposals* (Minneapolis: Fortress Press, 1991); Rebecca Chopp, *Saving Work: Feminist Practices of Theological Education* (Louisville, KY: Westminster John Knox Press, 1995).

39. R. Ruard Ganzevoort, introduction to *Religious Stories We Live By: Narrative Approaches in Theology and Religious Study*, ed. Ruad Ganzevoort, Maaike de Haardt, and Michael Scherer-Rath (Leiden: Brill, 2014), 1–7.

40. Ibid.

41. Randall and McKim, *Reading Our Lives*, 262.

42. Ibid.

43. Ibid., 261.

44. Thomas King *The Truth about Stories: A Native Narrative* (Toronto, ON: House of Anansi Press, 2003), quoted in Randall and McKim, *Reading Our Lives*, 261–62.

45. Though this quotation is widely attributed to Winston Churchill, there is no credible source to prove the attribution. He did, however, remark in the House of Commons that history would find Prime Minister Stanley Baldwin wrong because "I shall write that history," according to Max Hasting in "History as Written by the Victor," *The Telegraph*, Nov. 2, 2004, accessed July 8, 2015, http://www.telegraph.co.uk/culture/books/3626376/History -as-written-by-the-victor.html.

46. For more information, see Joerg Rieger, *Opting for the Margins: Postmodernity and Liberation in Christian Theology* (New York: Oxford University Press, 2003).

47. For more information, see Lamin O. Sanneh, *Whose Religion Is Christianity? The Gospel beyond the West* (Grand Rapids, MI: Wm. B. Eerdmans, 2003) and J. S. Cummins, *Christianity and Missions, 1450–1800*, Expanding World, vol. 28 (Aldershot, Great Britain, Brookfield, VT: Ashgate/Variorum, 1997).

48. Randall and McKim, *Reading Our Lives*, 262.

49. Ibid., 50.

50. Stephen Crites, "The Narrative Quality of Experience," *Journal of the American Academy of Religion* 39, no. 3 (1971): 291.

51. Though I am drawing on Crites's term, I am using it in a slightly different way.

52. Glenn Memorial Church, http://www.glennumc.org/purpose, accessed March 16, 2015. (URL content of this page has been changed. This content no longer appears.)

53. I have left out pneumatology—theology of the Holy Spirit—primarily due to space restrictions. Other doctrinal loci could be added as well. This chart is not intended to be exhaustive of all the various or possible theological narratives in the Christian tradition.

54. Dave Brunn, *One Bible, Many Versions: Are All Translations Created Equal?* (Downers Grove, IL: InterVarsity Press, 2013), 77–80.

55. Mark Lewis Taylor, "Anthropology," in Musser and Price, *New and Enlarged Handbook of Christian Theology*, 30.

56. E. Brooks Holifield, *A History of Pastoral Care in America: From Salvation to Self-Realization* (Nashville: Abingdon Press, 1983), 61–65.

57. Full Gospel Baptist Church, "What We Believe: Our Mission Statement," http://www.changingagenerationministries.org/pages/page.asp?page_id=33802.

58. Otto Maduro, "Liberation Theology," in Musser and Price, *New and Enlarged Handbook*, 299.

59. Other forms of liberation theology from the experiences of other marginalized groups can be added to this list as well.

60. See for example, James H. Cone, "Black Theology in American Religion," *Journal of the American Academy of Religion* 53, no. 4 (1985): 755.

61. Abraham Lincoln issued the Emancipation Proclamation on January 1, 1863, in the third year of the US Civil War. This document declared "that all persons held as slaves" within the rebellious states "are, and henceforward shall be free." There were limits, however, to the freedoms established and it took some time before those held as slaves were freed. For more information, see www.archives.gov/exhibits/featured_documents/emancipation_proclamation.

62. Cone, "Black Theology," 756–57.

63. Ibid., 758.

64. Ibid.

65. See ibid. for a further discussion of oppression as sin, as well as James Cone's books *My Soul Looks Back: Journeys in Faith* (Nashville: Abingdon, 1982) and *God of the Oppressed* (New York: Seabury Press, 1975).

66. "Our Covenant," Oakhurst Baptist Church, accessed October 11, 2015, http://www.oakhurstbaptist.org/join-in/our-covenant.

4. A Love Story

1. "Do You Love Me," lyrics by Sheldon Harnick, composed by Jerry Bock, from the musical *Fiddler on the Roof,* book by Joseph Stein, based on the stories of Sholom Aliechem, first produced in 1964. For more information, see Alisa Solomon, "On Jewishness, as the Fiddle Played," *New York Times*, October 17, 2013, http://www.nytimes.com/2013/10/20/theater/fiddler-on-the-roof-its-production-heritage.html?pagewanted=all&_r=0.

2. Thomas Lewis, Fari Amini, Richard Lannon, *A General Theory of Love*, 1st ed. (New York: Random House, 2000), 5.

3. See Yudit Greenberg, ed., *Encyclopedia of Love in World Religions*, vol. 1 (Santa Barbara, CA: ABC-CLIO, 2008).

4. Ibid., "Preface," xxviii.

5. For example, see Werner G. Jeanrond, *A Theology of Love* (London: T and T Clark International, 2010) and Thomas J. Oord's books *Defining Love: A Philosophical, Scientific, and Theological Engagement* (Grand Rapids, MI: Brazos Press, 2010) and *The Nature of Love: A Theology* (St. Louis: Chalice Press, 2010).

6. Oord, *Nature of Love*, 2.

7. Diana Eck, "Foreword," ibid., xxiii.

8. Jeanrond, *A Theology of Love*, 31.

9. Ibid.

10. Ibid., 31–32.

11. Ibid., 30.

12. Ibid.

13. Ibid., 32.

14. Ibid.

15. Ibid., 34.

16. Ibid., 35.

17. William Madges, "Love," in *The New and Enlarged Handbook of Christian Theology*, ed. Donald W. Musser and Joseph L. Price (Nashville, TN: Abingdon Press, 2003), 313.

18. Ibid.

19. Ibid.

20. Oord, *The Nature of Love*, 57–58.

21. Carter Lindberg, *Love: A Brief History through Western Christianity* (Malden, MA: Blackwell Publishing, 2008), 58.

22. Ibid.,59.

23. Ibid., 59.

24. Ibid.

25. Ibid.

26. Ibid.

27. Augustine, *Enchiridion 31:117* cited in Michael McCarthy, "Church Fathers" in Greenberg, *Encyclopedia of Love*, 117.

28. Michael McCarthy, "Church Fathers" in Greenberg, *Encyclopedia of Love*, 117.

29. Ibid.

30. Ibid.

31. McCarthy, "Church Fathers" cited in Greenberg, *Encyclopedia of Love*, 117. See also Saint Augustine's *City of God* trans. George E. McCracken et al., 7 vols. (Cambridge, MA: Harvard University Press, 1957–1972).

32. Lindberg, *Love: A Brief History*, 64.

33. Ibid.

34. Thomas L. Humphries Jr., *Ascetic Pneumatology from John Cassian to Gregory the Great* (Oxford, UK: Oxford University Press, 2013), 80.

35. Ibid.

36. Lindberg, *Love: A Brief History*, 66.

37. Ibid., 67.

38. Ibid., 68.

39. Ibid., 69–70.

40. Ibid., 72.

41. Ibid., 103.

42. Ibid., 107.

43. Ibid.

44. Greenberg, "Medieval Christian Philosophy," in Greenberg, *Encyclopedia of Love*, 102.

45. Lindberg, *Love: A Brief History*, 119.

46. Ibid.

47. Ibid.

48. Lewis, Amini, and Lannon, *A General Theory of Love*, 7.

49. Oord, *Defining Love*, 66.

50. Ibid.

51. Ibid., 67.

52. Christopher Peterson, *A Primer in Positive Psychology* (Oxford: Oxford University Press, 2006), 58, 249.

53. Christopher Peterson and Martin E. P. Seligman, *Character Strengths and Virtues: A Handbook and Classification* (Washington, DC: New York: American Psychological Association, Oxford University Press, 2004), 303–24.

171

54. See Oord, *Defining Love*, 74–84, for a further discussion of this research.

55. Ibid., 80.

56. Ibid., 97–136, for a further discussion of scientific explorations into love.

57. For more, see *World Values Study Wave 4 1999–2004*, Official Aggregate Version v. 20140429, World Values Survey Association (Aggregate File Producer: Asep/JDS, Madrid Spain, 2014), www.worldvaluessurvey.org.

58. Ibid.

59. Also see the *General Social Survey, Cumulative Datafile, 1972–2012*, items 480–487, 560–561, 946–950, 1016 for the high value of unselfish love, including "Altruism and Empathy in America: Trends and Correlates," 2006 paper based on GSS data. For additional information see Tom Smith "About the General Social Survey," http://www3.norc.org/GSS+Website/. Smith is the director of the General Social Survey and the National Opinion Research Center.

60. Jeanrond, *A Theology of Love*, 90.

61. Ibid.

62. Ibid., 91.

63. Ibid.

64. Ibid., 92.

65. Ibid.

66. Ibid.

67. See, for example, Catherine Lacugna, *God For Us: The Trinity and Christian Life* (San Francisco, CA: HarperSanFrancisco, 1991), for a discussion of trinitarian theology.

68. Dennis Doyle, *Communion Ecclesiology* (Maryknoll, NY: Orbis Press, 2000), 13.

69. Augustine quoted in Jeanrond, *A Theology of Love*, 52.

70. Ibid., 45.

71. Ibid., 67–103.

72. Oord, *The Nature of Love*, 84–86.

73. Ibid., 35.

74. Jeanrond, *A Theology of Love*, 115.

75. Ibid., 105.

76. Oord, *The Nature of Love*, 41.

77. See for example ibid. and Michael Lodal and Thomas Jay Oord, *Relational Holiness: Responding to the Call of Love* (Kansas City: Beacon Hill Press, 2005).

78. Oord, *The Nature of Love*, 53.

79. Jeanrond, *A Theology of Love*, 243.

80. Oord, *The Nature of Love*, 17.

81. Ibid.

82. Ibid., 18.

83. Ibid., 19.

84. Ibid., 20.

85. Ibid.

86. Ibid., 21.

87. Ibid., 25, 28.

88. Ibid., 25.

89. Ibid., 29–30.

90. Ibid., 27.

91. Defining the purpose of pastoral care in forming persons for love will also require us to consider the distinctions and overlaps between pastoral care and religious education, though that is beyond the scope of this chapter. My basic premise is that while religious education attends to the ongoing formation of persons in the Christian life, pastoral care attends to this formation at pivotal moments in life. These pivotal moments may be moments of suffering, healing, joy, or sorrow.

92. See, for example, Dorothy C. Bass and M. Shawn Copeland, *Practicing Our Faith: A Way of Life for Searching People* (San Francisco: Jossey Bass, 2010).

93. Karen Scheib, *Challenging Invisibility: Practices of Care with Older Women* (St. Louis, MO: Chalice Press, 2004), 50.

94. Jeanrond, *A Theology of Love*, 5.

95. While the terms *praxis* and *practice* are not identical, conversations about Christian practices in practical and pastoral theology have been influenced by the recovery of the concepts of practical wisdom and praxis. See Jeanrond, *A Theology of Love*, for a further discussion of praxis and practical wisdom.

96. Ibid., 43.

97. Ibid., 34.

98. Ibid., 2.

99. Ibid., 243.

100. Ibid.

101. Ibid., 247.

102. Oord, *Defining Love*, 81.

103. Jeanrond, *A Theology of Love*, 249.

104. Ibid.

105. Ibid., 216.

106. Ibid., 259.

107. Oord, *The Nature of Love*, 179.

108. Ibid., 132.

109. Oord, *Defining Love*, 190.

110. Ibid.

111. Ibid., 192.

112. Ibid., 195.

5. Becoming Story Companions

Epigraph 1: William Carlos Williams as recorded in an interview in Robert Coles's book *The Call of Stories* (Boston, MA: Houston Mifflin Company, 1989), 30.

Epigraph 2: Graeme M. Griffin *Coming to Care: An Introduction to Pastoral Care for Ordained Ministers and Lay People* (Parkville, Victoria: Uniting Church Theological Hall, 1995), 48.

1. "Companion," as defined in *Merriam-Webster's Collegiate Dictionary,* 11th ed. (Springfield, MA: Merriam-Webster, 2003).

2. *Susan* and *Diane* are pseudonyms, and some of the details have been changed to protect confidentiality.

3. Nelle Morton, *The Journey Is Home* (Boston: Beacon Press, 1985), 202.

4. Mindy McGarrah Sharp, *Misunderstanding Stories: Toward a Postcolonial Pastoral Theology* (Eugene, OR: Pickwick Publications, 2013), 5.

5. Jerome Brunner, *Acts of Meaning* (Cambridge, MA: Harvard University Press, 1990), 11.

6. Ibid., 13.

7. Steven Madigan, *Narrative Therapy* (Washington, DC: American Psychological Association, 2010) 37.

8. "Hear," as defined in *Oxford Dictionaries*, http://www.oxforddictionaries.com/us/definition/american_english/hear.

9. "Listen," as defined in ibid.

10. Griffin, *Coming to Care*, 48.

11. Martin L. Hoffman, *Empathy and Moral Development: Implications for Caring and Justice* (Cambridge, UK: New York: Cambridge University Press, 2000), 29.

12. Arthur W. Frank, *The Wounded Storyteller: Body, Illness, and Ethics* (Chicago: University of Chicago Press, 1997), 158.

13. Ibid.

14. Sharp, *Misunderstanding Stories*, 5, 133–37.

15. Griffin, *Coming to Care*, 50–61.

16. Ibid.

17. Judith Lewis Herman, *Trauma and Recovery*, rev. ed. (New York: BasicBooks, 1997), 1–4.

18. Ibid., 34–35.

19. Robert R. Carkhuff, Michael M. Pierce, and John R. Cannon, *The Art of Helping III*, 3rd ed. (Amherst, MA: Human Resource Development Press, 1977), 80.

20. Ibid.

21. Ibid., 79.

22. See, for example, Carrie Doehring, *The Practice of Pastoral Care: A Postmodern Approach*, rev. ed. (Louisville, KY: Westminster John Knox Press, 2015), 37–41; Howard Clinebell and Bridget Clare McKeever, *Basic Types of Pastoral Care and Counseling: Resources for the Ministry of Healing and Growth*, 3rd ed. (Nashville: Abingdon Press, 2011), 66–67.

23. Doehring, *Practice of Pastoral Care*, 37–41.

24. Clinebell and McKeever, *Basic Types of Pastoral Care*, 66.

25. David K. Switzer, *The Minister as Crisis Counselor*, rev. ed. (Nashville: Abingdon Press, 1986). For more on crisis intervention methods, see Lee Ann Hoff, *People in Crisis: Understanding and Helping*, 4th ed. (San Francisco: Jossey-Bass, 1995).

26. John Winslade, Gerald Monk, and Alison Cotter, "A Narrative Approach to the Practice of Mediation," *Negotiation Journal* 14, no. 1 (1998): 4.

27. Alice Morgan, *What Is Narrative Therapy? An Easy to Read Introduction* (Adelaide, SA: Dulwich Centre Publications, 2000), 3.

28. For more information on the theory and importance of listening in narrative therapy, see Wendy Drewery and John Winslade, "The Theoretical Story of Narrative Therapy," in *Narrative Therapy in Practice: The Archaeology of Hope*, ed. Gerald Monk, John Winslade, Katie Crocket, and David Epson (San Francisco, CA: Jossey-Bass, 1997), 32–52.

29. Randall, *The Stories We Are*, 25.

30. Ibid.

31. I draw on the work of both Graeme Griffin and Burrell David Dinkins to inform my definition of pastoral conversation. Griffin, *Coming to Care* and Burrell David Dinkins in *Narrative Pastoral Counseling* (Longwood, FL: Xulon Press, 2005).

32. Dinkins, *Narrative Pastoral Counseling*, 32.

33. Jean Stairs, *Listening for the Soul: Pastoral Care and Spiritual Direction* (Minneapolis: Fortress Press, 2000), 15.

34. Griffin, *Coming to Care*, 27.

35. Madigan, *Narrative Therapy*, 81.

36. For a discussion of the use of written documents in narrative therapy, see Michael White and David Epston, *Narrative Means to Therapeutic Ends* (New York: W. W. Norton and Company, 1990) and Jill Freedman and Gene Combs, *Narrative Therapy: The Social Construction of Preferred Realities* (New York: Norton, 1996).

37. In the United States, various state boards and professional organizations, such as the Association of Marriage and Family Therapists, generally administer licensing exams.

38. Griffin, *Coming to Care*, 50.

39. Shane J. Lopez and Matthew W. Gallagher, "A Case for Positive Psychology," in *The Oxford Handbook of Positive Psychology*, 2nd ed. (Oxford, New York: Oxford University Press, 2009), 4.

40. I first heard the term *pastoral consultation* from Christie Neuger, who may assign a slightly different meaning to it.

41. Dinkins, *Narrative Pastoral Counseling*, 33.

42. William L. Randall, *The Stories We Are: An Essay in Self Creation*, 2nd ed. (Toronto: University of Toronto Press, 2014), 17.

43. Ibid., 17–18.

44. Gary M. Kenyon and William Randall, *Restorying our Lives: Personal Growth through Autobiographical Reflection* (Westport, CT: Praeger, 1997), 2.

45. Griffin, *Coming to Care*, 49.

46. The United Methodist Church, *The Book of Discipline of the United Methodist Church 2012* (Nashville, TN: The United Methodist Publishing House, 2012). For more, see Reuben P. Job, *Three Simple Rules: A Wesleyan Way of Living* (Nashville: Abingdon Press, 2007), 23–24.

47. Child Welfare Information Gateway, "Mandatory Reporters of Child Abuse and Neglect," https://www.childwelfare.gov/topics/systemwide/laws-policies/. See also United States Department of Justice, "Elder Justice Statutes," http://www.justice.gov/elderjustice/prosecutors/statutes.html.

48. Doehring, *Practice of Pastoral Care*, 60.

49. See for example http://umcma.org/#/about-us/code-of-ethics for the United Methodist code of ethics for campus ministers. See also http://cciwdisciples.org/wp-content/uploads/2013/06/Min_Ethics_document-2011 for a code of ethics for the Disciples of Christ denomination and http://www.eocumc.com/sexual-ethics-policy/index.html for a code of ethics of the East Ohio Annual Conference of The United Methodist Church.

50. "The Order for the Ordination of Elders" and "The Order for the Ordination of Deacons," in *The United Methodist Book of Worship* (Nashville, TN: United Methodist Publishing House, 1992).

51. See Marie Fortune, *Love Does No Harm: Sexual Ethics for the Rest of Us* (New York: Continuum, 1995).

52. "Boundary," as defined in *The Merriam-Webster Online Dictionary,* http://www.merriam-webster.com/dictionary/boundary.

53. Ibid.

54. Doehring, *Practice of Pastoral Care*, 19.

55. Ibid. For a further discussion of fusion and disengagement, see also Ronald Richardson, *Creating a Healthier Church: Family Systems Theory, Leadership, and Congregational Life* (Minneapolis: Augsburg Fortress Press,1996).

56. Doehring, *Practice of Pastoral Care*, 19.

6. Reading Stories

1. Rita Charon, *Narrative Medicine: Honoring the Stories of Illness* (New York: Oxford University Press, 2006).

2. Ibid.

3. Anton T. Boisen, *Problems in Religion and Life: A Manual for Pastors* (New York: Abingdon-Cokesbury Press, 1946), 38.

4. Charon, *Narrative Medicine*, 9.

5. Ibid.

6. Ibid.

7. Ibid., 10.

8. William L. Randall, *The Stories We Are: An Essay in Self Creation*, 2nd ed. (Toronto: University of Toronto Press, 2014), 57.

9. Ibid., 57. A play on the word *stereotype*, Randall's term "story-o-types" refers to the often-unconscious process through which we create sketchy stories about others built on our preconceived assumptions and external observations, rather than on extensive experience and dialogue.

10. William A. Randall and A. Elizabeth McKim, *Reading Our Lives: The Poetics of Growing Old* (New York: Oxford University Press, 2008), 50.

11. Thomas Jay Oord, *The Nature of Love: A Theology* (St. Louis: Chalice Press, 2010), 17.

12. The term *therapoetic* is from Gary W. Kenyon and William Randall, *Restorying our Lives: Personal Growth through Autobiographical Reflection* (Westport, CT: Praeger, 1997), 2, 113, 131.

13. Ibid., 138.

14. Antonio Damasio, *The Feeling of What Happens: Body and Emotion in the Making of Consciousness* (Orlando, FL: Harcourt, 1999), 198.

15. Randall and McKim, *Reading Our Lives*, 50.

16. Ibid., 98.

17. Ibid., 50.

18. Ibid., 54.

19. Randall, *The Stories We Are*, 57.

20. Randall and McKim, *Reading Our Lives*, 50.

21. Ibid., 53–54.

22. Ibid., 50.

23. Ibid.

24. Dan P. McAdams, *The Stories We Live By: Personal Myths and the Making of the Self* (New York: Guilford Press, 1993), 47.

25. Ibid.

26. Ibid.

27. Randall and McKim, *Reading Our Lives*, 51.

28. John Paul Eakin, *Living Autobiographically: How We Create Identity in Narrative* (Ithaca, NY: Cornell University Press, 2008), 26.

29. Randall and McKim, *Reading Our Lives*, 54.

30. Ibid., 52.

31. Ibid., 54.

32. Vyduna-Haskins, "Growing Up with Dick and Jane," *History of Literacy*, http://history literacy.org/scripts/search_display.php?Article_ID=144.

33. Randall and McKim, *Reading Our Lives*, 52.

34. Ibid., 51.

35. Ibid., 52.

36. Ibid.

37. Ibid., 55.

38. Ibid., 55–56.

39. Debie Thomas, "First Words," *Journey with Jesus*, May 10, 2015, http://www.journey withjesus.net/theeighthday/142-first-words.

40. Randall and McKim, *Reading Our Lives*, 56.

41. See Nell Bernstein, *Burning Down the House: The End of Juvenile Prison* (New York: The New Press, 2014).

42. Gemma's name is fictional and this case is a composite based on conversations with and research about women trafficked as children and later imprisoned as adults for prostitu-

tion, including women who have been a part of the Magdalene Community of Thistle Farms in Nashville, Tennessee.

43. Ibid.

44. Ibid.

45. Ibid.

46. See, for example, Jean Kilbourne, "Beauty…and the Beast of Advertising," Center for Media Literacy, http://www.medialit.org/reading-room/beautyand-beast-advertising; Jean Kilbourne, "Women's Bodies in Advertising," *Our Bodies Ourselves*, February 13, 2012, http://www.ourbodiesourselves.org/health-info/womens-bodies-in-advertising/.

47. Centers for Disease Control and Prevention, "The National Intimate Partner and Sexual Violence Infographic," *Centers for Disease Control and Prevention*, September 8th, 2014, http://www.cdc.gov/violenceprevention/nisvs/infographic.html.

48. FaithTrust Institute, "Our Mission and Guiding Principles," *FaithTrust Institute*, http://www.faithtrustinstitute.org/about-us/guiding-principles.

49. Some resources for churches are Al Miles, *Domestic Violence: What Every Pastor Needs to Know*, 2nd ed. (Philadelphia: Fortress Press, 2011) and *Violence in Families: What Every Christian Needs to Know* (Philadelphia: Augsburg Books, 2002). See also Catherine Clark Kroeger and Nancy Nason-Clark, *Biblical and Practical Resources to Counteract Domestic Violence,* rev. ed. (Downers Grove, IL: IVP Press, 2010). Additional resources can also be found at http://www.faithtrustinstitute.org/.

50. Randall, *The Stories We Are*, 57.

51. While this case is fictionalized, it is based on an actual person.

52. Randall, *The Stories We Are*, 57.

53. Kenyon and Randall, *Restorying Our Lives*, 35.

54. Randall, *The Stories We Are*, 102.

55. Karen Scheib, *Challenging Invisibility: Practices of Care with Older Women* (St. Louis, MO: Chalice Press, 2004,) 64.

56. Ibid.

57. Randall and McKim, *Reading Our Lives*, 57.

58. Ibid.

59. See Michael White and David Epston, *Narrative Means to Therapeutic Ends* (New York: W. W. Norton and Company, 1990), 18–28.

60. Ibid.

61. Ibid., 22.

62. Ibid., 27.

63. Ibid., 31.

64. Scheib, *Challenging Invisibility*, 63.

65. Randall and McKim, *Reading Our Lives*, 50.

66. See Jill Freedman and Gene Combs, *Narrative Therapy: The Social Construction of Preferred Realities* (New York: Norton, 1996) for a further discussion of deconstructive questioning.

67. Jesmyn Ward, *Men We Reaped: A Memoir* (New York: Bloomsbury, 2013).

68. Ibid., 7.

69. Ibid., 8.

70. Ibid.

71. Kevin Nance, "Where the Writing Will Take Her," *Poets & Writers Magazine* 41, no. 5 (2013): 42–48.

72. Ibid.

73. Ibid.

74. Ward, *Men We Reaped*, 34.

75. Ibid.

76. Ibid., 38.

77. Ibid.

78. Ibid.

79. Ibid.

80. Ibid., 2.

81. Ibid.

82. Ibid.

83. Ibid., 2–4.

84. Ibid., 211.

85. Ibid.

86. Ibid.

87. Ibid., 212.

88. Ibid., 44.

89. Ibid.

90. Ibid., 45.

91. Ibid.

92. Ibid.

93. Ibid., 44.

94. Ibid., 52.

95. Ibid.

96. Ibid, 208.

97. Ibid

98. Ibid.

99. Ibid., 236.

100. Ibid.

101. Ibid.

102. Ibid., 237.

103. Ibid.

104. Ibid., 43.

105. Ibid., 250.

106. Ibid., 250–51.

107. Ibid

108. Ibid., 251.

109. Randall and McKim, *Reading Our Lives*, 59.

110. Ibid.

111. Dan P. McAdams, *The Person: A New Introduction to Personality Psychology*, 4th ed. (Hoboken, NJ: John Wiley and Sons, 2006), 425.

112. Mark Howe and M. L. Courage, "The Emergence and Early Development of Auto-biographical Memory," *Psychological Review* 104 (1997) 499–523, quoted in McAdams, *The Person*, 408.

113. McAdams, *The Person*, 408.

114. Ibid.

115. Ibid.

116. Ibid., 409.

117. Ibid.

118. Ibid., 407–8.

119. Ibid., 209, 409.

120. McAdams, *The Stories We Live By*, 75.

121. Ibid., 77.

122. Ibid, 78.

123. Ibid.

124. Ibid., 91.

125. Dan P. McAdams, *The Redemptive Self: Stories Americans Live By*, rev. ed. (New York: Oxford University Press, 2013), 31, 62.

126. Erik Erikson, *Identity: Youth In Crisis* (New York: W. W. Norton, 1968). See *Child-hood and Society*, 2nd ed. (New York: Norton, 1963) for a description of Erikson's eight stages of development: basic trust versus mistrust; autonomy versus shame; initiative versus guilt; industry versus inferiority; ego identity versus role confusion; intimacy versus isolation; gen-erativity versus stagnation; ego integrity versus despair.

127. Randall and McKim, *Reading Our Lives*, 62.

128. Ibid., 61.

129. Ibid.

130. Ward, *Men We Reaped*, 250.

131. McAdams, *The Redemptive Self*, 31.

132. Ibid.

133. Ibid.

134. Ibid.

135. Ibid., xii.

136. Ibid. See also Erikson, *Childhood and Society.*

137. McAdams, *The Redemptive Self,* 37.

138. Ibid.

139. Ibid.

140. Ibid., 39.

141. Ibid., xiii.

142. Ibid., xvii.

143. Ibid.

144. Ibid., 23–27, for a discussion of the six forms of redemptive narratives.

145. Ibid., 68.

146. Ibid.

147. Ibid.

148. Ibid.

149. Ibid., 47.

150. Ibid., 69.

151. Ibid., 70.

152. Ibid.

7. Reading Lifestories

Epigraph: Lisa Cron, *Wired for Story: The Writer's Guide to Using Brain Science to Hook Readers from the Very First Sentence* (Berkeley, CA: Ten Speed Press, 2012), 66.

1. William A. Randall and A. Elizabeth McKim, *Reading Our Lives: The Poetics of Growing Old* (New York: Oxford University Press, 2008), 74.

2. Ibid.

3. Cron, *Wired for Story*, 47.

4. Ibid., 45.

5. Jonah Lehrer, *How We Decide* (Boston and New York: Houghton Mifflin Harcourt, 2009), 13, cited in Cron, *Wired for Story*, 45.

6. Gerry Everding, *"Readers Build Vivid Mental Simulations of Narrative Situations, Brain Scans Suggest,"* January 6, 2009, http://news.wustl.edu/news/Pages/13325.aspx, quoted in Cron, *Wired for Story*, 67.

7. Cron, *Wired for Story*, 67.

8. Ibid.

9. Rita Charon, *Narrative Medicine: Honoring the Stories of Illness* (New York: Oxford University Press, 2006), 40.

10. Ibid., 107.

11. William L. Randall, *The Stories We Are: An Essay in Self Creation*, 2nd ed. (Toronto: University of Toronto Press, 2014), 209.

12. Maurice Sendak, *Where the Wild Things Are* (New York: Harper and Row, 1963); Margaret Wise Brown, *Goodnight Moon* (New York: Harper, 1947); Margret Rey and H. A. Rey, *The Complete Adventures of Curious George* (Boston: Houghton Mifflin, 2001).

13. Molly Andrews, *Narrative Imagination and Everyday Life* (New York: Oxford University Press, 2014), 1.

14. Ibid., 3.

15. Ibid., 3–4.

16. Ibid., 11.

17. Ibid., 11–12.

18. Martin Luther King Jr., "I Have a Dream," speech delivered at the Lincoln Memorial, Washington, DC, August 28, 1963, http://www.americanrhetoric.com/speeches/mlki haveadream.htm.

19. Douglas Fisher and Nancy Frey, *Engaging the Adolescent Learner: Setting the Stage for 21st-century Century Learning* (Newark, DE: IRA, 2012) quoted in Scott Filkins, "Strategy Guide: Close Reading of Literary Texts," *ReadWriteThink*, National Council of Teachers of English, http://www.readwritethink.org/professional-development/strategy-guides/close-read ing-literary-texts-31012.html.

20. Ibid.

21. Ibid.

22. Kip Wheeler, "Close Reading of a Literary Passage," August 5, 2015, https://web.cn.edu/kwheeler/reading_lit.html.

23. Charon, *Narrative Medicine*, 107–14.

24. Ibid., 11.

25. Ibid. Charon's rubric of close reading for training medical students attends to five aspects of narrative texts: frame, form, time, plot, and desire.

26. John Hayes and Carl Holladay, *Biblical Exegesis: A Beginner's Handbook*, 3rd ed. (Louisville, KY: Westminster John Knox Press, 2007), 1.

27. Ibid.

28. Ibid.

29. Ibid., 12–15.

30. Thomas G. Long, *The Witness of Preaching*, 2nd ed. (Louisville, KY: Westminster John Knox Press, 2005), 70.

31. Ibid., 71–73.

32. Ibid., 73.

33. Ibid., 75.

34. Ibid.

35. Ibid., 76.

36. Ibid., 77–81.

37. National Institute of Mental Health, "Schitzophrenia and Violence," December 10, 2006, http://psychcentral.com/lib/schizophrenia-and-violence/711/.

38. Ibid.

39. Long, *The Witness of Preaching*, 81.

40. Ibid.

41. Ibid., 82.

42. Ibid., 84.

43. David Denborough, *Retelling the Stories of Our Lives: Everyday Narrative Therapy to Draw Inspiration and Transform Experience* (New York: W. W. Norton and Co., 2014), 26.

44. Ibid., 28.

45. Ibid., 27.

46. Michael White and David Epston, *Narrative Means to Therapeutic Ends* (New York: W. W. Norton and Company, 1990), 40.

47. Denborough, *Retelling the Stories*, 36. See also Jill Freedman and Gene Combs, *Narrative Therapy: The Social Construction of Preferred Realities* (New York: Norton, 1996), 58–63, for a discussion of questions used in the process of externalization.

48. This is my recollection rather than a direct quotation.

49. Long, *The Witness of Preaching*, 89.

50. Ibid.

51. Questions adapted from William L. Randall, *The Stories We Are: An Essay in Self Creation*, 2nd ed. (Toronto: University of Toronto Press, 2014), 118–38.

52. Charon, *Narrative Medicine*, 112.

53. Long, *The Witness of Preaching*, 96.

54. *Groundhog Day*, screenplay by Harold Ramis and Danny Rubin, directed by Harold Ramis, 1998; Columbia TriStar.

55. Long, *The Witness of Preaching*, 97.

56. Ibid.

57. William A. Randall and A. Elizabeth McKim, *Reading Our Lives: The Poetics of Growing Old* (New York: Oxford University Press, 2008), 104.

58. Ibid., 110.

59. Ibid.

60. Ibid.

61. Ibid.

62. The first six criteria are from Dan P. McAdams, *The Person: A New Introduction to Personality Psychology*, 4th ed. (Hoboken, NJ: John Wiley and Sons, 2006), 243. The final criterion, "truth value," is from Randall and McKim, *Reading Our Lives*, 111.

63. McAdams, *The Person*, 423.

64. Ibid.

65. Ibid.

66. Randall and McKim, *Reading Our Lives*, 111.

67. McAdams, *The Person*, 423.

68. Ibid., 425.

69. Ibid.

70. Ibid.

71. Ibid.

72. Ibid.

73. Ibid.

74. Randall and McKim, *Reading Our Lives*, 111.

75. Ibid.

76. Ibid.

8. Restorying in Transition and Trouble

1. Gary M. Kenyon and William Randall, *Restorying Our Lives: Personal Growth through Autobiographical Reflection* (Westport, CT: Praeger, 1997), 1.

2. Ibid., 99.

3. Ibid., 100.

4. Ibid., 101.

5. Ibid.

6. William A. Randall and A. Elizabeth McKim, *Reading Our Lives: The Poetics of Growing Old* (New York: Oxford University Press, 2008), 99.

7. M. Freeman, "When the Story's Over: Narrative Foreclosure and the Possibility of Self Renewal" in *Lines of Narrative: Psychosocial Perspectives*, ed. Molly Andrews, Shelly D. Slater, Corinne Squire, and Amal Treacher (London: Routledge, 2000), 81–91, quoted in Randall and McKim, *Reading Our Lives*, 126.

8. Randall and McKim, *Reading Our Lives*, 189.

9. Michael White and David Epston, *Narrative Means to Therapeutic Ends* (New York: W. W. Norton and Company, 1990), 16.

10. Steven Madigan, *Narrative Therapy* (Washington, DC: American Psychological Association, 2010), 14.

11. See Christie Cozad Neuger, *Counseling Women: A Narrative Pastoral Approach* (Philadelphia: Fortress Press, 2001); Burrell David Dinkins *Narrative Pastoral Counseling* (Longwood, FL: Xulon Press, 2005); Suzanne M. Coyle, *Uncovering Spiritual Narratives* (Minneapolis: Fortress Press, 2014) as examples of adaptations of narrative therapy theory to pastoral care and counseling.

12. E. T. Bohlmeijer, G. J. Westerhof, W. Randall, T. Tromp, and G. Kenyon, "Narrative Foreclosure in Later Life: Preliminary Consideration for a New Sensitizing Concept," *Journal of Aging Studies,* 25 (2011): 364–70.

13. Mark Freeman cited in Bohlmeijer et al., "Narrative Foreclosure," 364–70.

14. Ibid., 367.

15. Ibid., 365.

16. Ibid., 367.

17. Ibid., 369.

18. Ibid.

19. Randall and McKim, *Reading Our Lives,* 126.

20. Ibid.

21. Ibid.

22. See Andrew Lester, *Hope in Pastoral Care and Counseling* (Louisville, KY: Westminster John Knox Press, 1995).

23. M. Katherine Shear, Paul A. Boelen, and Robert Niemeyer, "Treating Complicated Grief: Converging Approaches" in *Grief and Bereavement in Contemporary Society: Bridging Research and Practice,* ed. R. A. Neimeyer, Darcy L. Harris, Howard R. Winokuer, and Gordon F. Thornton (New York: Routledge, 2011), 143.

24. Freeman as cited in Bohlmeijer et al., "Narrative Foreclosure."

25. Kenneth R. Mitchell and Herbert Anderson, *All Our Losses, All Our Griefs: Resources for Pastoral Care* (Philadelphia: Westminster Press, 1983). Mitchell and Anderson name the six types of loss as material, relational, functional, role, systemic, and intrapsychic. I prefer the use of *loss of a dream* or Andrew Lester's term *future story* to the term *intrapsychic loss.* Terese Rando's term *symbolic loss* is used in place of *intrapsychic loss.* See also Therese Rando, *Treatment of Complicated Mourning* (Champaign, IL: Research Press, 1993) cited in Kenneth J. Doka and Terry L. Martin, *Men Don't Cry...Women Do: Transcending Gender Stereotypes in Grief* (Philadelphia: Taylor and Francis, 2002), 12. See Lester, *Hope in Pastoral Care and Counseling,* for a further discussion of future story.

26. Doka, *Men Don't Cry,* 12.

27. Adapted from Mitchell and Anderson, *All Our Losses, All Our Griefs*.

28. Ibid. The definitions I have assigned to their terms differ slightly from Mitchell and Anderson's definition.

29. Melissa M. Kelley, *Grief: Contemporary Theory and the Practice of Ministry* (Minneapolis: Fortress Press, 2010), 8.

30. Elizabeth Berg, "Departure from Normal" in *Ordinary Life: Stories* (New York: Random House: 2002), 30.

31. Ibid., 32.

32. Ibid., 33–34.

33. Ibid., 34.

34. Neimeyer et al., *Grief and Bereavement*, xi.

35. Colin Murray Parkes, "Introduction: The Historical Landscape of Loss: Development of Bereavement Studies," in Neimeyer et al., *Grief and Bereavement*, 1.

36. Ibid., 2.

37. Ibid.

38. Kelley, *Grief: Contemporary Theory*, 38.

39. George H. Pollock, *The Mourning-Liberation Process*, vol. 1 (Madison, CT: International Universities Press, 1989) quoted in Kelley, *Grief: Contemporary Theory*, 38.

40. Parkes, "Introduction," in Neimeyer et al., *Grief and Bereavement*, 3–4.

41. Ibid.

42. Kelley, *Grief: Contemporary Theory*, 22.

43. Ibid.

44. Ibid.

45. Ibid.

46. Nigel P. Field and Carol Wogrin, "The Changing Bond in Therapy for Unresolved Loss: An Attachment Theory Perspective," in Neimeyer et al., *Grief and Bereavement*, 37.

47. Kelley, *Grief: Contemporary Theory*, 23, 25.

48. Field and Wogrin, "The Changing Bond in Therapy," in Niemeyer et al., *Grief and Bereavement*, 38.

49. Ibid.

50. Ibid.

51. Ibid.

52. Robert A. Neimeyer and Diana C. Sands, "Meaning Reconstruction in Bereavement: From Principles to Practice," in Neimeyer et al., *Grief and Bereavement*, 10.

53. Kelley, *Grief: Contemporary Theory*, 78–79.

54. Robert A Neimeyer, *Meaning Reconstruction and the Experience of Loss* (Washington, DC: American Psychological Association, 2001), xii, quoted in Kelley, *Grief: Contemporary Theory*, 71.

55. Neimeyer and Sands, "Meaning Reconstruction," in Niemeyer et al., *Grief and Bereavement*, 10.

56. Kelley, *Grief: Contemporary Theory*, 75.

57. Neimeyer and Sands, "Meaning Reconstruction," in Niemeyer et al., *Grief and Bereavement*, 11.

58. Berg, "Departure from Normal," in Niemeyer et al., *Grief and Bereavement*, 32.

59. Ibid., 35.

60. Neimeyer and Sands, "Meaning Reconstruction," in Niemeyer et al., *Grief and Bereavement*, 11.

61. J. William Worden, *Grief Counseling and Grief Therapy: A Handbook for the Mental Health Practitioner*, 4th ed. (New York: Springer Publishing, 2009), 57–77.

62. Neimeyer and Sands, "Meaning Reconstruction," in Niemeyer et al., *Grief and Bereavement*, 11.

63. Jesmyn Ward, *Men We Reaped: A Memoir* (New York: Bloomsbury, 2013) in Niemeyer et al., *Grief and Bereavement*, 8.

64. Kelley, *Grief: Contemporary Theory*, 49.

65. Ibid., 65.

66. For a discussion of the theological function of funerals, see Thomas G. Long, *Accompany Them with Singing: The Christian Funeral* (Louisville, KY: Westminster John Knox Press, 2009).

67. Kelley, *Grief: Contemporary Theory*, 84–85.

68. David Denborough, *Retelling the Stories of Our Lives: Everyday Narrative Therapy to Draw Inspiration and Transform Experience* (New York: W. W. Norton and Co., 2014), 207–43.

69. Kelley, *Grief: Contemporary Theory*, 84.

70. Cheryl Strayed, *Wild: From Lost to Found on the Pacific Crest Trail* (New York: Random House, Inc., 2012).

71. Kelley, *Grief: Contemporary Theory*, 84.

72. Ibid.

73. Ibid.

74. Ward, *Men We Reaped*, 20–41.

75. Kelley, *Grief: Contemporary Theory*, 108–10.

76. See Shear, Boelen, and Neimeyer, "Treating Complicated Grief: Converging Approaches," in Niemeyer et al., *Grief and Bereavement*, 143, for a discussion of the absence of social support as a risk factor for poor grief outcomes.

77. Denborough, *Retelling the Stories*, 207.

78. Ibid.

79. Ibid., 212.

80. Ibid., 211–12.

81. Neimeyer and Sands, "Meaning Reconstruction," in Niemeyer et al., *Grief and Bereavement*, 12.

82. Ibid., 13.

83. The terms *critical awareness* and *ironic awareness* are Randall and McKim's terms, which were discussed in more detail in chapter 7. See Randall and McKim, *Reading Our Lives*, 110.

84. Michael White, *Re-Authoring Lives: Interviews and Essays* (Adelaide, SA: Dulwich Centre Publications, 1995), 82.

85. Ibid., 83.

86. Tim Harker, "Therapy with Male Sexual Abuse Survivors: Contesting Oppressive Life Stories," in *Narrative Therapy in Practice: The Archaeology of Hope*, ed. Gerald Monk, John Winslade, Kathie Crocket, and David Epston (San Francisco: Jossey-Bass, 1997), 197–98.

87. Ibid., 198.

88. Ibid., 199.

89. Some resources for churches are Al Miles, *Domestic Violence: What Every Pastor Needs to Know*, 2nd ed. (Philadelphia: Fortress Press, 2011) and Al Miles, *Violence in Families: What Every Christian Needs to Know* (Philadelphia: Augsburg Books, 2002). See also Catherine Kroeger and Nancy Nason-Clark, *Biblical and Practical Resources to Counteract Domestic Violence*, rev. ed. (Downer's Grove, IL: IVP Press, 2010); Marie Fortune, *Keeping the Faith: Guidance for Christian Women Facing Abuse* (New York: HarperOne, 1995). Additional resources can be found at http://www.faithtrustinstitute.org/ and http://www.cdc.gov/violenceprevention/intimatepartnerviolence/.

90. The National Domestic Violence Hotline, http://www.thehotline.org/.

91. Karen Scheib, *Challenging Invisibility: Practices of Care with Older Women* (St. Louis: Chalice Press, 2004), 61.

92. Sarah Bailey, "Christianity Faces Sharp Decline as Americans Are Becoming Even Less Affiliated with Religion," *Washington Post*, May 12, 2015, https://www.washingtonpost.com/news/acts-of-faith/wp/2015/05/12/christianity-faces-sharp-decline-as-americans-are-becoming-even-less-affiliated-with-religion/.

93. Granberg-Michaelson,"Think Christianity Is Dying? No, Christianity Is Shifting Dramatically?," *Washington Post*, May 20, 2015, https://www.washingtonpost.com/news/acts-of-faith/wp/2015/05/20/think-christianity-is-dying-no-christianity-is-shifting-dramatically/.

94. There is a growing body of literature on narrative leadership, much of it coming out of the Narrative Leadership Project of the Alban Institute. https://alban.org/ See, for example, Larry A. Goleman, *Finding Our Story: Narrative Leadership and Congregational Change* (Rowan and Littlefield Publishers, 2010); Larry A. Goleman, *Living Our Story: Narrative Leadership and Congregational Culture* (Washington, DC: Rowan and Littlefield Publishers, 2010); Richard L. Hester and Kelli Walker Jones, *Know Your Story and Lead with It: The Power of Narrative in Clergy Leadership* (Washington, DC: Rowan and Littlefield Publishers, 2009).

Afterword

1. Daniel Stern, *The Interpersonal World of the Infant* (New York: Basic Books, 1985), 182.

2. These are functions of pastoral care commonly cited in pastoral care texts. Seward Hiltner first identified the first three of these functions in *A Preface to Pastoral Theology* (Nashville: Abingdon Press, 1958), 89–172. The functioning of reconciling was introduced by William A. Clebsch and Charles Jaekle in *Pastoral Care in Historical Perspective* (New York: Jason Aronson, 1975, 1983), 56–66. In this same text, Clebsch and Jaekle also provide their own take on the three functions that Hiltner identified (33–66). Howard Clinebell added the functioning of "nurturing" in *Basic Types of Pastoral Care*, rev. and enlarged (Nashville: Abingdon Press, 1984) 126. Liberation was added to the list by Carol Watkins Ali, *Survival and Liberation: Pastoral Care in African American Context* (St. Louis, MO: Chalice Press, 1999), 112. Advocacy as a function of care is named by Nancy Ramsay, "A Time for Ferment and Redefinition" in

Pastoral Care and Counseling: Redefining the Paradigms, ed. Nancy J. Ramsay (Nashville: Abingdon Press, 2004), 4.

Exercises and Questions for Discussion

1. David Denborough, *Retelling the Stories of Our Lives: Everyday Narrative Therapy to Draw Inspiration and Transform Experience* (New York: W. W. Norton and Company, 2014).

2. David Burrell Dinkins, *Narrative Pastoral Counseling* (Longwood, FL: Xulon Press, 2005).

3. Elizabeth Berg, "Departure from Normal" in *Ordinary Life: Stories* (New York: Random House, 2003).

Selected Bibliography

American Psychiatric Association. Diagnostic and Statistical Manual of Mental Disorders: *DSM-5*. Arlington, VA: American Psychiatric Association, 2013.

Anderson, Herbert and Edward Foley, eds. *Mighty Stories, Dangerous Rituals: Weaving Together the Human and the Divine*. San Francisco: Jossey-Bass, 1998.

Andrews, Molly. *Narrative Imagination and Everyday Life* (New York: Oxford University Press, 2014).

Andrews, Molly, Shelly D. Sclater, Corinne Squire, and Amal Treacher, eds. *Lines of Narrative: Psychosocial Perspectives*. London: Routledge, 2000.

Anselm. *Why God Became Man* = *Cur Deus Homo*. Edited by Jasper Hopkins and Herbert Warren Richardson. Lewiston, NY: E. Mellen Press, 1974.

Augustine. *City of God*. Translated George E. McCracken et al. 7 vols. Cambridge, MA: Harvard University Press, 1957.

Bass, Dorothy C., and M. Shawn Copeland. *Practicing Our Faith: A Way of Life for a Searching People*. 2nd ed. San Francisco, CA: Jossey-Bass, 2010.

Berg, Elizabeth. *Ordinary Life: Stories*. New York: Random House, 2002.

Bernstein, Nell. *Burning Down the House: The End of Juvenile Prison*. New York: The New Press, 2014.

Bohlmeijer, E. T., G. J. Westerhof, W. Randall, T. Tromp, and G. Kenyon. "Narrative Foreclosure in Later Life: Preliminary Considerations for a New Sensitizing Concept." *Journal of Aging Studies* 25, no. 4 (2011): 364–70.

195

Boisen, Anton T. *Problems in Religion and Life: A Manual for Pastors.* New York: Abingdon Press, 1946.

Bolz-Weber, Nadia. *Pastrix: The Cranky, Beautiful Faith of a Sinner & Saint.* New York: Jericho Books, 2013.

Brown, Margaret Wise. *Goodnight Moon.* Illustrated by Clement Hurd. New York: Harper, 1947.

Browning, Don S. *A Fundamental Practical Theology: Descriptive and Strategic Proposals.* Minneapolis: Fortress Press, 1991.

Bruner, Jerome S. *Acts of Meaning.* Cambridge, MA: Harvard University Press, 1990.

Brunn, Dave. *One Bible, Many Versions: Are All Translations Created Equal?* Downers Grove, IL: InterVarsity Press, 2013.

Calvin, Jean. *Institutes of the Christian Religion.* Philadelphia: Westminster Press, 1960.

Carkhuff, Robert R., Michael M. Pierce, and John R. Cannon. *The Art of Helping III.* 3rd ed. Amherst, MA: Human Resource Development Press, 1977.

Charon, Rita. *Narrative Medicine: Honoring the Stories of Illness.* Oxford: Oxford University Press, 2008.

Chopp, Rebecca. *Saving Work: Feminist Practices of Theological Education.* Louisville, KY: Westminster John Knox Press, 1995.

Clebsch, William A., and Jaekle, Charles. *Pastoral Care in Historical Perspective.* New York: Jason Aronson, 1975, 1983.

Clinebell, Howard. *Basic Types of Pastoral Care.* Rev. and enlarged ed. Nashville: Abingdon Press, 1984.

Clinebell, Howard John. *Basic Types of Pastoral Care and Counseling: Resources for the Ministry of Healing and Growth.* Edited by Bridget Clare McKeever. Updated and rev. ed. Nashville: Abingdon Press, 2011.

Cobley, Paul. *Narrative*. London: Routledge, 2001.

Coles, Robert. *The Call of Stories*. Boston, MA: Houston Mifflin Company, 1989.

Combs, Gene, and Jill Freedman. "Narrative, Poststructuralism, and Social Justice." *The Counseling Psychologist* 40, no. 7 (2012): 1033–60.

Compton, William C., and Hoffman Edward. *Positive Psychology: The Science of Happiness and Flourishing*. 2nd ed. Belmont, CA: Wadsworth, Cenage Learning, 2013.

Cone, James. "Black Theology in American Religion." *Journal of the American Academy of Religion* 53, no. 4 (1985): 755–771.

———. *God of the Oppressed*. New York: Seabury Press, 1975.

———. *My Soul Looks Back: Journeys in Faith*. Nashville: Abingdon, 1982.

Coyle, Suzanne M. *Uncovering Spiritual Narratives: Using Story in Pastoral Care and Ministry*. Minneapolis: Fortress Press, 2014.

Craighead, W. Edward, and Charles B. Nemeroff, eds. *The Concise Corsini Encyclopedia of Psychology and Behavioral Science*. Hoboken, NJ: Wiley& Sons 2004.

Cron, Lisa. *Wired for Story: The Writer's Guide to Using Brain Science to Hook Readers from the Very First Sentence*. New York: Ten Speed Press, 2012.

Crossley, Michele L. *Introducing Narrative Psychology: Self, Trauma, and the Construction of Meaning*. Buckingham: Open University Press, 2000.

Cummins, J. S. *Christianity and Missions, 1450–180*. Vol. 28, *An Expanding World*. Aldershot, Great Britain: Ashgate/Variorum, 1997.

Daly, Gerard J. P. *Augustine's Philosophy of Mind*. London: Duckworth, 1987.

Damasio, Antonio R. *The Feeling of What Happens: Body and Emotion in the Making of Consciousness*. New York: Harcourt Brace, 1999.

Denborough, David. *Retelling the Stories of Our Lives: Everyday Narrative Therapy to Draw Inspiration and Transform Experience*. New York: W. W. Norton & Company, 2014.

Dinkins, Burrell David. *Narrative Pastoral Counseling*. Longwood, FL: Xulon Press, 2005.

Doehring, Carrie. *The Practice of Pastoral Care: A Postmodern Approach*. Louisville, KY: Westminster John Knox Press, 2006.

———. *The Practice of Pastoral Care: A Postmodern Approach*. Rev. and expanded ed. Louisville, KY: Westminster John Knox Press, 2015.

Doka, Kenneth J., and Terry L. Martin. *Men Don't Cry... Women Do: Transcending Gender Stereotypes in Grief*. Philadelphia: Taylor and Francis, 2002.

Doyle, Dennis. *Communion Ecclesiology*. Maryknoll, NY: Orbis Press, 2000.

Dulles, Avery. *Models of the Church*. Expanded ed. Garden City, NY: Image Books, 1987.

Dykstra, Craig R. *Growing in the Life of Faith: Education and Christian Practices*. Louisville, KY: Geneva Press, 1999.

Eakin, John Paul. *Living Autobiographically: How We Create Identity in Narrative*. Ithaca, NY: Cornell University Press, 2008.

Erikson, Erik. *Childhood and Society*. 2nd ed. New York: Norton, 1963.

———. *Identity: Youth in Crisis*. New York: W. W. Norton, 1968.

Filkins, Scott. "Strategy Guide: Close Reading of Literary Texts." *ReadWriteThink*. National Council of Teachers of English, http://www.readwritethink.org/

professional-development/strategy-guides/close-reading-literary
-texts-31012.html.

Fortune, Marie M. *Love Does No Harm: Sexual Ethics for the Rest of Us*. New York: Continuum, 1995.

Frank, Arthur W. *The Wounded Storyteller: Body, Illness, and Ethics*. Paperback ed. Chicago: University of Chicago Press, 1997.

Freedman, Jill, and Combs, Gene. *Narrative Therapy: The Social Construction of Preferred Realities*. New York: Norton, 1996.

Freud, Sigmund. *Civilization and Its Discontents*. New York : W. W. Norton 1962.

Ganzevoort, Reinder Ruard, Maaike de Haardt, and Michael Scherer-Rath. *Religious Stories We Live By: Narrative Approaches in Theology and Religious Studies*. Leiden, The Netherlands: Brill, 2014.

Giddens, Anthony. *Modernity and Self-Identity: Self and Society in the Late Modern Age*. Stanford, CA: Stanford University Press, 1991.

Golemon, Larry A. *Finding Our Story: Narrative Leadership and Congregational Change*. Herndon, VA: Alban Institute, 2010.

———. *Living Our Story: Narrative Leadership and Congregational Culture*. Herndon, VA: Alban Institute, 2009.

Greenberg, Yudit Kornberg, ed. *Encyclopedia of Love in World Religions*. Santa Barbara, CA: ABC-Clio/Greenberg, 2008.

Griffin, Graeme M. *Coming to Care: An Introduction to Pastoral Care for Ordained Ministers and Lay People*. Parkville, Victoria: Uniting Church Theological Hall, 1995.

Groundhog Day. Screenplay by Harold Ramis and Danny Rubin. Directed by Harold Ramis. Columbia TriStar, 1998.

Guralnik, David B. *Webster's New World Dictionary of the American Language.* Second college ed. New York: Simon and Schuster, 1980.

Harnick, Sheldon, and Jerry Bock. "Do You Love Me." *Fiddler on the Roof,* musical. Capitol/EMI Records, 1964.

Hayes, John H. *Biblical Exegesis: A Beginner's Handbook.* Edited by Carl R. Holladay. 3rd ed. Louisville, KY: Westminster John Knox Press, 2007.

Herman, Judith Lewis. *Trauma and Recovery.* Rev. ed. New York: BasicBooks, 1997.

Hester, Richard L., and Kelli Walker-Jones. *Know Your Story and Lead with It: The Power of Narrative in Clergy Leadership.* Herndon, VA: Alban Institute, 2009.

Hickman, Hoyt L. *Worship Resources of the United Methodist Hymnal.* Nashville: Abingdon Press, 1989.

Hiltner, Seward. *A Preface to Pastoral Theology.* Nashville: Abingdon Press, 1958.

Hodgson, Peter Crafts, and Robert Harlen King. *Christian Theology: An Introduction to Its Traditions and Tasks.* Newly updated ed. Minneapolis: Fortress Press, 1994.

Hoff, Lee Ann. *People in Crisis: Clinical and Diversity Perspectives.* Edited by Bonnie Joyce Hallisey and Miracle Hoff. 6th ed. New York: Routledge, 2009.

Hoffman, Martin L. *Empathy and Moral Development: Implications for Caring and Justice.* Cambridge, UK: Cambridge University Press, 2000.

Holifield, E. Brooks. *Health and Medicine in the Methodist Tradition: Journey toward Wholeness.* New York: Crossroad, 1986.

———. *A History of Pastoral Care in America: From Salvation to Self-Realization.* Nashville: Abingdon Press, 1983.

Howe, Mark, and M. L. Courage. "The Emergence and Early Development of Autobiographical Memory." *Psychological Review* 104 (1997): 499–523.

Holland, Scott. *How Do Stories Save Us? An Essay on the Question with the Theological Hermeneutics of David Tracy in View.* Louvain, Belgium: Peeters, 2006.

Humphries, Thomas L. *Ascetic Pneumatology from John Cassian to Gregory the Great.* Oxford, UK: Oxford University Press, 2013.

Hunter, Rodney J., H. Newton Malony, Liston O Mills, and John Patton, eds. *Dictionary of Pastoral Care and Counseling.* Nashville: Abingdon Press, 1990.

Jeanrond, Werner G. *A Theology of Love.* London: T & T Clark, 2010.

Job, Reuben P. *Three Simple Rules: A Wesleyan Way of Living* . Nashville: Abingdon Press, 2007.

Kelley, Joseph, F. *The Ecumenical Councils of the Catholic Church: A History.* Collegeville, MN: Michael Glazier, 2009.

Kelley, Melissa M. *Grief: Contemporary Theory and the Practice of Ministry.* Minneapolis, MN: Fortress Press, 2010.

Kenyon, Gary M,. and William Lowell Randall. *Restorying Our Lives: Personal Growth through Autobiographical Reflection.* Westport, CT: Praeger, 1997.

King, Martin Luther, Jr. *I Have a Dream.* New York: Schwartz & Wade Books, 2012.

King, Thomas. *The Truth about Stories: A Native Narrative.* Toronto, ON: House of Anansi Press, 2003.

Kroeger, Catherine Clark, and Nancy Nason-Clark. *Biblical and Practical Resources to Counteract Domestic Violence.* Rev. ed. Downers Grove, IL: IVP Press, 2010.

Lacugna, Catherine. *God For Us: The Trinity and Christian Life.* San Francisco, CA: HarperSanFrancisco, 1991.

Lehrer, Jonah. *How We Decide.* Boston: Houghton Mifflin Harcourt, 2009.

Lerer, Seth. *Children's Literature: A Reader's History, from Aesop to Harry Potter*. Chicago: University of Chicago Press, 2008.

Lester, Andrew D. *Hope in Pastoral Care and Counseling*. Louisville, KY: Westminster John Knox Press, 1995.

Lewis, Thomas, Fari Amini, and Richard Lannon. *A General Theory of Love*. New York: Random House, 2000.

Lieblich, Amia, Dan P. McAdams, and Ruthellen Josselson. *Healing Plots: The Narrative Basis of Psychotherapy*. Washington, DC: American Psychological Association, 2004.

Lindberg, Carter. *Love: A Brief History through Western Christianity*. Malden, MA: Blackwell Publishing, 2008.

Lopez, Shane, and C. R. Snyder, eds. *The Oxford Handbook of Positive Psychology*. 2nd ed. Oxford, UK: Oxford University Press, 2009.

Long, Thomas G. *Accompany Them with Singing: The Christian Funeral*. Louisville, KY: Westminster John Knox Press, 2009.

———. *The Witness of Preaching*. 2nd ed. Louisville, KY: Westminster John Knox Press, 2005.

Madden, Deborah. *"Inward and Outward Health": John Wesley's Holistic Concept of Medical Science, the Environment and Holy Living*. London: Epworth, 2008.

Maddox, Randy L. *Responsible Grace: John Wesley's Practical Theology*. Nashville: Kingswood Books, 1994.

Madigan, Stephen. *Narrative Therapy*. Washington, DC: American Psychological Association, 2010.

McAdams, Dan P. *The Person: A New Introduction to Personality Psychology*. 4th ed. New York: Wiley, 2006.

———. *The Redemptive Self: Stories Americans Live By*. Rev. and expanded ed. Oxford: Oxford University Press, 2013.

———. *The Stories We Live By: Personal Myths and the Making of the Self.* New York: W. Morrow, 1993.

McGarrah Sharp, Melinda A. *Misunderstanding Stories: Toward a Postcolonial Pastoral Theology*. Eugene, OR: Pickwick Publications, 2013.

Merriam-Webster, Inc. *Merriam-Webster's Collegiate Dictionary*. 11th ed. Springfield, MA: Merriam-Webster, Inc., 2003.

Migliore, Daniel L. *Faith Seeking Understanding: An Introduction to Christian Theology.* Grand Rapids: W. B. Eerdmans, 1991.

Miles, Al. *Domestic Violence: What Every Pastor Needs to Know*. 2nd ed. Philadelphia: Fortress Press, 2011.

———. *Violence in Families: What Every Christian Needs to Know*. Philadelphia: Augsburg Books, 2002.

Mitchell, Kenneth, and Herbert Anderson. *All Our Losses, All Our Griefs: Resources for Pastoral Care*. Philadelphia: Westminster Press, 1983.

Mitchell, William John Thomas, ed. *On Narrative*. Chicago: University of Chicago Press, 1980.

Monk, Gerald, John Winslade, Kathie Crockett, and David Epston, eds. *Narrative Therapy in Practice: The Archaeology of Hope*. San Francisco: Jossey-Bass Publishers, 1997.

Morgan, Alice. *What Is Narrative Therapy? An Easy-to-Read Introduction*. Adelaide, South Australia: Dulwich Centre Publications, 2000.

Morton, Nelle. *The Journey Is Home*. Boston: Beacon Press, 1985.

Musser, Donald W., and Joseph L. Price, eds. *New and Enlarged Handbook of Christian Theology*. Nashville: Abingdon Press, 2003.

Nance, Kevin. "Where the Writing Will Take Her." *Poets & Writers Magazine* 41, no. 5 (2013): 42–48.

Neimeyer, Robert A, Darcy L. Harris, Howard R. Winokeur, and Gordon F. Thornton, eds. *Grief and Bereavement in Contemporary Society: Bridging Research and Practice*. New York: Routledge, 2011.

Neuger, Christie Cozad. *Counseling Women: A Narrative, Pastoral Approach*. Minneapolis: Fortress Press, 2001.

Nygren, Anders. *Agape and Eros*. London: S.P.C.K., 1957.

Oord, Thomas Jay. *Defining Love: A Philosophical, Scientific, and Theological Engagement*. Grand Rapids, MI: Brazos Press, 2010.

———. *The Nature of Love: A Theology*. St. Louis, MO: Chalice Press, 2010.

———. *Relational Holiness: Responding to the Call of Love*. Edited by Michael E. Lodahl. Kansas City, MO: Beacon Hill Press of Kansas City, 2005.

Patton, John. *Pastoral Care in Context: An Introduction to Pastoral Care*. Louisville, KY: Westminster/John Knox Press, 1993.

Peterson, Christopher, and Martin E. P. Seligman, eds. *Character Strengths and Virtues: A Handbook and Classification*. American Psychological Association. New York: Oxford University Press, 2004.

———. *A Primer in Positive Psychology*. Oxford: Oxford University Press, 2006.

Pollock, George H. *The Mourning-Liberation Process*. Vol. 1. Madison, CT: International Universities Press, 1989.

Ramsay, Nancy J., ed. *Pastoral Care and Counseling: Redefining the Paradigms*. Nashville: Abingdon Press, 2004.

Rando, Therese. *Treatment of Complicated Mourning.* Champaign, IL: Research Press, 1993.

Randall, William L. "The Importance of Being Ironic: Narrative Openness and Personal Resilience in Later Life." *Gerontologist* 53, no. 1 (2013): 9–16.

———. *The Stories We Are: An Essay on Self-Creation.* Toronto: University of Toronto Press, 1995.

Randall, William, and Gary Kenyon. *Ordinary Wisdom: Biographical Aging and the Journey Of Life.* Westport, CT: Praeger 2001.

Randall, William Lowell, and Elizabeth McKim. *Reading Our Lives: The Poetics of Growing Old.* New York: Oxford University Press, 2008.

Rey, Margret, and H. A. Rey. *The Complete Adventures of Curious George.* Boston: Houghton Mifflin, 2001.

Richardson, Ronald. *Creating a Healthier Church: Family Systems Theory, Leadership, and Congregational Life.* Minneapolis: Augsburg Fortress Press, 1996.

Rieger, Joerg. *Opting for the Margins: Postmodernity and Liberation in Christian Theology.* New York: Oxford University Press, 2003.

Ricoeur, Paul. *Time and Narrative.* Vol. 1. Chicago: The University of Chicago Press, 1984.

Roberts, Alexander, James Donaldson, and A. Cleveland Coxe. *The Ante-Nicene Fathers: Translations of the Writings of the Fathers down to A.D. 325.* Vol. 1. Buffalo: The Christian Literature Publishing Company, 1895.

Russell, Norman. *The Doctrine of Deification in the Greek Patristic Tradition.* New York: Oxford University Press, 2006.

Runyon, Theodore. *The New Creation: John Wesley's Theology Today.* Nashville: Abingdon Press, 1998.

Sanneh, Lamin O. *Whose Religion Is Christianity? The Gospel beyond the West.* Grand Rapids, MI: W. B. Eerdmans Pub., 2003.

Scalise, Charles J. *Bridging the Gap: Connecting What You Learned in Seminary with What You Find in the Congregation.* Nashville: Abingdon Press, 2003.

Scheib, Karen D. *Challenging Invisibility: Practices of Care with Older Women.* St. Louis, MO: Chalice Press, 2004.

Sendak, Maurice. *Where the Wild Things Are.* New York: Harper and Row, 1963.

Snyder, C. R., and Shane J. Lopez. *Oxford Handbook of Positive Psychology.* New York: Oxford University Press, 2009.

Stairs, Jean. *Listening for the Soul: Pastoral Care and Spiritual Direction.* Minneapolis: Fortress Press, 2000.

Stern, Daniel. *The Interpersonal World of the Infant.* New York: Basic Books, 1985.

Sternberg, Robert J., and Michael L. Barnes, eds. *The Psychology of Love.* New Haven: Yale University Press, 1988.

Stone, Howard W., and James O. Duke. *How to Think Theologically.* 2nd ed. Minneapolis: Fortress Press, 2006.

Strayed, Cheryl. *Wild: From Lost to Found on the Pacific Crest Trail.* New York: Vintage Books, 2012.

Swinton, John, and Richard Payne. *Living Well and Dying Faithfully: Christian Practices for End-of-Life Care.* Grand Rapids, MI: William B. Eerdmans, 2009.

Switzer, David K. *The Minister as Crisis Counselor.* Rev. ed. Nashville: Abingdon Press, 1986.

Tracy, David. *Blessed Rage for Order: The New Pluralism in Theology.* New York: Seabury Press, 1997.

Tillard, J.-M. R. *Church of Churches: The Ecclesiology of Communion.* Collegeville, MN: Liturgical Press, 1992.

United Methodist, Church. *The Book of Discipline of the United Methodist Church, 2000.* Nashville: United Methodist Publishing House, 2000.

———. *The United Methodist Book of Worship.* Edited by Andy Langford. Nashville: Abingdon Press, 1992.

Van Huyssteen, J. Wentzel. *Encyclopedia of Science and Religion.* New York: Macmillan Reference USA, 2003.

Volf, Miroslav. *After Our Likeness: The Church as the Image of the Trinity.* Grand Rapids, MI: William B. Eerdmans, 1997.

Ward, Jesmyn. *Men We Reaped: A Memoir.* New York: Bloomsbury USA, 2013.

Watkins Ali, Carol. *Survival and Liberation: Pastoral Care in African American Context.* St. Louis, MO: Chalice Press, 1999.

Wesley, John. "The Christian's Pattern." In *The Works of John Wesley*, edited by Thomas Jackson, 14:202–205. 3rd ed. 14 vols. London: Wesleyan Methodist Book Room, 1872. Reprinted, Grand Rapids, MI: Baker, 1979.

———. *John Wesley.* Edited by Albert Cook Outler. New York: Oxford University Press, 1964.

———. *Journal and Diaries.* Edited by W. Reginald Ward and Richard P. Heitzenrater. Vols. 18–24 in The Bicentennial Edition of the Works of John Wesley. Nashville: Abingdon Press, 1988.

Wesleyan Reform Union. *Christian Words.* London: Oxford University Press, 1868.

White, Michael. *Re-Authoring Lives: Interviews and Essays.* Adelaide, SA: Dulwich Centre Publications, 1995.

White, Michael, and David Epston. *Narrative Means to Therapeutic Ends.* New York: Norton, 1990.

Wimberley, Edward P. *African American Pastoral Care*. Rev. ed. Nashville, TN: Abingdon Press, 2008.

Winslade, John, Gerald Monk, and Alison Cotter. "A Narrative Approach to the Practice of Mediation." *Negotiation Journal* 14, no. 1 (1998): 21–41.

Worden, J. William. *Grief Counseling and Grief Therapy: A Handbook for the Mental Health Practitioner*. 4th ed. New York: Springer Pub., 2009.

World Conference on Faith and Order. *On the Way to Fuller Koinonia: Official Report of the Fifth World Conference on Faith and Order*. Edited by Thomas F. Best and Günther Gassmann. Geneva: WCC Publications, 1994.

Zizioulas, Jean. *Being as Communion: Studies in Personhood and the Church*. Crestwood, NY: St. Vladimir's Seminary Press, 1985.

Index

CPSIA information can be obtained
at www.ICGtesting.com
Printed in the USA
LVHW051939060619
620437LV00005B/17